THIS IS THE PULI
leslie benis

Cover:
Ch. Templomkerti Suba (Int. Ch. Pusztai Furtos Ficko **X** Fajdosi Cigany) with one of the puppies he sired. Suba is the most recent FCI International Champion. He was bred by the retired president of the Hungarian National Puli Club, Reverend Anzelm Barany, and was imported by Florence and Michael Weissmann of New York.

Frontispiece:
Pici Star of Hunnia (Ch. Cinkotai Csibesz **X** Shagra Margitka). Owner is Mrs. Evelynn Miller.

Back cover:
Nagykunsagi Hohanyo (Cegledi Fifi **X** Csillagkerti Aliz). Owner; E. Peter Munchheimer.

ISBN 0-87666-368-4

Distributed in the U.S.A. by T.F.H. Publications, Inc., 211 West Sylvania Avenue, P.O. Box 27, Neptune City, N.J. 07753; in England by T.F.H. (Gt. Britain) Ltd., 13 Nutley Lane, Reigate, Surrey; in Canada to the book store and library trade by Clarke, Irwin & Company, Clarwin House, 791 St. Clair Avenue West, Toronto 10, Ontario; in Canada to the pet trade by Rolf C. Hagen Ltd., 3225 Sartelon Street, Montreal 382, Quebec; in Southeast Asia by Y.W. Ong, 9 Lorong 36 Geylang, Singapore 14; in Australia and the south Pacific by Pet Imports Pty. Ltd., P.O. Box 149, Brookvale 2100, N.S.W., Australia. Published by T.F.H. Publications Inc. Ltd., The British Crown Colony of Hong Kong.

Contents

Ch. Skysyl Harvey J. Wallbanger (Ch. Skysyl Up And Away X Ch. Skysyl Sketched in Shaded Gray). Harvey is the finest example of the efforts of Mrs. Owens' Skysyl Kennels. He is a second generation descendant of an outcross breeding between the long established Skysyl lines and the Kennedy's "PuliKountry" imported lines. Harvey is the second Skysyl owned Puli to go Best In Show in the U.S. Shown here with co-owner Anne Bowley. Photo: Ashbey.

ACKNOWLEDGMENTS

There are many people to thank for helping me with this book, as the creation of a technical book is rarely if ever the work of one author, and this book is no exception.

My greatest appreciation goes to Erno Kubinszky, DVM, on whose knees I learned that just to love a dog is not enough—much more is needed to do a real service to the individual dog or to its breed in general. He guided my interest in dogs throughout many years, and continues helping me every time I am in need, even though thousands of miles have separated us for more than a decade.

My immeasurable gratitude goes to Dr. Sandor Palfalvy for his kind permission to reference the research material that he has been collecting for a lifetime on the ancient history of the Puli.

I am greatly indebted to Mrs. Margaret Curran for her invaluable work in researching and writing the section, "The Puli In America." Margaret's love for the breed is evidenced by her very objective reporting of its progress in America—a sometimes very controversial subject.

Many of my Puli-loving friends read one or more chapters of my manuscript, offered advice, and kept me from making many mistakes. Judy Mischka was the very first to brave the pages of the manuscript. I am particularly grateful to Barry Becker for his careful reading of the manuscript and for correcting my innumerable outrages against the English language, and to Bill Pohlmann for his review of and comments on the book and for catching the passages that were technically sloppy from a scientific point of view. However, in some instances I have disagreed with their recommendations for fear that the points in question would lose something by being re-stated differently; for all such and remaining errors I am clearly responsible.

My sincere thanks are extended also to those who contributed photographs to this book.

Among the photographs of the many unrelated dogs, I have included three series of well-known bloodlines to illustrate how quality and uniformity can be maintained with careful selection of breeding stock and the cooperation of breeders.

Champion Cinkotai Csibesz and his relatives are shown in photographs to illustrate the standard in some detail.

Champion Nagykunsagi Csorgo, C.D. and his line and Champion Gyalpusztai Kocos Burkus and his relatives are portrayed in the photographs illustrating selective breeding.

Last, but by no means least, I am very deeply indebted to my wife, Klara, for her untiring patience and encouragement throughout my lengthy labor: Without her support and enthusiasm, this book would not have been written, as her love for the Puli was the inspiration that kept me going during the times when I was ready to give up the entire project.

PREFACE

This book was written for all of the past, present, and future fanciers of the Puli breed. It is intended to fill the information gap (about the Puli) of some 50 years for the English-speaking dog fancy.

It is my hope that this book leads the reader's mind from a superficial knowledge of the Puli into a deeper insight and understanding of the breed. Additionally, I would like to draw the attention of those breeders who have through the years inadvertently entangled themselves in the less important details of Puli characteristics, becoming "head or coat hunters" or specializing in a single structural detail within their own blood lines, overlooking the breed in its entirety. A certain degree of "kennel blindness" comes to all but a gifted few who seem to be able to see the "whole" in spite of the results of yesterday's dog shows and the ever present fashion trends.

This book is not intended to be an all-inclusive general dog book, but rather an encouragement to read and learn more and more about dogs through the initiation the fancier would get by reading this. Each of the chapters is highly specialized in a particular aspect of the breed, and is very condensed. I know I have oversimplified given subjects in some parts to make the book suitable for a general readership, knowing that each of the chapters could be expanded to book length to satisfy the more scientific minded. I am delighted to say that a sizeable number of people: breeders, dog show judges, and even scientists in various parts of the world are becoming interested in the Puli on an almost academic level. On the other hand, and in order that those interested should have the opportunity to learn where the various Puli topics now stand, more details are included than some readers would like.

During this present decade, our young people are heading back to a less complicated and "earthy" way of life, and we hear their loud cries for all to protect Nature in her virginal state. Since it has remained unchanged since the beginning of recorded history, the Puli is a living symbol for ecology and a challenge to the scholars of genetic survival. The destiny of the breed might parallel the destiny of the new age of the 1970's, becoming a golden era for the Puli.

This text might never have been written if I had known at the outset how much time it would require. I mistakenly thought that I could produce this book by merely editing the articles and illustrations that I had prepared through the years for various dog magazines, and by inserting new sentences in parts of the books I had co-authored on various dog subjects. But, soon after I began,

American, Mexican, F.C.I. International Champion Cinkotai Csibesz.

American, Hungarian, and Mexican Champion Gyalpusztai Kocos Burkus.

We are deeply indebted to Dr. Imre Bordacs of Budapest for making available to us   these two Pulis who were outstanding examples of their breed even in Hungary. That he could be persuaded to part with them has been our good fortune. I cannot claim any credit for their beauty and quality. They came to the U.S. fully matured, ready to walk into the show rings of the new country in which they would make their home. It has been my privilege to own them at a time when fresh blood was badly needed and was at a premium. The impact they have made on the American Puli scene is as definite as the one they have left behind in their native land. Photographs by: Joan Ludwig.

I had to face the realization that such procedure would not work, and I must start afresh.

Any person writing on his own breed tends to become involved in every tiny detail, and through long months this book truly became a labor of love—every subject I researched presented a new challenge and required more and more work. After many vacations spent in the seclusion and solitude of the High Sierras, and countless evenings at home writing late into the night, I finally realized that a book is never really finished. It is just a matter of where the author draws the line beyond which there is no more research nor waiting for additional information or photographs.

The names of the three types of Hungarian sheep dogs are Puli, Komondor, and Kuvasz; the plural forms of these names are Pulik, Komondorok, and Kuvaszok, but the Anglicized forms Pulis and Komondors will be used extensively herein.

The motto I have tried to convey throughout this book is to make all Puli enthusiasts aware of the fact that in the long run IT IS NOT MY PULI; IT IS NOT YOUR PULI, BUT THE PULI BREED THAT IS IMPORTANT.

Leslie Benis
Tarzana, California

Chapter 1

THE HISTORY OF THE PULI

ANCIENT HISTORY

I am sure that most of you readers have seen dog genealogy charts of various origins showing the "family tree of dogs," of how they are related, and how the different breeds descended from their ancestors. If you look hard enough you may find the Puli in a corner, in a separate box with a remark: "Origin Unknown." Well, just because genealogists fail to prove the Puli's relationship to any of today's known breeds, its origin is far from being unknown. It is not surprising that they failed to find connections with today's dogs since the Puli dates back about eight thousand years to the beginning of recorded history. In other words, it is believed that the Puli was domesticated about two thousand years before any of the four basic canine families were.

Researchers have more or less agreed for a long time that the Puli migrated with the Magyars over one thousand years ago into what is now Hungary. They also agreed that the Magyars came from eastern areas. Archeological findings traced their horses, cattle, and their language back that far. Most of the canine researchers followed this logic as well, and we can find books and articles on the theories of how and where the Magyars and their Pulis have spent the last one thousand years. I do not want to bore the reader with the hundreds of names and their publications on the subject, but there are two books that condense most of these writings, and quote all the significant ones to date. Both published in Hungarian, the first is: *The Hungarian Sheep Dogs*, by Felix Geza Buzzi, published in 1915. The other, which is even more precise is *The Hungarian Sheep Dogs and Their Foreign Relatives* (Amagyar Pasztorkutyak Es Azok Kulfoldi Rokonai), by Dr. Geyza

Csaba Anghi, published in 1936. These two books alone reference in their bibliographies over a hundred publications by various historians, archeologists, canine researchers (Cynologists), and scientists. Although they disagree somewhat in the details, they all traced the Magyar migration as having been westward to present-day Hungary.

Some researchers even maintained that the area from which they migrated was beyond the Ural Mountains of western Russia. This gave birth to the theories of the possible Lhasa Apso-Puli and Tibetan Terrier-Puli relationship.

But, east of the Urals, between the Ural Mountains and the Karpathian (Carpathian) Mountains, all these theories seemed to run into deadlock, as that is where the history of the Hungarian nation and the ancestry of the Puli seemed until very recently to end.

Historians working for some time in several unrelated areas have agreed that such records of the past did not end there, but World War II came along before they could gather enough proof. English, French, and German archeologists who were working toward tracing the complete history and the writings of the ancient Sumerian people unearthed more articles in villages in the area of what was once called Mesopotamia. Hungarian scientists, who fled their native country before the end of the war, went back to work on the history of the Hungarian nation after settling down in their adopted countries. They discovered a wealth of information that completely fitted the pattern of their earlier research. Today there is unquestionable proof that links Hungarians with Sumerians. Linguists have traced back to the Sumerian language over two thousand words used in today's Hungarian. Among these words that are just about unchanged in spelling or meaning are the names of three ancient Hungarian working dogs: the Puli, Komondor, and Kuvasz.

Independent from the research already described, Dr. Sandor Palfalvy, a Hungarian born physicist, was collecting similar data regarding the Puli. After he published his initial findings, with the help of Dr. Fred Thardy's newsletter, "The Puli," he found himself connected with a well-advanced, wide-open research project. His findings fitted nicely into the puzzle, and after his work has been verified by other scientists we will be able to say with confidence that the history of the Puli has been extended another six thousand years. Dr. Palfalvy's research findings, which have been partially introduced in the monthly publication *The Puli*, will be published in his forthcoming book. Other disputations have been advanced from time to time regarding the Puli's ancient history, but they do not appear to have the validity of these findings.

Included here is only a small part of Dr. Palfalvy's discovered data.

During the years of 1890 to 1894 a Hungarian archeologist, Count Jeno Zichy, headed various expeditions to different parts of Russia searching for ancient Scythian cities. At one of these excavations, located in the Csegem River Valley, on the north side of Caucasus Mountain in the Bagszan area, Zichy found among hundreds of other items a broken legbone of a horse bearing ancient

This broken leg bone, unearthed by Count Zichy in 1890, is from the year 2000 B.C. and bears a primitive Scytha inscription: *1 PULI— 200 KOJLY*. Photo courtesy Dr. S. Palfalvy.

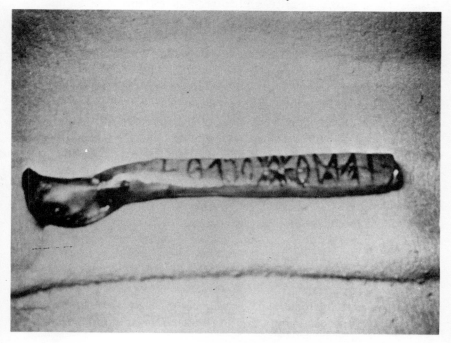

runic inscriptions. After careful examination of the findings it was concluded that the excavated items, among them the broken leg-bone, were dated about the era of 2000 B.C. Since Scythian writing was undeciphered at the time, this legbone was of no interest to the museums, and was retained in Count Zichy's private collection.

In 1944, Professor Lechner found that these runic inscriptions were the writings of the ancient Magyars and discovered the key to the language. With this knowledge, he examined the legbone again, and found that the inscription translated into "1 Puli 200 Kojly." "Kojly" is still used in the high country of Hungary to describe one species of sheep. Added to this is the fact that even at the beginning of the twentieth century it was an accepted form of book-keeping between shepherd and the flock's owner to inscribe on the ends of a thick stick (usually a hazelnut branch that they would break in half) the number of sheep the shepherd accepted for his care for the summer months. The shepherd took one end, the other end stayed with the owner. When the shepherd returned with the flock from the summer pastures, they matched the broken ends of the stick to assure identity, and to account for the sheep.

During an 1896–1899 expedition by German and Russian scient-ists excavating in an ancient cemetery of Csigirin (in the vicinity of today's Russian towns of Cherkassy and Kremenchug) there was found in one of the opened graves the 4000-year-old skeleton of a 20-to-25-year-old man, and the bones of a medium-sized dog near his right hand. Various items were turned up in the same grave, among them a very small, flat piece of polished bone with a small hole at one end and inscribed with one of the same words found on the legbone: PULY. From the position of this bone in relation to the human skeleton, it was evident that it had been worn by the man as a neckpiece. The details of these excavations were published under: *Friedhofe Und Graber Im Alterman*, by Altmann, Hertl, Pavlok, Zacharv; Berlin, 1904 (pages 97 to 124).

Other excavations of the same nature revealed that most of the men in graves of this era were buried with their horses, or at least with their saddles and arrows, among other everyday items. Some-times in the excavations of entire cemeteries only one or two buried men were found without saddles and arrows, and it was concluded that these were the "on foot" men of the community, which unquestionably points to the shepherds, especially since the two items mentioned above came from graves without arrows and saddles.

The code of Hammurabi is probably better known than the previously mentioned excavated findings. Hammurabi was king of the ancient nation of Babylon. His laws and the happenings of everyday life of the Babylonians were carved on stone monuments which were discovered in January, 1902 on the Acropolis of the city of Susa, Mesopotamia. Some segments of this monument are now in the Louvre Museum in Paris, and the remaining parts of it are in the Asmolean Museum in Bagdad, Iraq. After the secrets of the characters on this monument were learned, we can find many Sumerian words that still exist in the Hungarian language, and are spelled identically in both the Sumerian and Hungarian languages. Below are listed two such words with the English translation:

SUMIR	HUNGARIAN	ENGLISH
Agg	Agg	old
Saru	Saru	sandal

Words with a slight difference in spelling, but similar sound are:

Nab	Nap	sun
Nab Ur	Nap Ur	Sun God
Zim	Szem	Eye

In relation to the Puli, scientists find two different places in the code of Hammurabi relating the word "Puli" definitely to a dog. First in column number XLII, lines 63 to 66, decoded and translated to English suggest: "Run away horse—Puli helps me—to turn back smartly—by confusing it. . . ." Further down in Column number XLIII, lines 51 to 55, decoded and translated: ". . . Say out loud—again—who are you—who are you—if the Puli is scaring you—I will calm (him) from you—if your business to me is sparkling (clear). . . ."

As fantastic as it seems after decoding the ancient characters of the huge stone tablets, and expressing them with Latin letters or words, almost entire lines can be read in Hungarian without translation, by those who are familiar with Old Hungarian.

In 1886 the Royal British Academy of Science under the leadership of Sir H. J. McDonald and Sir A. C. Simon conducted excavations of the ancient city of Assur, in the vicinity of today's city of Mosul, Iraq. The findings are published in Sir McDonald's book, *Ruin City of Assur*, published in London, 1895. Among the items they unearthed were clay tablets found in the temple of the Sun God, that were written by a priest named Zamoly of the Sun God, whom the Chuz people worshipped from 3000 B.C. These clay tablets contain simple sentences of primitive observations of nature, their surroundings, and everyday events. Some of these "golden" sayings can be heard from Hungarian villagers even today: "Air becomes still before a storm"; "Sun God ripens the crop"; "Red setting of Sun God brings wind"; "The flock is crowding when the storm comes". The word *Puli* is mentioned in two different places on these tablets, as follows: "Puli barking always have reason," and "Through his hair Puli can see further than you."

From another expedition (lasting through the 1920's and 1930's) for the Royal British Academy and headed by Sir C. Leonard Wooley, English archeologists brought back clay tablets and stone cuttings from the old-world cities of Ur and Lagash, dating from 3500 B.C. The city of Ur is mentioned in the Bible, and is spelled the same, although other spellings are also used. These plates are stored in the British Museum in London. Plates number 307 and 863 are of special interest to us since these tablets introduce two family names; one is "Kuth," the other "Bana." Both of these names spelled the same way, are very common family names in Hungary today. They also show the now familiar words KOJ LY (sheep), ABA LY (cattle), and PU LY. These plates also introduce two more signs: KU MUN DUR (Komondor), and KUAS SA (Kuvasz). Combining all the listed belongings on the tablets, it is evident that some kind of an ancient version of an inventory is presented in the following form: "The Family of Kuth had 216 horses with 8 Kuvaszok, 167 cattle with 6 Komondors, and two flocks of sheep, 620 in all with 6 Pulis. The family of Bana had 72 horses with 2 Kuvaszok, 436 cattle with 6 Komondors and 2 Pulis, 840 sheep taken care of by 2 Komondors and 3 Pulis."

In this overly condensed form it sounds childlishly easy to put two and two together, to see the connection between the Hungarians and the Sumerian people, as well as the present day Puli and the Sumerian shepherd's PU LY.

One of the major breakthroughs that led to these findings was the "breaking" of the code of those runic writings.

16

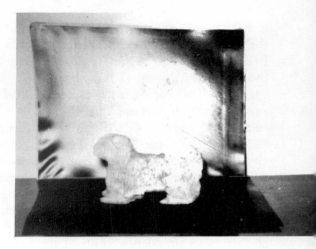

A miniature sculpture from 3900 B.C. found during the excavations of the ancient city Eridu of the Mesopotamian area. The original is in the National Museum of Iraq, Bagdad. Photo courtesy Dr. S. Palfalvy.

Up to this point Dr. Palfalvy and his colleagues showed that the name Puli was connected to the Hungarians, Magyars, and Sumerians. The name was also associated with sheep, sheepherding and to the shepherd, dating back roughly 5500 years. But to this point we do not know if it referred to the same Puli or even to a dog similar to the Puli as we know it today.

Two German archeologists working together between 1882 and 1887 on the unearthing of the ruins of the city of Erdiu, in the area of Mesopotamia, published their findings in two separate books. One was Friederich Muller's *Altertum,* published in Leipzig, Germany, 1891; the other was Martin Tellmann's *Archaisce Texts aus Eridu,* printed in Dresden, Germany, 1894.

Both of these books discuss in detail the opening of the stone burial vault of IL-Di, the ten-year-old daughter of the ruler TAR MOG UR. (IL-Di is a name popular for girls in Hungary even today). The vault was lavishly decorated for the age of 3900 B.C. The objects recovered from the vault could fill a room in a museum. Around the remains of the skeleton were well-detailed miniature sculptures of a cow, a cat, two birds, a sheep, and a dog. The sculptured dog is now in the National Museum of Iraq, Bagdad. It is a lifelike replica of our present-day Puli.

In 1911 a book was published in London by C. R. C. Thompson: *Foundations for Civilization.* In it he writes about the expedition he led to the ancient city of Jarmo. A photograph of a clay tablet, *c.* 4500 B.C., shows the carved representation of a Puli-like dog; at the top of the tablet are included the words ABA LY (cattle) and PU LY (dog). The original of this clay tablet can be seen today in the National Museum of Iraq, Bagdad.

French Professor Maurice Espreaux wrote in *Le Peuple des Sumirienne*, a book published in 1906 in Paris, about examining the ruins of the city "BOGHAZKO" during archeological excavations he conducted in the Anatolia Province of today's Turkey. (This city name is such a clear-cut Hungarian word that if you wrote it down and placed it in front of any Hungarian today, he would swear to you that it must be an existing Hungarian town or village.) On page 126 of his book, Espreaux introduces a photograph of a sunbaked, carved clay figure found in the ruins of BOGHAZKO and dated its production at about the year 6000 B.C. The author

French professor Maurice Espreaux found this tablet during the excavations of the ancient (6000 B.C.) city of Boghazko; it shows a Sumerian shepherd and his Puli. Photo courtesy Dr. S. Palfalvy.

A clay tablet from the ruins of the city of Jarmo, 4500 B.C. Photo reproduction from the book *Foundation for Civilization* by C.R.C. Thompson, printed in London in 1911. Photo courtesy Dr. S. Palfalvy.

writes that the "tablet now belongs to the Anatolian Museum of Turkey, and it pictures a Sumer shepherd with his dog, and in one corner it shows a bull of those days." Not only is the representation of the dog a definite Puli-like dog, but the shepherd's clothing is strikingly similar to the costumes worn by the "folk active" of the Hungarian villagers, even including the shepherd's stick.

MODERN HISTORY

The written evidence of the present-day Puli dates back as far as 1751, when a livestock expert named Heppe wrote about the "Hungarian Water Dog," closely describing today's Puli. The German book *Der Schaferhund, Der Hirtenhund* by Buffon, published in 1773 by Phylax, lists among the known herding dogs a small, mostly black-colored, heavily coated dog which is best known as being very able to direct the herd. Unfortunately, in this early writing there is no mention of the dog's exact size. Dr. Emil Raitsits states in his 1924 book that in the late 1800's is to be found the first more-or-less technical description of the Puli and the Pumi: "The Puli used around sheep is described as always lower than the highest point of the shepherd's boots," which is roughly 40 centimeters or 15¾ inches.

The Hungarian book *The World of the Animals*, published in 1901 by Ludwig Mehely, places the Puli in first place as the best-known Hungarian sheep dog. He quotes detailed listings of the qualities he finds in the Pulis, which he had the opportunity to study in larger numbers than the Komondors and Kuvaszok. He found that the height of the Puli varied between 34 cm (13⅜ inches) and 42 cm (16½ inches). "Small in size, rather short in body, with rounded skull, its tail curls over the back with its heavy coat creating an umbrella-like mass over its hindquarters. The color is almost always pure black with the exception at times when they throw their coat and look sun-beaten dull black." As one can see, the earliest-published measured sizes and descriptions are completely in line with today's known standard for the breed, just as the 7000–8000 year old clay tablet pictures the Puli exactly the way we know it today.

The unfortunate history of the Hungarian nation is greatly responsible for letting its thousand years of hard-earned livestock values and dogs diminish to zero. The Turkish invasion during the 1500's was a period in which herds of the famous longhorn Hungarian cattle and Racka sheep were stolen, along with work-dogs, and herded south toward Turkey. Later, under the occupation of the Austrians, everything Hungarian in origin was forbidden. Even the official language of the country became German. Much of the Hungarian cattle that was still left was replaced with the much smaller Western European breeds, as competition at the market with the Western lamb was desired. The populace were also forced to change their sheep breeding program. During the Austro-Hungarian coalition period, life was somewhat easier. Austrians were more forgiving, and the ancient live stock was on the increase again, if for no other reason than for being Hungarian. These same up-and-down periods can be observed in the history of the Hungarian horse, cattle, sheep, and the different dog breeds the Magyars brought with them into the meadows of the Karpathian Mountains of Hungary.

We refer to the period up to the late 1800's as being the "unorganized" breeding period. During this time, however, the shepherds were protecting their Pulis the best way they knew how. (Today, to protect a bitch in season is considered to be the basic step in maintaining the pure bred dog.) The shepherds of the 17th, 18th, and 19th centuries are now known to have done much more than to have just protected their dogs; they did what some of today's breeders sometimes refuse to do, and that is to take the time to arrange the best matings. The shepherd sometimes spent days riding to the distant parts of the country to breed his Puli bitch to the best male. But we now talk about that era as "unorganized" because they did not keep records of their breedings.

In those days the price of a good Puli was just about equal to the shepherd's earnings for a full year. But only the good one, the fast working, easy to teach Puli was considered more than "just a dog." The shepherd was very proud of his reliable, hard-working helper, but if the Puli did not fulfill his requirements the shepherd degraded him to being "just a dog" and got rid of him. This makes it understandable that among all the qualities that today's Pulis possess, the working capability and willingness to learn are the most dominant and the most obvious. The Puli does not require long training in herding. (Even today shepherds in Hungary teach their new Pulis to herd by merely exposing them to older working Pulis. If the young Puli works with an experienced dog for a few days, he will perform the same job perfectly when left alone.) Shepherds of past times paid attention to proportion, size, and color of a good-herding Puli, having learned from the horsemen of the same plains, who used their Pulis for rounding up horses, what were the structural requirements for a dog of endurance and speed.

Although in the last 40 to 50 years breeders have been concentrating more on show quality, size, and color, and less on working capabilities, the Pulis born in the big cities today adapt to herding instantly after being exposed to it, unless they have been changed by selection through generations for other than their original physical characteristics. Naturally a Puli that has been bred to be twice the size, or twice the weight, of the original herding Puli cannot adapt to light-footedness, speed, or tireless activity.

The era of "organized" breeding in Hungary is considered to have begun at the turn of this century. The early 1900's produced numerous scientists, veterinarians, and breeders whose names have become forever connected with the Puli. Books and dog magazines began to explore the value of the Hungarian sheep dog. The general public began to compare the values of the foreign imported breeds with the more intelligent but less impressive Hungarian breeds.

In the early days of dog shows it was difficult to convince the shepherds to participate. It was important that the Puli be presented by the shepherds the way they preferred them. But the shepherds had their herding trials among themselves and were not interested in taking part in the "childish play of the aristocracy". This attitude hindered the complete mapping of the dogs of different regions of the country. With impressive prices, booths, clothes, and useful articles, the interest in dog shows began to grow. It is recorded that in 1911 at a Budapest dog show one of the invited English judges offered 1000 Hungarian crowns to purchase one of the exhibited Kuvaszok, Komondors, or Pulis. A shepherd's yearly salary was from 12 to 20 crowns. The writer does not mention if the English gentleman was able to buy any of the dogs or not, but this and other similar instances created enough interest so that the shepherds and breeders started to show their Pulis to the general public. The further popularization of the Puli and the other Hungarian breeds came through the untiring efforts of Dr. Emil Raitsits, a professor at the Hungarian University of Veterinary Medicine, as he realized the need of more organized efforts to save the Hungarian breeds from extinction in the fast modernization of agriculture. He spent much of his time traveling the countryside trying to locate all of the Pulis available for registration and attempting to persuade shepherds and farmers to register their stock and maintain registrations for future litters. His first devoted helper was Adolf Lendl, the director of the Budapest Zoo, and he managed to locate small funds to be spent for the conservation of these breeds. He remodeled part of the zoo to have a special section for an experimental breeding program. At the same time he helped to popularize these breeds by exhibiting them in the same general area of the zoo where other ancient, but almost extinct, domesticated and wild animals were kept. This experimental breeding program was widened considerably and later acquired the kennel name "Allatkert" (Animal Garden) and furnished the foundation stock for many of the kennels that were founded. This section of the Budapest Zoo still exists, but on a much more limited basis. For those who are not familiar with the immeasurable contributions this program provided with its first scientifically-based breeding program, the sight of friendly dogs behind bars and next to wild beasts is shocking. The present director of the zoo comforted us with the assurance that those Pulis get more exercise and are better fed than many of the Pulis from well-known kennels.

Dr. Raitsits founded the Hungarian Herding Dog Breeders Association and became its first president. This organization was solely responsible for the creation of a nation-wide interest in the revival of the Hungarian breeds. World War I, because it was not extensively fought on Hungarian territory, did not affect the breed, per se, although it affected the long range programs. But the Trianon peace treaty following the war cut Hungary to less than half of its original size. The portion not retained was divided between Czechoslovakia, Rumania, Russia, and Serbia (now part of Yugoslavia). The high Karpathian mountain region was given to Czechoslovakia on the northern border, and to Rumania on the southeastern border. This was Hungary's primary mountain plateau and sheep pasturage. Although the original sheep country in Hungary was considered to be the central flat land or the "Puszta," the Hungarians or Magyars occupied the entire Karpathian mountain area for over a thousand years, and eventually established sheep breeding in the high parts of the country. It is impossible to estimate the number of the working Pulis lost as a result of the peace treaty. Hungarians living in these areas were treated as enemies by the forces that occupied them. Sooner or later they were forced to leave their homes, and their livestock. Under such circumstances it is easily seen that many Pulis were lost forever. However, forty years after Czechoslovakia gobbled up the northern part of Hungary, the Czechoslovakian Kennel Club in the late 1950's accepted and inaugurated in their registry a coarser-boned, Puli-size, Puli-like sheep dog as a new "national breed".

Marcsa, an actual working Puli, the first Puli Champion in Hungary.

A dog show was held in Budapest in 1916; although the records do not indicate how many Pulis were exhibited, we found that the first "Grand Victor" title was awarded to Marcsa, a Puli that later became the Allatkert kennel's best-known foundation bitch. Even today some of the oldtimers claim there has never been another Puli like her.

Records indicate that the first kennel names registered to Puli breeders following the Allatkert were Betyarvilag, Fertopart, Hajdusagi, and Torokvesz. Of these first registered kennels, only the Allatkert (the Budapest Animal Garden or Zoo) and the Betyarvilag kennel (owned by the widow of its original founder, Antal Rajna) survived to the post World War II era.

These kennel names are important for those who want to trace their Pulis back that far. One or more of these kennel names can be found on most current Puli pedigrees.

To further help these breeds in 1924, Dr. Raitsits founded a separate registration body for Hungarian breeds only. In those days it was common (in some European countries it is still fashionable) that the breed clubs handle their own registrations under National Kennel Club supervision. Dr. Raitsits handled all registrations personally until his medical school assistant, Miss Ilona Orlay, took over. This was at first on a voluntary basis, but she subsequently became the secretary of the Hungarian Breeds section of the kennel club and handled all registrations and correspondences connected with these breeds until her very recent retirement. (Much of the data in this chapter was contributed by her.)

A popularization movement not only revived the Puli but slowly helped it to a position where it became a thing of national pride for a Hungarian to own a Puli or a dog of any of the other Hungarian breeds. Many government officials and social dignitaries lent their names to help publicize and popularize these breeds.

The Puli became established in the cities and suburbs and began to challenge the popularity of the Kuvasz, which had been brought to the cities much earlier by virtue of having been the favorite guard dogs of the Hungarian nobility.

The first herding trials organized by the kennel club were held in conjunction with an agricultural fair in 1932. Shepherds would come to sell, trade, or buy livestock and were accompanied by their Pulis. These trials were repeated at most of the agricultural fairs and exhibits.

In accordance with the aim to popularize the breed, the standard was somewhat looser than we know it today. Although the structural and proportion requirements were clear-cut and well-known, more color variety and size disparity became permissible. To gain some kind of government subsidy, Dr. Raitsits tried to arouse interest in using the Puli for police work. The vigor and intelligence of the Puli readily adapted the breed for such work, but police authorities maintained that he was too small to be effective. In one of the first issues of the Ebtenyesztes (Dogbreeding) magazine, Dr. Raitsits claimed: "We succeeded to breed *out* the 50 cm (19½ inches) large or Police Puli." We found evidence of a somewhat limited but active Puli breeding program within the police department in the following years. The highlight of the police Puli activities came in Vienna, Austria, when a Hungarian Police Puli in 1933 became the star of the International Police Dog

Competition (helping the breed to international recognition) by winning over a large number of German Shepherds, Dobermans, and Boxers. Only one local Hungarian Police Department left any marks in the records of the breed. Kispest is an industrial suburb of Budapest, and the local police department received the registered kennel name Kispesti Orszem (The Patrol of Kispest). Activities continued there until the number of police dogs had to be reduced during the 1950's to give way to modern tracking and patroling methods.

Shortly after the untimely death of Dr. Raitsits in 1935, his closest associates introduced the modernized Puli standard. This standard was named after its authors: Dr. Abonyi, Dr. Anghy, and Dr. Muller, and established a point scale, a very detailed percentage table, and four separate size groups for the Puli.

I. Large or Police Puli   50 cm ($19\frac{1}{2}$ inches and above)
II. Medium-sized Puli   40–50 cm ($15\frac{3}{4}$ inches to $19\frac{1}{2}$ inches)
III. Small Puli   30–40 cm ($11\frac{7}{8}$ inches to $15\frac{3}{4}$ inches)
IV. Miniature or Toy Puli   below 30 cm ($11\frac{7}{8}$ inches)

This standard was specifically designed to help the Puli get into the apartment type environment with smaller size and give way before the Police Puli which brought most of the government funds for the cause. The point system introduced at the same time emphasized that only the medium and small Pulis were to receive the maximum available points for size and general impression, since only this size group was considered ideal with respect to the ancient requirements of the shepherds. All size groups were to be judged separately as were the different colors. Counting only the black, gray, and white colors, this system created twelve individual varieties for registration and dog shows. It soon became apparent that the breed was not going to become popular enough within the foreseeable future to necessitate the additional paperwork for such a large number of varieties. Although the point system was supposed to create an interest among breeders to work from each size group toward the medium-sized Puli, city breeders with limited experience neglected this goal, much to the frustration of the authors of the standard. Extensive study into the history of the dog shows held in Hungary failed to turn up evidence to prove that there ever was a show in which all varieties were represented. As a matter of fact, shows held outside of Budapest almost never had an entry in either the Police or the Toy Puli class.

The Puli arrived at its pre-World War II peak in popularity, achievements, and fame through its own inherent characteristics: playfulness, intelligence, and the ability to win everyone's heart, and not through a standard designed to make it popular.

This author had the opportunity to interview Dr. Abonyi in person regarding the four-size standard. Dr. Abonyi said: ". . . the point system, and the percentage table related to the details of the Puli, proved to be the best thing that ever happened to the Puli. Looking back through the years the four size allowance had some merits for a short time, but in the long run it was a mistake, and I can see it now. . . ." Dr. Abonyi became involved in efforts to change the Puli standard back to a relatively wide scale but with a single size requirements model, as detailed in the next section.

The outbreak of World War II found the breed in a relatively secure position. It was well-established in Hungary and other European countries. But, had it not been for the fact that the Puli was then at its peak in popularity, it could not have survived as a breed through the long years of the war.

THE PULI IN HUNGARY TODAY

The years of the Second World War left their mark on the breed. Food was scarce and rationed, even for people. Worming medicine and insecticides were forgotten luxuries of the pre-war times. Kennels had to give up their priceless breeding stock or reduce it to a bare minimum. Because of military duties, the frequent bombing of cities and other turmoils of war, many Puli owners had to place their dogs with friends who were not as dog-oriented as would have been ideal. The end of the war found the Puli in its saddest historical state. First the German occupation forces and later the Russian invaders killed by the hundreds the faithful protectors of their masters' private property. Pulis, with their special alertness, became the most sought-out enemies of the ransacking military personnel; loud-voiced Pulis could attract attention for miles, so they were marked for elimination before they could cause trouble. My favorite Puli was killed by a Russian bullet because he would not let an enemy soldier go from the kitchen into the part of the house where the female members of the family were hiding.

Hundreds of Pulis were scattered all over Europe with their fleeing owners. Most of them never returned to Hungary, and for all practical purposes were lost. A few of them found their way into foreign stud books. Pulis with pre-war Hungarian registrations were found in Argentina, arriving there after 1945 with migrating refugees.

The collation of available material about the breed could not be accomplished for a long time as postal services were suspended for many months. Gatherings of people for any reason were forbidden by the occupation forces. The hardest period was between 1945 and 1948 when people exhausted their energies just to feed themselves. The number of Pulis decreased because Puli owners, with a small number of exceptions, were unable to meet the extra financial and nutritional requirements that a litter of puppies would have imposed upon them. Then, too, no one in the country wanted a dog to add to his daily troubles, and placing the puppies would have been impossible.

The hero of the breed in 1945 was undoubtedly Miss Ilona Orlay, the Secretary of the Hungarian Kennel Club. Only hours after the eight-week-long battle of Budapest, she walked from her house in the eastern suburbs of the city to the centrally-located general offices of the H.K.C., and gathered all the records of the Hungarian breeds and loaded them into a large two-wheeled cart. This load she pulled through the still-burning rubble of the city to her home 15 to 20 miles distant. These records proved to be priceless in the later re-establishment of the Puli and other Hungarian breeds.

The efforts of the dog fancy were further hampered by the fact that the occupying Russians and the new Hungarian regime looked upon the dog sport as the luxury hobby of the "aristocracy" and tended to treat it accordingly. They burned the non-table cuts of meat from the slaughter houses rather than make it available to dog owners. Unnecessary "red tape" was attached to any paper work connected with dogs. The official department to handle dog registration and pedigrees became part of a useless bureaucratic government agency of the Department of Agriculture and, like an unwanted toy, it was passed from department to department and from one building to another. A very small dog show was held in March, 1948, mainly to get some idea of the surviving breeding stock. Some progress was evident for the Hungarian dog fanciers by about 1950. General membership meetings were held, and soon a reorganized Hungarian Kennel Club emerged. Dr. Erno Kubinszky was named acting Secretary and President. The registration procedure was brought back under the Club's jurisdiction, and a new era began with two full-time paid employees in the office.

The first kennels to receive registration or renew activity to help the breed through its worst loss were Kondorosi, Cigany Szinhaz, Allatkert, Kispesti, Orszem, Betyarvilag, and Miss Orlay's own Dunagyongye. Though these were the only kennels, many

Nagykunsagi Ragyogo Ricsi, owned and bred by Dr. Imre Bordacs. This Puli bitch imprinted her name on the post-W.W. II history of the breed. This photograph was taken after she had whelped and shows her in bad coat condition, but from her stand and proportions one can see why she became one of the favorites at the time.

individuals and Puli owners were instrumental in pulling the breed through these hard years. As soon as times became more nearly normal, other persons again became interested in the Puli. Other well-known kennels emerged, such as Nagykunsagi (owned by Dr. Imre Bordacs), Arpadligeti, and Barnavari, just to mention a few, became known through their exports to the United States.

It is worthwhile to mention here that the hard years had one merit. Common troubles and common enemies make the best friends and this became true of the H.K.C. After reorganization, the breed clubs became chapters of the H.K.C. and all registration and pedigree services were performed by the same office, instead of the individual breed clubs fighting to keep their own records and pedigrees.

The Puli, being the smallest and least-demanding of the Hungarian breeds, was the most fortunate in securing first place in the upsurge of the dog sport in its native country. In 1955, the Puli growth in population percentage was almost back to normal, although still very low in actual number. After the 1956 revolution, life became somewhat easier. Enough so that some people could sacrifice time and some money to their interest in dog breeding.

The change of the four-size variety standard was long overdue. In 1959 the officers of the Puli Club, under Dr. Bordacs' leadership, finally decided to create a Puli standard that would not have to be adjusted with the constant changes in popularity, one that would incorporate the best up-to-date material on the breed and take into consideration the newer, scientifically-based breeding methods and achievements. Dr. Abonyi, a former student of the late Dr. Raitsits and then a professor at the University of Veterinarian Medicine, and also having been one of the authors of the four-size standard, gave much very valuable help to the committee. Through the years he collected data, measurements, and charts on the variations of the size of the Puli. After long discussion, deliberation, and the careful examination of old registration records, it became apparent that although four sizes were permitted for the Puli the number of registrations were negligible in two of the four classes. The "toy" size, under 30 cm ($11\frac{7}{8}$ inches), and the large or "police" size, above 50 cm ($19\frac{1}{2}$ inches), were eliminated. The remaining sizes were included in one category in the new proposal. With the full cooperation of

The first Hungarian-owned Puli to become F.C.I. International Champion after W.W. II was Ch. Aranyhegyi Fustos. He is shown here (reproduced from a Hungarian postcard) not yet in full coat, at the age of 20 months.

the Hungarian National Puli Club, the Hungarian Kennel Club, and with the help of the Hungarian Dog Show Judges Organization, the new Puli Standard was printed in 1960 by the Office of Standardization. The new 30-page illustrated Standard gave breeders the basis for their breeding programs and the ability to meet the ever-increasing demand for good Pulis. Seventeen listed disqualifications helped to speed clearing faults and unwanted qualities from the breed.

Many of the refugees of the revolution, finding new and better lives in their adopted countries, started to import Pulis and other

Hungarian breeds mainly for sentimental reasons. With these imports, the breed became better known in many foreign countries and created a demand from the Hungarian breeders. In 1962 the American Kennel Club re-established contact with the Hungarian Kennel Club and the Hungarian pedigrees were once again acceptable for registration in the United States. The fast-growing demand created a new danger for the Hungarian National Puli Club. They faced the possible dilution of quality by those who would breed the Puli only for the profit to be gained. This critical situation was cleverly handled by the newly-elected officers of the H.K.C. They made an agreement with the official state-owned export-import company stipulating that dogs could not be taken out of the country without the permission of the Hungarian Kennel Club. Before a dog could be offered for export through the export-import company, it had to be shown to a panel of expert judges of its respective breed. If the dog qualified, a stamp of approval was put on its pedigree, and only with this stamp would the export-import company consider the dog for export. This one step imposed the best quality control, and together with the renewed national pride that the majority of Hungarian breeders feel about their ancient breeds, the Puli is enjoying an unprecedented upgrading in quality.

Not until the 1960's did the Puli again reach its pre-war popularity. Since then a steady increase in interest in the breed, and a constant growth in quality and increase in number can be observed. At the International Show in Budapest the number of Pulis exhibited increases year by year, and the number of regional chapters of the Hungarian National Puli Club continues to grow. With the renewed interest by enthusiasts in the breed, and the constant modernization of agriculture, the Puli has reached the point where shepherds are acquiring their herding Pulis from well-known breeders. State-owned farms are setting up their own Puli breeding programs. At the world-famous horse farm in Hortobagy, which is also a tourist attraction, the folk-dressed horsemen demonstrate for the spectators their horsemanship and the ability of their Pulis to round up the half-wild horses scattered over the open fields of the puszta.

This tremendous increase in the number of Pulis created a new workload for the Hungarian Kennel Club. New litter inspectors

Typical Pulis
from recent
Hungarian dog
shows.

had to be educated and placed into service. More personnel were needed to handle just the Hungarian breeds. Breeding-stock and pre-registration inspections had to be held more frequently, and more judges had to be qualified to handle the increasing number of dog shows and proliferation of entries. The quality control is mainly in the hands of the litter inspectors, breeders, exhibitors, and dog show judges. To make the judging requirements uniform, the Hungarian Kennel Club periodically holds seminars for future judges and holds a very strict closed-book written and oral examination for each prospective judge. When I took these examinations, the oral part alone involved six hours of cross-examination by seven interrogators.

To retain the working ability of the Puli, the Hungarian Kennel Club encourages obedience training. The H.K.C. owns large pieces of property on which they hold training classes, field trials, and terrier trials. The latest news from Hungary is that the Puli Club is creating interest with their herding demonstrations, and that they hope this interest will develop into herding trials, exhibiting genuine herding Pulis.

THE PULI OUTSIDE HUNGARY

In the early 1930's the breed became best established outside its native country in Germany. Dr. Erna Mohr, a geneticist and a well-known veterinarian, later the director of the Munich Zoo, became interested in the Puli and soon was one of the most respected authorities on the breed in Central Europe. She had published numerous scientific articles on the Puli and two books related to the Hungarian sheep dogs. Until her death in 1968, she was very active in the club for Ungarishe Hirtenhunde (German Puli, Komondor, Kuvasz Club). As the head of the West German delegation to the World Congress of the Breeders of Hungarian Sheep Dogs, she visited Hungary a number of times, the last time in 1966. Germany was also the home of the first F.C.I. International Puli Champions. Because of its central location within Europe and

Reproductions from the albums of the Hungarian Kennel Club's Registration Department. Pulis approved for final registration are photographed with their registration numbers and are being filed with the H.K.C.

International Ch. Csengo von Rexhof (Int. Ch. Nuckos Ajasch **X** Cinka Panna). Note: Pulis photographed with hanging tail appear to have a longer body. Csengo measured 44 cm. (17 3/8 inches) square in reality.

its location outside of the Iron Curtain, Germany still leads in the number of International Puli Champions.

The first nine Pulis taken from Hungary for breeding purposes were owned by a Hungarian family migrating to Brazil in 1931.

Switzerland is a close second to Germany in Puli activities, and has an active club for all "Foreign Sheep Dogs." The Puli group is the largest and most active in this club. I had the opportunity to participate in their 1963 annual show in Basel, and I was much surprised that there were 18 Pulis entered in a show wherein the native Swiss Saint Bernard was represented by 43 entries.

Now practically all of the countries of Europe have Pulis, but they do not have enough to call for the registration of a breed

Cacilie vom Lechgau, a typical Puli bitch in Germany in 1935. Photograph courtesy of the late Dr. Erna Mohr.

Alibaba von Lillienthal, a German Champion in 1947. Photograph courtesy of the late Dr. Erna Mohr.

Top-winning German Puli bitch of her time; Bogar von Rexhaf (Furge Macko X Cinka Panna).

club. Austria, Holland, and Sweden have more than the other countries, but we do not have records of the actual numbers of dogs available.

Surprisingly, in the number of Pulis registered outside of Hungary, Israel is second to the United States, and far ahead of third place Germany. This position was achieved in a relatively short time. In 1952, Miss Elizabeth Csengeri, who at the time had a well-established Puli kennel in Hungary, emigrated to Israel taking her four best dogs. Later she imported a number of others from Hungary and exchanged a few with German and Swiss breeders. Through her efforts, Pulis were placed with shepherds on sheep farms, where their abilities were soon recognized. Since then, Pulis have been sought by many Israeli shepherds. She also helped to form the Puli Club of Israel for the purpose of helping the breeding and show-minded Puli owners. As a result, there exists

Europa Winner: Int. Ch. Zumm of Lechgau, owned and handled by Mrs. Marietta Martin, President of the Swiss Puli Club. Zumm collected 16 CACIB awards in various countries of Europe.

Left, Immerzu Belzebub Csutora;
right, Immerzu Pusztai Butykos
Csuhaj, the first Puli pair of
Immerzu, the newest kennel to
become interested in the Puli in
England. Photograph courtesy of
Immerzu Kennels.

Borgvale Pusztai Marok Marcsa ▶
(Hungarian import), a new
addition to the international Puli
scene in England and the first
Puli in England to win top
honors for the breed. Owner:
Mrs. Pat Lanz. Photograph
courtesy of Mrs. Lanz.

The owners of the Immerzu Kennel, Mr. and Mrs. Horan, showing their first English-born Puli litter. Photograph courtesy of IMMER-ZU Kennels.

Miss Elizabeth Csengeri of Israel with one of her favorite Pulis.

On the international scene in the mid 1960's. From left to right: Cirokai Lurko, representing Hungary; Ch. Cinkotai Csibesz, top-winning Puli in the U.S., at that time; and Int. Ch. Csengo v. Rex-hof, the top-winning Puli in Western Europe. The three rivals competed in Brno, Czechoslovakia under judge Dr. Lajos Abonyi of Hungary. (The international CACIB award went to "Csibesz," shown by the author.) Cirokai Lurko is presently owned by Mrs. Judith Radocsai of Pennsylvania.

in Israel today an ideal balance between working Pulis, those kept as house pets, and show dogs. Her foundation stud, one of the most famous post-war Pulis, named "Buksi" (Hungarian registration number 190) can be found in the background of many of today's Pulis in the United States, along with some other Bukkabranyi Pulis from her kennel.

Many of us had the pleasure of meeting this remarkable woman when she traveled to this country in 1969 on a combined visit and tour judging dog shows. She was the keynote speaker at the 2nd National Puli Fanciers' Convention in Santa Monica, California, in 1969. She won the hearts of many of us with her frank, straightforward remarks and criticism regarding the Puli stock she had seen and judged while in the United States. She is one of the remaining symbols of the old Hungarian school, in whose eyes "Only the excellent Puli is a Puli, the remaining are just dogs." Her strong influence and judgement are quite evident in the overall quality of Pulis in Israel, where they are more uniform in type, size, and color than dogs of any other country in the world.

THE PULI IN AMERICA
(Margaret H. Curran)
"... THE PULI—

truly a part of your heart ..."

This is as true for owners of Pulis today as it was in the past. It is a fine tribute to this wonderful dog that Americans have taken him to their hearts with the same devotion the Hungarians have given him for centuries.

In the beginning—and a new breed in a new country a world away from that of its origin would have to have a beginning—the first official knowledge of a superior sheepherding breed of dog came with the observations of Nicholas Roosevelt when he was U.S. minister to Hungary in the early 1930's. This was the Puli, already a legend in his own time. His existence had been closely guarded by shepherds in the remote areas of the grazing lands and his almost uncanny intelligence had given rise to the shepherd's words "He's not a dog, he is a Puli." This simple designation still sets the Puli apart from other sheepherding dogs even today.

This phrase that has been so widely quoted is found in an article on the Puli written in 1940 for the *Hungarian Quarterly* by the Hungarian novelist Zsolt Harsanyi. While visiting with a shepherd on the great Hungarian plain he asked the man to show him what his Puli could do. "Pengo" obeyed the shepherd's quiet commands, given without emphasis, gesture, or even a glance. He understood the sound of the words.

"A very intelligent dog," Harsanyi said to the shepherd.

"That's not a dog, Mister," replied the man, "that's a Puli!"— "That, of course," writes the author, "explained everything."

This picture of historical importance shows one of the first Pulis arriving in the United States, in the early 1930's. Note the squarely built body, straight front legs and the round head. This dog is identical in proportions and every detail with today's imports arriving from Hungary. Photograph: 1937 Yearbook, U.S. Department of Agriculture.

Time has eroded much of the history of the Puli, not only in the United States but also in its homeland. Some of the available material from private sources is of questionable veracity; some of it is blatantly false and biased; all of it has gaps which have never been filled except through conjecture. We have only within the past decade begun to put together the fragments extant.

The Puli first came to the attention of Americans through the United States Department of Agriculture. Agriculturalists had the problem of herding dogs that sometimes killed the very animals they were entrusted to protect. When word came of the existence of a breed of sheepherding dog, the Puli, that had never harmed anything it was called upon to protect, the Agricultural Department arranged to import these dogs to the national experimental facilities in Beltsville, Maryland, and by breeding them not only with each other but with various other breeds it was hoped to instill into American farm dogs this quality as well as heightening the intelligence and natural herding instincts that this breed possessed.

The experiment was started in the fall of 1935 with the importation of four Pulis from Hungary. They were bred among themselves and crossed with the German Shepherd, the Border Collie, the Chow Chow, and perhaps also with the two Turkish sheepdogs which were quartered there at the time. The tests were inconclusive and never published, and, when World War II put an end to them, the Pulis were auctioned off to professional breeders and thus became absorbed into America's breeds of dogs.

Two of the known breeders who got foundation stock from the experimental station at Beltsville were Bronson Williams and Louis Kiss. Not a great deal has been written about either one, nor are any details on the Pulis available. "Tony" Williams was interviewed (July 20, 1946) by *The New Yorker* reporter who had noticed his ad in a newspaper misquoting a reference to the Puli that had appeared in the column a year or so before. The reporter found out that Tony Williams, who lived in Frenchtown, New Jersey, also had Siamese cats, Muscovy ducks, and brown eggs for sale as well as Pulis. He had bought his first Pulis just before the war (had registered some forty of them to that date) when the Department of Agriculture discontinued their experimental program and put the Pulis up for auction. "Williams," the columnist wrote, "bought three of them, a dog and two bitches, third-generation descendants of the Pulis originally imported from Hungary." To keep his Pulis from running herd on his two children when they went out to play he even bought a small herd of sheep. "A puli," states the article, "usually spends the night stretched across the front doorway of his master's house; this is thought to be a holdover from his hereditary position as guardian of the shepherd's tent. If you have two pulis, the second naturally stretches himself by the back door." Since the two men had been discussing the intelligence of the Pulis, it seemed only natural that the reporter should include the fact that Pulis, being grammarians, expect to be ordered about with full sentences—"Go into the next room until we finish dinner"—"Go around to the back door and get your feet wiped."

Mr. Louis Kiss farmed in Marlboro, New York. There is a photo of his daughter and two Pulis in a December, 1941 issue of *The National Geographic Magazine* in an article "Working Dogs of the World" by Freeman Lloyd. The caption is "A Little Dog With a Huge Fur Coat is the Hungarian Puli." The shaggy little dog is named Zsoka and the puppy the young girl is holding is no doubt one of Zsoka's offspring. Here again, we have mention of the U.S. Department of Agriculture experiments, this time in tests of inheritance of intelligence and temperament. "Some of the little dogs made high scores in a 'whistle test' of obedience and in sheep-herding, but individuals varied widely. Some were actually afraid of the sheep."

Most Puli owners are familiar with Walter A. Weber's original painting of the Puli on the back of a runaway sheep, riding it like a broncobuster. It was painted for the last of a series of seven articles on the world's principal breeds of dogs as recognized by the American Kennel Club (*National Geographic*, Sept., 1944). The article is by Stanley P. Young, Senior Biologist, Fish and Wildlife Service, U.S. Department of the Interior. It mentions the experimental breeding of the Agriculture Department with the four imported Pulis, stating that "it was hoped to ascertain differences in temperament, intelligence, aptitude, and suitability as herd dogs among different crosses with the Puli." It mentions the fact that in the breeding experiments the Puli had litters as large as ten, as small as four. The average seemed to be six or seven. The tests proved the Pulis to be willing workers. "One astounded its trainers by a climbing leap over a six-foot fence overlaid with barbed wire."

World War II put an end to these breeding experiments; they were not just discontinued for the time being, the dogs were sold. There were never any official reports compiled that would be considered definitive, only reports of individual veterinarians whose knowledge has filtered down to us by bits and pieces. As far as the Department of Agriculture was concerned, the experiments were inconclusive, and they have never been resumed. It is doubtful that in this age of automation such an experiment would serve any useful purpose. The preservation of the true Puli characteristics lies in the integrity and the responsibility of the breeders of today.

Because these first four imported Pulis and their progeny are the beginning of the recorded history of this Hungarian sheepherding dog in the United States, this agricultural experiment has been given wide mention but no results. So many diverse statements have grown up around it that even now it is almost impossible to separate fact from fiction. There are only faint traces, of names and of places, and of kennels and faces of Pulis long gone.

The claim has been made that this foundation Puli stock produced excellent quality offspring as these Pulis were excellent representatives of the breed. This information, which seems to vary slightly even in its own accounting, is often colored by descriptions that are more superlative than factual. However, if one considers the purpose for which they were brought into this country, the claim is certainly true—the Puli was and still is a working dog of superior intelligence, stamina, and ability. There is nothing to substantiate the claim of superior qualities of conformation. In the years that followed the abandonment of the experimental project, the breeders were limited to a relatively few strains and as is so often the case with prolonged inbreeding, the Puli began to drift farther away from its original appearance and even its personality.

An excellent statement of this view is given by Philip Mahan, a law professor at the University of Alabama in 1966. In his "Commentary" in the December issue of *The Puli* he writes, in part:

"Aware of the great danger of broad generalizations, I will make one and say the American bred Puli has suffered badly in the last twenty years from excessive inbreeding and a consequent deterioration. One of our early litters was whelped when we were living in the Pacific Northwest and three of the pups were sold to sheep ranchers. I learned they did quite well. I would hesitate to predict that some of the dogs I have seen in the last couple of years would perform adequately.

"I have hopes the addition of new blood will render the breed more attractive to a number of people who now never get to know the fine qualities that are there, but are never available to the outsider.

"I know I must be wrong as to individual dogs but we have moved about considerably in the last twenty years and I have seen a fairly representative sampling of Pulis from California to New York. I think we Puli owners have come to think of the breed as it has developed in the United States as being 'just that way.' I have recognized in myself and detected in others a defensiveness, and I think we should make a careful and objective evaluation of the American dogs in comparison with the Hungarian stock. Presumptively, it is dangerous to have produced so many dogs from such a limited number of original dogs.

"My family raised and showed Italian Greyhounds; I had Terhune Collies and later Irish Terriers. The Puli is different. I like the difference and want to see it presented at its best to those persons who truly are interested in acquiring a dog that can make a positive contribution to their lives.

"My original interest in the breed stemmed from the article in *The New Yorker* in 1946, describing the experiments of the Department of Agriculture and the intelligence of the Puli. We acquired a pair at that time and since have purchased four other dogs, and raised several litters. Personality traits have varied widely but always included was some hard-to-describe form of intelligence that distinguishes the Puli from other dogs I have had. Each owner, of every breed, has his own description of his dog's

Ch. Magyars Bodri (Mereg Duda X Donald's Droopy) is a fine example of the early interest within the U.S. in retaining the true Puli type. This Puli could easily compete for top honors in today's dog shows. Note the head and tail carriage and the "ready for action" stand.

personality, and as to this, I'll leave each Puli owner on his own. We can agree the Puli has a distinctive flair, a different something."

The Magyar Puli Kennels in Far Hills, New Jersey were owned by Donald Cook, a star of the Broadway stage ("The Moon is Blue"). Magyar Pulis were from both the Williams and the Kiss strains. They will always be remembered in the history of the Puli in the United States because from this kennel came the first Champion of Record: Ch. Magyar's Bundaz. He was whelped May 26, 1946, and got his championship on October 10, 1948. His sire was Mereg Duda; his dam was Ulla. Mereg Duda was at stud at Williams' Trinity Farm. There was a German import, Dorgo von Barengrund, at the Magyar Kennels that was the sire of Skysyl's first litter. The outcross breeding was recommended by Williams for Juli II. This stud was used only twice, by both Cook and Williams, and there is no further information about him that is now available aside from the fact that his sire was Assyvonder Kaaswaldhutte and his dam was Anya von Balaton.

The individual more responsible than anyone else for America's awareness of the Puli was Nicholas Roosevelt, whose enthusiasm for the unusual qualities of the little herding Pulis he had seen in Hungary led him to bring a pair back to the United States when he returned from his tour of ministerial duty.

Roosevelt was an American journalist, soldier, diplomat, and writer. Throughout his entire public life he was a newspaper man who somehow managed to have a front row seat wherever history was in the making. His appointment as U.S. minister to Hungary was to last only two and a half years (from 1930–33) but he came home not only with two Pulis but also with a sincere regard for the diligence, self-discipline, and contentment of the industrious peasants who cared for the animals on the big estates. He resumed his newspaper career with the New York papers, married a Californian, Tirzah Maria Gates, in 1936, and made his home in Hewlett, New York.

After a third bout with pneumonia, Roosevelt gave up his job with the *New York Times* and its radio station WQXR, and he and his wife made the decision to move from the pressures of the big city to their vacation home on the Californian coast at Big Sur, where they could enjoy good health, the beauty of nature, and have time for writing. This was in October of 1946.

There is no doubt but that their Pulis were a part of this new household. Nikkito (so named by Mrs. Ben Vezerian, who became his owner) was whelped on February 24, 1947. His sire was Sandor, his dam was Erzi. That this pair was not, as has been reported, the original pair Mr. Roosevelt imported from Hungary is quite evident from their pedigrees. Nikkito's grandparents were (from Sandor) Samoz and Duna; (from Erzi) Mereg Duda and Duna. Samoz and Duna had the same sire and dam: Tarcsai Bikfic and Celia. Mereg Duda was from Bakonyi Toncsi out of Juli II. Bakonyi Toncsi and Juli II had the same sire and dam: Szikancsi Buksi and Zsuzsi Pasztor. (Tarcsai Bikfic was also the sire of Drava as well as Duna. His sire was Istenhegyi Almos Bago and his dam was Somogyi Ciganylany.) It is not surprising that Bronson Williams recommended that Mrs. Owen chance an outcross with a German stud for Juli II when she acquired her as Skysyl's foundation bitch.

Early Puli owners in the California area do not recall the Roosevelt Pulis having more than one litter, and that one was not arranged for profit. However, others were added to the Roosevelt household many years later.

The American Kennel Club recognized the Puli as a member of the Working Group of Pure-bred Dogs in the year 1936. Shown in numbers for the first time at the Westminster show, there was an entry of 8 Pulis, combined sexes, and it was a 5-point major. Reports of entries at this show vary from 23 to 40. Statistics of AKC registration belie these astounding figures. The first Puli to be registered (September 15, 1936) with the AKC was the bitch Torokvesz Sarika, owned by Louis Kiss. In all, there were 12 registered in 1936, 5 in '37, 9 in '38 and 12 each in '39 and '40. (Total Puli registrations through the end of 1967 reached 3,662.)

However, important as these first Puli breeders were to our Puli history in the United States, they would have still remained virtually unknown had it not been for a little grey Puli that captured the hearts of Sylvia and Schuyler Owen and set in motion the publicity that is still in evidence today.

Most Puli owners are familiar with the story of this Puli, named Juli II, that became the foundation bitch of the Owens' Skysyl Puli Kennels. Until Juli came into their lives, they had never heard of a Puli, much less seen one. She had been bred by Bronson

Williams at his Trinity Farm and had been sold at the age of two months to his friend Archibald Clark for tryout as a stock herder on his large Pennsylvania cattle and sheep farm. She worked there for over two years and, when Clark sold his farm, he decided that Juli would make some family a good watch dog and pet. He took her to a man of his acquaintance who was the owner of a tomato-canning plant and lived next door to the Owen family in Hope, New Jersey. This man took one look at this "mongrel-looking, filthy-smelling dog," as Mrs. Owen describes her, and wanted no part of her. He did, however, send Mr. Clark on to the old grist mill, a part of the Owen family homestead where Schuyler Owen worked. And that was the beginning of a love affair that lasted until Juli died at the age of seventeen-and-a-half. Juli, washed and combed and fed, was a welcome addition to the Owen household. Perhaps this is where the brushing and combing began. Certainly from that moment on it never ceased to be considered a primary part of Mrs. Owen's picture of the Puli.

There is a head study of Juli II in the November 1951 issue of *Popular Dogs*. There is also a picture of Ch. Skysyl Apeter-Pan, one of the litter of nine from Juli's mating with Dorgo von Barengrund. Mrs. Owen bought a bitch, Magyar's Bodri, made her a champion and then mated her with Apeter-Pan. He was to be at stud at Skysyl for some time, as was a later-acquired Swiss import, Ch. Baber Buksi von Bukkabranyi, bred by Elisabeth Csengeri and sired by her prize Buksi.

From the time the Skysyl Kennel name was first granted in October of 1949, Mrs. Owen began a publicity campaign that was to result in the organization of the Puli Club of America in 1951. *The American Kennel Gazette* of that time describes it in this way: "Meeting in one of the club rooms on the second day of the West-minster show at Madison Square Garden, a group of Puli fanciers organized the Puli Club of America. While much work still remains to be done, this meeting set the wheels in motion toward the fashioning of a strong parent body of a breed that is still comparatively new to America. Already there is envisioned a broad educational program that will make Pulik nationally known for their many sterling qualities—particularly usefulness to farmers.

"The new club's officers are: George E. McCartney, Pine Ledge Kennels, Box 14, Greenville, R.I., president; Donald Cook,

Magyar Kennels, 62 E. 83 St., New York City, and Mrs. Rudolph de Wardener, West Arlington, Vt., vice-presidents; Mrs. Edna Kaehele, Kraal Kennels, Box 14, Station A, Columbus 1, O., treasurer; and Mrs. Schuyler Owen, Skysyl Kennels, Oyster Bay, L.I., N.Y., secretary."

Four years later, in 1955, after several preliminary meetings, the first official meeting of the Puli Club of California was held. It was to be separate from the Puli Club of America, but intentions were to affiliate at a later date. (There were 13 votes for and 6 against affiliation at that time.) Elected officers were Mrs. Alice Preinitz, president; Earl Pearce, vice-president; Mrs. Zelda Reynolds, secretary; John R. Fletcher, treasurer. Directors were Larry Byrne (3 yr.), Mrs. Clarice Vezerian (2 yr.), and Mrs. Luella Gray (1 yr.).

It is interesting to note that the Pulis of the '40's and '50's were a working breed that had the opportunity of earning in a new country the high esteem which they had been accorded for centuries by shepherds in ancient lands. At West Wind Farm in Lyme, New Hampshire, Mrs. Owen advertised her Skysyl Pulis as "We Breed and Show what we Work—We Work and Breed what we Show."

There was a series of articles in *Popular Dogs* in 1958 on Stock Dogs of the United States by William Southern of Clifton Hill, Missouri (Southern's Collie Farm). The article for September had as a guest writer Mrs. Schuyler Owen, who had written several interesting columns on "The Working Puli." She mentions the fact that herding is very deeply inbred, the shepherding instinct showing in litters under six months old. Citing examples of the fortunate Pulis that were having a chance to prove their versatility, we get a glimpse of "John Shag" in Cameron, Mo., master of 240 acres of cattle, sheep, chicks, and kittens, and of "Witch" who tagged after her sire and dam, Doctor Erdos and Skysyl Borcsa, working cattle at the Bauer farm so that she was prepared for life on a sheep ranch at Little Falls, Idaho. Also made known were many Pulis at farms near the village of Penn Yan in New York, and the story of an Israeli farmer's Puli that was aptly named Hero and safely took a hundred ailing steers down through the mountain passes to the home of the veterinarian when his master could not leave the rest of the herd.

Vacationing Puli owners in Canada and the United States, as well as the friends of Puli owners, report seeing Pulis in various places throughout the countryside. On the Navajo reservation in Colorado, Pulis were seen herding in various areas. Many shepherds there are reported to be Basques from Spain.

The Theodore Stenslands of Lone Oak Puli Kennels in Howardsville, Virginia, got an inquiry one day from Roy May for two or more Pulis to be used for herding sheep on a ranch at Wendover, Utah. Mr. May was chief herder for Carson Brothers, who ran twenty herding dogs the year round for 20,000 head of sheep. A neighboring Basque herder possessed a wonderful herding animal of an unfamiliar breed. They went to a local veterinarian together and learned that this dog was a Puli. Mr. May wanted some like him, and the Stenslands sent him Marcsa, a bitch, Matyi, a 3-year-old male, and two seven-month-old puppies.

The story is told in diary form of their arrival just in time to start for the spring range, of the high passes and snowdrifts, and of the big blizzard that lasted three days and nights. About a hundred lambs were born during this period, and even a Puli puppy proved his worth. The complete account of their adaptability and the owner's delight in them is included in "The Incredible Puli," a long article by Mrs. R. D. McLellan in the November 1957 issue of *Dogs In Canada*.

The fabulous Mrs. McLellan of Montreal, Quebec, brought her Puli, Adolar Von Der Herlingsburg ("Pooch"), with her from Germany in January of 1948. He was, in November of 1948, the first representative of the breed to be recognized by the Canadian Kennel Club. He not only got his championship but earned his CDX as well. His son, Csiko, was also a fine testimonial to the worth of his sire. Both of them made exhibition appearances in the United States. Csiko was entered at Westminster in 1959 and went Best of Winners.

It was due to Mrs. McLellan's untiring efforts that the Associated All Hungarian Breed Club of North America was founded in 1959. As secretary, she also edited the club's newsletter. Other dedicated breeders joined with her in setting the standard because they wanted it to be the FCI International Puli Standard and it was accepted as such.

The first Puli to be registered in Canada, Ch. Adolar von Der Herlingsburg, C.D.X. Owner: Mrs. M. McLellan. Photograph: Mrs. McLellan.

Perhaps the most famous of the Canadian directors was Dr. Guenther Voss, Director of the Assiniboine Park Zoo in Winnipeg. Visitors from all over the world were charmed by his little Puli that was allowed to run free. American directors were D. A. Foster of Richland, New Jersey; Mrs. W. M. Loewenthal of Washington, D.C.; Mrs. John Silny of Portland, Oregon; and Mrs. Francis Benedek of Palo Alto, California (who imported Pulis to the West Coast as early as 1949). Foreign consultants from Hungary, Germany, and Israel made accurate information available. Many United States Puli breeders and owners were members of this club, primarily to avail themselves of the accessibility of information on the Puli and for imported stock.

About ten years ago, a sheepherding Puli owned by J. C. Anderson of Sydney, British Columbia, went Best in Show at

Regina, Saskatchewan, thus finishing a Canadian championship in a blaze of glory. This was an import from Germany named Zumpel von Lechgau. There are still Pulis herding sheep on the western and northwestern plains of the Rockies where they have proved their heritage.

Statistics are readily available on pure-bred show dogs, as those entered in shows in the United States must be AKC registered. The Stud Book of the American Kennel Club is not a book at all but filing and cross-filing information cards that can be fed into the computer for comprehensive data on every dog registered. The American Kennel Gazette, the official publication of the AKC, reports on every breed in every show in the U.S. every month.

Anne Kennedy (PuliKountry Pulis, formerly of San Bernardino, now of Victorville, California) and Ruthlee Becker have extensive

Ch. Csiko von der Herlingsburg, son of Ch. Adolar, was a frequent visitor at American dog shows. He is pictured here going BOW at Westminster in 1959 under judge Mr. Albert Van Court.

files on Pulis entered in show competition in the United States, and, thanks to their cooperation, some little-known facts have come to light.

The first Puli to be shown in an AKC show was Louis Kiss' Torokvesz Sarika. It was on December 6, 1936, at the 24th show of the Newark Kennel Club, Newark, New Jersey; the judge was R. Vagt, and she was the only Puli entry.

The 61st Westminster show on February 10, 11, and 12, 1937, had an entry of 8 Pulis (for a 5-point major). Best of Breed went to Andrashazi Zsuzsi (A-133931), owned by N. Molnar, formerly by Dr. Eichhorn. There were three Kiss Pulis entered in American-bred: Kati De Betyar, Csiba De Vitez, and Ficko De Flotas. In Open class there were (also in order of winning) Andrashazi Zsuzsi (Molnar), Csiba De Vitez (Kiss), Torokvesz Sarika (Kiss), and Matyashegyi Shubas (Molnar).

At the 11th show of the elite Morris and Essex in May of 1937, there were 3500 dogs. Four of them were Pulis. Judged by M. R. Korshin as Best of Breed and Winners Dog was Molnar's Matyashegyi Shubas. Reserve Dog was J. Thury's Kullancs. Winners Bitch and Reserve Bitch were both owned by Kiss; Winner was Zsuzsi (A-127848) and Reserve was Macko De Morgos.

The first AKC recorded show on the West Coast with a Puli entry was in Pasadena on October 29 and 30, 1938. The judge was A. Mitchell and there were two entries, both in the Open class. Best of Breed honors were won by Pusztafia Kormos (listed), owned by Miss F. Weif. Second was Ravasz, owned by H. S. Brandstatter.

At the 18th annual show of the Del Monte Kennel Club (California) there were 456 entries. Three of them were Pulis. Judged by Mrs. S. D. Wall, Best of Breed was given to Fella, owned by W. Parker; Best of Opposite went to Muggins, owned by Mrs. M. E. Pinckard. The third Puli, Dusty, was disqualified.

At the San Mateo (California) show of July 27, 1941, Fella, under D. Shuttleworth, again took the honors, being the only Puli entry.

Pulis owned by Kirst were the first to be shown in Texas in 1940. Also in 1940, there were three Pulis at International in Chicago to be judged by E. Meyer. Two were entered in American-bred. First and Best of Breed went to Yonchee (A-356,590), owned by Mrs. P. J. Gaffney. Second went to Betyar (Szerpusztai), owned by Mrs. W. L. Friedman. Open bitch went to Szerpusztai Csitri (A-295,865), whose owner was R. S. Calt.

Mrs. Alice Preinitz, whose name is synonymous with that of the Puli in Southern California, had a Kiss-bred male, Sobri Joska, whelped in December of 1947. His sire was Bogancs (from Samoz and Duna) and his dam was Kacer-Zsuzsika (from Stefan and Coca—Stefan was by Mereg Duda out of Duna and Coca was from a Drava-Duna mating). Records show that Sobri Joska went Best of Breed at the Los Angeles Kennel Club show in 1950. However, there were few Pulis in competition at that time and it was not until four years later that he got his championship. Mrs. Preinitz was also the organizer of the Puli Club of California and its first president.

Kennels that contributed to Puli history in the United States in the late 1950's and early 1960's, in addition to Skysyl and Cedwood in the East, Gooseberry Hill in the Midwest, and Shagra and Sczyr in California (still existing today) were Pinepath, Kylend, Marlise, Anka, and Woodsyl (all in the East).

Marlise Kennel stock was acquired for the most part from Joseph de Lengyel. Mr. de Lengyel is even at the present time importing Pulis from Hungary, mostly blacks and a few whites.

Top dog of the sixteen Pulis at the Alma Nemes farm in Naperville, Illinois, for many years was Titzko, whelped in 1942 and bred by Louis Kiss. Mrs. Nemes, one of the first breeder-exhibitors, had show horses and sheep as well as show Pulis. She owned the first champion bitch in the United States: Ch. Czigany Tanczos, C.D. (Suzy), bred by Bronson Williams, whelped March 8, 1946 (Duna x Mereg Duda). Suzy got her C.D. in 1948, her AKC championship in 1949, her Canadian championship in 1950. She was also the first Puli to place in the Working Group—a Group 4th.

Pulis that flashed all too briefly across the scene were Dr. Andrew Peterson's Black Primadonna in the East and Nikkito in the West. Black Primadonna was the dam of Skysyl's Peterson's Best, whose picture headed the Puli column in the *Gazette*, written by Sylvia Owen for several years. Nikkito, Roosevelt-bred in California, was from all accounts a beautiful silver in color. His claim to posterity lies in the fact that he was the foundation stud of the Garshun Puli Kennels of Mrs. Ben Vezerian in Monrovia, California. From

Nikkito came Arpad, owned by Stewart and Zelda Reynolds of Bakersfield, California, and beginning of the Arpad strain on the West Coast.

Reynolds was the envy of others as well as Puli owners at the dog shows. He idly watched the Puli judging through all the classes with Inky (Ch. Arpad) relaxing under his chair, then only to enter the ring and walk out with a Best of Breed trophy. Inky was not only an American champion but a Mexican one also, with a CDX, as was Babe (Ch. Sczyr's Zrinyi). A son Ike and a daughter Princess (Ch. Kiraly) and Ch. Sczyr's Suzi B were good representatives of the Arpad line.

The four Pulis representing the Reynold's "Sczyr" kennel are: Ch. Arpad (Inky) and Ike seated on top; lying down below are Mami and Ch. Kiraly (Princess). Photograph courtesy of Sczyr kennel.

Ch. Rodney's Twinkle (Molnar's Trefa X Molnar's Tercsi) one of the early West Coast champions. Owner: Mrs. Luella Gray.

Reynolds didn't stay for group judging in those days because judges weren't paying much attention to the Puli. Group placings for many, many years on the West Coast in the Working Group were consistently awarded to the more familiar German Shepherds, the Doberman Pinschers, the Great Danes, and the Boxers.

An outstanding example of Inky's progeny was Ch. Arpad Vitez, owned by Thomas and Irene Adler, a Puli that was to figure prominently in California-bred pedigrees in the first half of the 1960's. This champion, known as Champ, was used prolifically at stud because of his owner's enthusiasm about bringing the Puli to public notice. Unfortunately, the majority of his offspring were not of his quality.

"Tris" (Ch. Rodney's Twinkle), the only champion then owned by the Shagra Kennels of Luella Gray, was by Molnar's Trefa out of Molnar's Tercsi. However, the breeding program at the Shagra Kennels was extensive and most of the Pulis that were sold

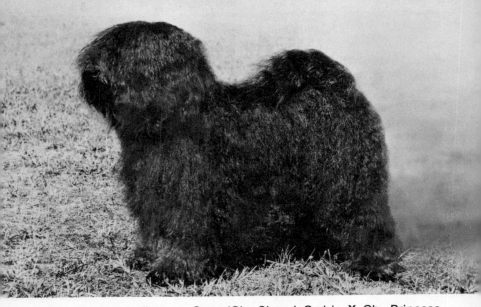

Ch. Cedwoods Antony Gray (Ch. Skysyl Cedric **X** Ch. Princess Woodsmoke). The most famous Puli of his time, he can be found in many of today's Puli pedigrees. Owner: Mrs. Ellanor Anderson, Connecticut.

were not shown. A notable exception, especially in Obedience, was Ch. Shagra's Tasha, who was shown to her UD by owner Sandra Ohrenberger. Later, with the use of imported Hungarian studs, Shagra Kennels bred some outstanding Pulis that won honors in the show ring. Among them were Ch. Shagra's Clown Prince and Ch. Shagra Scaramouche.

Perhaps every kennel has had Pulis that have become headliners in the dog world. Among those that have received wide publicity are Ch. Skysyl Apeter-Pan and Ch. Skysyl Birrichina, who placed in the Working Group (4th) in the early 1950's. Cedwood's superb Ch. Anthony Gray was the first Puli to win the Working Group. He had a remarkable show career under the expert handling of Eric Thomee. In 1966 Ch. Cinkotai Csibesz (Hunnia Puli Kennels, reg.) went Best in Show in Mexico City (an FCI show) and now is the first and only International Puli Champion in the United States. PuliKountry's Ch. Nagykunsagi Csorgo, CD ("Kelly") was the top Puli in Canada for 1968 with a Best in Show. Best in Show honors in the United States were won by Ch. Skysyl Question Being Is It ("Monday"), a bitch owned by Dr. and Mrs. William Lilley. She twice attained this coveted award, shown and campaigned by the late Phillip Fairfield. Her dam, Ch. Kylend's Watch It, owned by Skysyl, was shown throughout her meteoric show career by Anne Hone Rogers. The most recent Best in Show winner, Ch. PuliKountry's Apro, CD, owned by Lois McManus of the Gooseberry Hill Kennels in Wisconsin, won his laurels at Catonsville, Maryland, on October 16, 1971.

The impartial observer of the 1960's found himself asking the question, "Why was there still such a variation in appearance—size, coat, and even color—after a period of almost thirty years?"

The answer is amazingly simple: American breeders didn't know enough about the breed. The reason why they didn't is understandable. Normally, as in other breeds, there would have been a

Ch. Pusztafi Jatszi CD. (Pusztafi Hajdu **X** Pusztafi Dade). Owner: Mrs. Benninger.

63

Combining the best from the East and West are PuliKountry's Impact (Ch. Nagykunsagi Csorgo C.D. X Zsuzsika) and Ch. Puli Too (Ch. Gay Impala X Zsazsa II), owned by Victor Stiff, president of the Puli Club of America. Photograph: C. Reif.

stud book; there would have been readily available information on the breed by recognized authorities in its land of origin; there would have been communication between Americans and Hungarians. But this was not the case with the Puli in the United States.

By the time the Puli came to the attention of the early breeders the world was at war and the ill-fated star of Hitler had already risen in Europe. Hungary was having her troubles and finally allied herself with the Axis powers, only to be taken over by Russia two years after the peace treaty was signed. For many years following, there was to be virtually no communication between Hungarians and people abroad.

The eminent Dr. Imre Bordacs of Budapest, internationally recognized authority on the Puli, spoke at the first National Puli Fanciers Convention in Los Angeles, California, in June of 1968. He gave an excellent statement of the reason for this lack of conformity in the United States Pulis as he discussed unrestricted practices in breeding in Hungary in the 1930's. These practices had to do with the early Puli standard in which there were four size divisions and the breeders did not separate their breeding stock. Had they done so, there would have been a real program and restrictions. (Color always remained the same, only restricting the size of the white spot.)

"Such unrestricted practices," said Dr. Bordacs, "were also found outside of Hungary where the dogs imported before the Second World War were bred without benefit of direction from the country of origin, without determined goals or flow of fresh bloodlines, and where breeding in an environment foreign to the Puli was often left to the whims and inclinations of individual breeders."

Looking at the 1960's we find a hodgepodge of things that shouldn't happen to any breed, but invariably do. On the one hand, we have outstanding individual examples of the breed making the kind of impression all Puli owners applaud. On the other hand, there are breeders who indiscriminately breed just to supply demands of the market.

Throughout all of these years, the Puli Club of America was static, publicized for the most part by the Skysyl Kennels, which in the ensuing years moved about the New England states. The club seemed to function only in the areas of grooming, stud service, show reports, and new litters whelped. Will Judy, editor of *Dog World*, had written Mrs. Owen at the club's beginning in April of 1951 that he hoped the new club would carry on actively and be more than just a paper organization. In his words, "To love the Puli is not enuf—these Puli folks must spend time, effort and money to keep the breed before the public." But, though Mrs. Owen spent time, effort, money, and love, the fact remains that her kennel records and her breeding became an individual effort, and the club remained primarily a paper organization.

About the year 1960 this club made a formal suggestion to the Puli Club of Southern California about incorporating with their organization, but the western Puli club, still recuperating from the "suggestion" of the American Kennel Club to change the club's name from Puli Club of California to Puli Club of Southern California, did not feel the eastern club had anything to offer its members at that time. In California, the PCSC was having monthly meetings and many activities where one could share the joy of ownership with other Puli fanciers. The Puli Club of America was only offering a yearly specialty held in the East with a concurring annual meeting and brief issues of "The Puli News." This situation gave rise to the activity on the West Coast and the following years' achievements which have dominated the history of the Puli in the United States from approximately 1963.

It is of primary importance that Puli owners know the main differences between the organization of dog breeds in the United States and that in other parts of the world. The governing body to whose regulations all owners of pure-bred dogs in the United States are subject is the American Kennel Club. Registration with the AKC is necessary before a dog can be shown at a purebred dog show. The only thing—and this is important to remember—that the AKC guarantees as far as registration is concerned is that the dog is pure-bred, as testified by an acceptable pedigree.

In Hungary there are procedures for controlling the bloodlines, the degree of inbreeding and line breeding, and the number of surviving progeny. This is in accordance with the procedures of the FCI (Federation Cynologique Internationale) and applies to all other countries outside Hungary, with the exception of the United States. The American Kennel Club, not being a member of the

Ch. Kylends Watch It (Skysyl Christopher Columbus, C.D.X. **X** Georgia Mese). Owner: Mrs. Sylvia Owen of the Skysyl Puli kennels. Photograph: E. Schafer.

FCI, exercises no control over the breeding of the Puli. That is the sole responsibility of the individual breeder.

Even before the AKC acceptance of Hungarian imports to the United States, the Puli Club of Southern California was making an effort to inform Puli owners of the Puli standard by having scoring matches. This was a totally new innovation and it was a successful one. Pulis were judged in four rings by four judges according to the AKC standard of excellence as correlated with the Hungarian point scale. The results were arrived at in much the same way as points in Obedience trials today. In obedience, a

Ch. Skysyl Up and Away (Ch. PuliKountry's Apro C.D. **X** Ch. Maro-
ebe's Anything Goes). Owners: Mrs. Sylvia Owen and Miss Anne
Bowley. Photograph: E. Schafer.

Ch. Skysyl Question Being Is It (Ch. Skysyl November Leaf X Ch. Kylends Watch It). Owners: William Lilley III and Beverly K. Lilley. The first Puli to win BIS in the U.S. (Florida, 1968). Photograph: E. Schafer.

dog is credited with 200 points and any deviation from an exercise is subtracted from this total. In these breed scoring matches, every Puli was entitled to 100 points, deviations in various categories of conformation being taken away from his score. There was an added restraint, however, with the notation that in Hungary a Puli with a score of under 70 points was not considered acceptable for registration.

The beginning of 1963 heralded an event that was to become so far-reaching in its importance and effect as to stand out as the most definitive factor of the last decade contributing to the recognition of the Puli as a contending force in American dog circles. This was when, on January 16, 1963, the American Kennel Club placed on their records the MEOE (Magyar Ebtenyesztok Orszagos Egyesu-

Ch. Skysyl Watch It Again (Ch. Skysyl Up and Away X Ch. Kylend's Watch It), owned by Mrs. Ellen M. Iverson. Photograph: J. Ludwig.

Ch. Cedwood's Hedy Gray (Ch. Cedwood's Pierre X Cedwoods Tina), owned by Mr. G. Allen Scruggs of New York. Photograph by E. Schafer.

lete), the Hungarian Kennel Club, with consideration given to those export pedigrees (governing 3 complete generations and bred in Hungary) issued by the MEOE on native breeds. (As always, the AKC reserves the right of rejecting an application in case of unacceptable entries in the pedigree.)

For many years this request had been desired by the Puli Club of America but it had always been impossible. Other breeds imported from Europe had experienced problems getting acceptance into the AKC Stud Book Register. Many difficulties were cleared upon receipt of up-to-date Stud Books. (For example, in 1949, imports from Belgium, Denmark, Norway, Sweden, and

Skysyl Watch Out (Ch. Skysyl Up and Away X Ch. Skysyl Sketch In Shaded Gray). Owners: Stanley H. and Betty Ann N. Dole. Note how the proper grooming has retained the excellent texture of the coat. Combing, when done properly, does not necessarily have to ruin the Puli's coat.

Switzerland were considered for registration in the name of the importer with proper import papers.)

It was through the efforts of the Puli Club of Southern California that this was accomplished. Credit is due primarily to Leslie Benis and June Kirkpatrick for implementing this correspondence with Mr. Neff, then Executive Vice-President of the American Kennel Club.

Research on the breed in the early 1960's yielded few returns and Puli owners were suffering from a lack of communication and information (much of which had been questionable as well as contradictory). It was essential that all Puli owners be reached, not only the breeders and exhibitors. So we had in March of 1963 the

Ch. Shagra Scaramouche (Ali Star of Hunnia X Shagra Margitka). Owners: W. Buell Jr. and Mrs. Luella Gray. No. 3 Puli in U.S. 1968, 1969 according to the Phillips rating system. Photograph by J. Ludwig.

first edition of *PuliKeynotes*, the official club publication of the Puli Club of Southern California, created and designed by its first editor, the author of this section. Breed columnist was Leslie Benis (now of the internationally known Hunnia Puli Kennels of Tarzana, California). Show reporter was Anne Kennedy, whose PuliKountry Pulis have enjoyed wide acclaim. Obedience columnist was Sandra Ohrenberger, whose Puli Tasha had both her breed championship and her UD. (She is now Mrs. Howard Cross and is still actively interested in obedience training, as is her husband, who is an instructor as well as an obedience judge.) The editor, determined to make the publication interesting for all Puli owners and prospective owners, interspersed such information and material as would give a lighter touch to keep the publication in balance.

The creation of an information outlet such as *PuliKeynotes* could not have been done at a more opportune time. Events were shaping that would have far-reaching effects upon the Puli in the United States.

With the AKC acceptance of Hungarian pedigrees, there were new recognized bloodlines to reinforce the Puli strain in this country. There is no question but that this achievement must surely stand as the most important milestone in the history of the breed since its acceptance by the American Kennel Club. It dominated the Puli scene to such an extent that the breed was revitalized and began its journey back to the breeding of the Puli characteristics that had so marked the specific traits of the Pulis of the late 1930's, 1940's, and the early 1950's.

At the time this was achieved, there was wide-spread approbation from breeders all over the country because it was a long-cherished hope that was finally realized. But with the advent of the first imports to Southern California, there was a diversified opinion regarding the wisdom of such a step. The differences in the imports were so marked as to size, weight, color, and coat as to create a great deal of dissension. But it was not until the imports with their corded coats began to become serious contenders for honors in the show ring that established breeders in the United States began to be stirred out of their lethargy and began denigrating the imports and perpetrating the myth of the "American version" of the breed with emphasis on the combed-out coat.

Ch. Shagra Piroska C.D. (Ch. Shagra Csiko X Shagra Trilby). Owner-handled by Barry Becker. Judge: the author. Photograph: J. Ludwig.

To the best of my knowledge, this is the only breed that numbers among its fanciers, and even breeders, some who persist in referring to the Puli in the United States as the "American version."

Do you hear mention of the "American version" of the Old English Sheepdog?, the Norwegian Elkhound?, the Irish Setter?, the Rhodesian Ridgeback?, or the Welsh Corgi? There are countless other breeds whose fanciers are proud of their breed's country of origin, and they try with dedication and true humility to maintain the breeds as close to their natural state as possible.

There is an analogy drawn by a perceptive Puli owner who paraphrased an old saw in this manner:

Official, filling out form for dog license: "It's an American Puli, isn't it?"

"No," replied the Puli owner. "All her ancestors were Hungarians, therefore she is Hungarian."

"But she was born in America?"

"Yes, but if she had her pups in my stable, I wouldn't call them horses."

It did not help the situation in the minds of American breeders that a wealth of Puli history which had been offered them and that they had rejected now appeared in published form. The year 1964 saw the publication of *The Puli*, edited by Dr. Sandor Palfalvy of Birmingham, Alabama. Dr. Palfalvy is a surgeon whose spare time away from his profession and his Pulis was spent researching the early history of the entry of the Puli into domestic life.

It was the late Dr. Fred Thardy of Tuscaloosa, Alabama, who, realizing the importance of Dr. Palfalvy's incredible gathering of data in twenty years of research, made him see that such knowledge must be shared. So the Thardys became the publishers of *The Puli*, and with the translation into English from the original Hungarian, all Puli owners had the privilege of, among other things, "Roaming on Ancient Puli Tracks." This is a compilation of his published information in *The Puli* and his search for facts that scientifically prove the Puli's existence as a shepherd dog from the Sumerian civilization of thousands of years ago. A linguist of great ability, Dr. Palfalvy has not only gathered books, drawings, and photostatic data from museums all over the world, but he also enjoys the cooperation of and correspondence with scientific research colleagues all over the world.

The Csardas Kennels' foundation stud Am./Mex. Ch. Matyasfoldi Kapuore Bitang (Burkus Picike X Bogancs). "Mishka" (Hungarian import) is pictured here with owner-handler Mrs. Mickey Breckenridge, going BOB. Photograph: L. Olson Studios.

"It is impossible that you would take all this information about Pulis and other Hungarian breeds to the grave with you," Dr. Thardy told Dr. Palfalvy, and so it was that *The Puli* came into being.

A severe heart attack prevented Dr. Palfalvy from continuing to edit *The Puli*; and, although plans had been made to revive publication, the untimely death of Dr. Thardy prevented its resumption. "Roaming on Ancient Puli Tracks" will, however, be a book in the near future. Archeology has always yielded information on ancient civilizations whose records had been lost in antiquity, about people, their mode of living, their dress, their animals, and their personal lives. Research is a slow and never-ending process, and each year adds to our knowledge.

There is not too much known about the Pulis in the far reaches of the United States. The first Puli in Hawaii, owned by Honolulu's famous Chief of Police, Dan Liu, was acquired from Alice Preinitz, the second from Luella Gray. The long quarantine in the Islands has had a deterrent effect on the animal import trade. The first appearance of a Puli in Alaska show rings was in June of 1959. The largest number of entries (11) was at the Anchorage show of May 1963. Subsequent shows were never as large. There are only two major shows a year in Alaska and it is difficult to develop champions.

The few families in Alaska that have Pulis live in Anchorage and nearby towns. Their original stock came from kennels of the eastern United States. There have been very few litters whelped in Alaska because, according to Catherine Donaho, "We just can't sell a puppy to someone who would treat it as if it were a dog." So the owners keep most of the puppies, having from two to eight as members of the family. They patrol the home grounds, guarding all the approaches, and especially taking care of the toddlers of the family. The Alaskan earthquake of March 27, 1964, with its seismic sea wave which damaged downtown Anchorage very heavily, brought out all the protective instincts of the Puli for family and property that had not been tested to that ultimate degree.

Mrs. Donoho's Arctic Pride was given the Anchorage SPCA award for his action when his master became ill at his home. The Puli raced to the road and refused to yield the right of way to traffic. He succeeded in forcing drivers to stop and then, by barking and leading the way, persuading them to follow him to the Donoho home. As fame of his heroism spread, Arctic Pride appeared on television, received broad newspaper publicity, and even participated in a fashion show.

There are Puli owners all over America who have been taking their Pulis to obedience training classes. Many of them have entered formal competition and have received their CD's (Companion Dog degree). The first Puli to get his CD was Dongo, owned by George McCartney, who was the first president of the Puli Club of

Mishka's number one champion son is Ch. Csardas' B'gosh of Sczyr (Ch. Matyasfoldi Kapuore Bitang **X** Sczyr's Grey Babe). Owner: Mr. Larry Jiminez, Stockton, California.

Ch. Csardas' Bandit of Sczyr (Ch. Matyasfoldi Kapuore Bitang **X** Sczyr's Grey Babe), owner-handled to his title by Michael Curran of Van Nuys, California. Judge: Mr. Robert Ward. Photograph: Henry Schley.

America. Many of the Puli breeders of the 1950's had obedience-trained Pulis, though there were relatively few that attained formal recognition. A notable exception was Georgia Putz; he won his UD in 1955, the first Utility Dog in the United States. He was bred, owned, and trained by Rudolph de Wardener at Bethany Farm in North Stonington, Connecticut. The de Wardeners often advertised puppies from their Georgia Kennels as "Not just a dog— but a Puli for I.Q." They also showed in the Canadian shows with high honors.

To Howard Trautwein, who has an obedience school in Buffalo, New York, the Puli is the undiscovered gold mine for the obedience ring. "To own a Puli and not train him to obey commands is like owning a Cadillac and not learning how to drive. In both cases a marvelous piece of machinery deteriorates and much pleasure is lost to the owner. Like the expensive car," says Mr. Trautwein, "your Puli is loaded with power and something more. He deserves to have a chance to use his retentive mind."

Familiar faces in the California rings were actor-director Bert Freed with CDXer Face and Sandy Ohrenberger with Tasha, who won her UD as well as her championship. Another outstanding Puli who was a Champion in both areas was Ch. Rongy Baba ("Pupa"), owned by Loretta Schoellenbach. Pupa not only had her American UD but also its equivalent in Mexico, the P.U. Another Puli owner with UD Pulis is Mary Jane Richert of San Diego. One of them, her Ch. Zelda Plunkett, is also a breed champion and has numerous trophies for high-scoring dogs in many California shows. The first UD in Canada for a Puli was won in 1968 by David Sly's Misha of Magyar Puszta. The latest UD of record at this time of writing is Mike Ruecker's Koshka's Ancsa of Hunnia. There are also several promising UD candidates that already have their CDX degrees. No "tracking" Puli has been reported yet, but that will, no doubt, be just a matter of time. Since that is the ulti-mate in Obedience degrees, a Puli will meet that challenge in his own inimitable way.

No history of the Puli in the United States would be complete without mention of the contributions to the knowledge of the breed made by the efforts of the Puli Club of Southern California and many of its outstanding members. Although its title is restric-tive, its scope is extensive, and Puli owners in the United States

Another fine example of new breeding efforts is Ch. Kara's Marco (Int. Ch. Cinkotai Csibesz X Ch. Barnavari Baba). Bred by Dr. and Mrs. Cornelius. Posed here by owner Barbara Edwards.

One of Marco's most promising sons, bred by Barbara Edwards and Constance Peterson, is Fekete Gurgi (Ch. Kara's Marco X Juhasz Pajtasa), owned by Patricia and Robert Coleman of Higganum, Connecticut.

and in many foreign lands share their information on the breed. Translations by Klara Benis from the original Hungarian into English have made material about the Puli available to all Puli owners. To others, who have translated from the German publications, we are also deeply indebted.

After the channels of communication had been opened once again with the Hungarian Kennel Club, plans were in the making for the first National Puli Fanciers Convention. It was conceived by the Puli Club of Southern California and was held the day before the PCSC Specialty. Judging the Puppy Sweepstakes at the show, and the featured speaker at the Convention, was Dr. Imre Bordacs, one of the most respected authorities in Europe on the Puli. As a representative of the MEOE, he presented the Puli Club of Southern California with a perpetual trophy for our Specialties of the future. It is a statue of a Hungarian shepherd by sculptor Beszedes. Dr. Bordacs' talk on the true Puli type was ably translated by Oscar Beregi and the question and answer period that followed was moderated by Klara Benis, as interpreter.

We have been privileged since that time to welcome other Puli authorities from foreign lands and they have added much to our knowledge of the breed. Among them were Elizabeth Csengeri of Israel and Sara Nagy of Budapest, both of whom judged the Puppy Sweepstakes and spoke at subsequent conventions. The interesting Erno Kubinszky, DVM, of Budapest and his wife Vally were honored guests at the 1970 PCSC special awards dinner in Santa Barbara, California. Dr. Kubinszky judged the Sweepstakes at our Specialty that year. All speeches (and translations of speeches) were published in *PuliKeynotes* so the information was available for all who could not attend. Puli people visiting Hungary were given the opportunity to see and film the Puli in his native land and to share their experiences upon their return home.

Not only did these conventions have speakers on the Puli but also authorities of other breeds who directed their abilities to specific fields in the world of dogs. Among them were Dr. James G. McCue, Jr. of Idaho Falls, Idaho, who lectured on genetics and its relation to successful breeding; Denver T. Dale (dog structure and motion); Mona Berkowitz (basic foundation for breeding better dogs); Robert Ward (descriptive terminology);

Hunnia's Vallalkozo Tancos (Ch. Star of Hunnia Attila **X** Hunnia's Huncut Hamis) at six months of age with owner-breeder Mrs. Maizelle H. Hart of Beverly Hills, California.

Ch. Hunnia Bator Fenyes Remenye C.D.X. (Int. Ch. Cinkotai Csibesz X Ch. Barnavari Baba). Owners: Mrs. Wilhelmina Ferrando and Mr. Gilbert Pearson of Santa Barbara, California. Photograph: H. Schley.

Yot Club Sobri of Shagra (Shagra Draga Gyongy X Shagra Heidi Pityke). Owners: Mrs. Ferrando and Mr. Pearson. Photograph: J. Ludwig.

Ch. Gyalmezei Pajtas, "Puli"; (Ch. Gyalpusztai Kocos Burkus X Nagykunsagi Mutyur). "Puli", following his sire's footsteps, started his show record late in his life. He won Best Of Breed at two of the Puli Club of America Specialty Shows at the age of eight years, and crowned his records with a Best In Show at the 1975 Plainview, Texas Show at the age of nine years.

William Koehler (temperament); and obedience panels of judges and handlers. Dr. Wilfrid Shuté from Canada, the PCSC Specialty judge in June 1971, decried the use of ambiguous terms in our Puli Standard and urged a revision that would include specifics. He admonished us (and though we have heard it again and again, it always bears repeating) to "keep the working characteristics of the breed for which they were intended."

To realize just to what great extent the Hungarian imports and their offspring have dominated the Puli scene since being accepted by the AKC, one has only to look at the Phillips rating charts of *Popular Dogs*. This is a special yearly feature based on the Best in Show wins and the Group placings of the ten top dogs in each breed. The points are based on the number of dogs over which the win was scored. Ch. Cinkotai Csibesz, owned by Leslie and Klara Benis of the Hunnia Kennels in Tarzana, California, was the top Puli in 1965, 1966, and 1967. He is not only an American Champion, but a Mexican one and an International one, and has won the highest international award (CACIB) five times.

In 1965, three out of six were imports. Second to Csibesz in points in 1965 and 1966 was Amer/Mex Ch. Matyasfoldi Kapuore Bitang (Miska), owned by the Breckenridges of Simi, California. In 1966, the first five out of six were imports or their offspring; in 1967, three out of five; in 1968, five out of seven; in 1969, seven out of ten. Ruthlee Becker, compiling the Puli list for the period 1960 - 70, finds the growth of the list significant in that there was only one Puli in 1960 but ten in 1969. Interesting also were the geographical changes from the East and Midwest to the Far West.

1960	1.	Ch. Cedwood's Anthony Gray
1961	1.	Ch. Gooseberry Hill Bandmaster
1962	1.	Ch. Gooseberry Hill Bandmaster
	2.	Ch. Cedwood's Anthony Gray
	3.	Ch. Puzstafi Jatszi, CD
1963	1.	Ch. Cedwood's Anthony Gray
	2.	Ch. Kylend's Watch It
1964	1.	Ch. Kylend's Watch It
	2.	Ch. Gooseberry Hill Inkling
	3.	Ch. Gooseberry Hill Bandmaster
1965	1.	Ch. Cinkotai Csibesz
	2.	Ch. Matyasfoldi Kapuore Bitang

3. Ch. Nagykunsagi Csorgo, CD   5. Star of Hunnia Ficko
4. PuliKountry's Apro, CD   6. Ch. Kylend's Kelly

1966 1. Ch. Cinkotai Csibesz
       2. Ch. Matyasfoldi Kapuore Bitang
       3. Ch. Nagykunsagi Csorgo, CD
       4. PuliKountry's Apro, CD
       5. Star of Hunnia Ficko
       6. Ch. Kylend's Kelly

1967 1. Ch. Cinkotai Csibesz
       2. Ch. Skysyl Question Being Is It
       3. Ch. Matyasfoldi Kapuore Bitang
       4. Ch. Shagra's Clown Prince
       5. Ch. Gyalpusztai Kocos Burkus

1968 1. Ch. Skysyl Question Being Is It
       2. Ch. PuliKountry's Apro, CD
       3. Ch. Cinkotai Csibesz
       4. Ch. Shagra Scaramouche
       5. Ch. Matyasfoldi Kapuore Bitang
       6. Magyar Murza, CD
       7. Ch. Nagykunsagi Csorgo, CD

1969 1. Ch. Skysyl Question Being Is It
       2. Ch. PuliKountry's Apro, CD
       3. Ch. Shagra Scaramouche
       4. Ch. Tiszaujfalui Pamacs
       5. Ch. Malou's Silver Cedric
       6. Ch. Gyalpusztai Kocos Burkus
       7. Ch. Star of Hunnia Bogancs
       8. Ch. Shagra's Clown Prince
       9. Ch. Matyasfoldi Kapuore Bitang
      10. Ch. Hortobagyi Pajtas Macko

1970 1. Ch. Gyalpusztai Kocos Burkus
       2. Ch. PuliKountry's Apro, CD
       3. Ch. Skysyl Question Being Is It
       4. Ch. Hortobagyi Pajtas Macko
       5. Ch. Skysyl Sketch in Shaded Gray
       6. Ch. Shagra's Clown Prince
       7. Ch. Morgo Csibesz
       8. Ch. Cedwood's Pierre
       9. Ch. Kakaspusztai Bogar Cigany

Another import of the early 1960's is Ch. Erdalsoi Adu Betyar Matyi (Sarlo X Nagykorosi Morcos), who was purchased by the author with hopes to demonstrate his excellent herding abilities. He is pictured here with raggedy coat as he arrived from the fields of Hungary. Because of the lack of herding trials in the California area, "Matyi" could not excel in herding, but he set the standard for pigmentation in a Puli for a long time to come. He possesses and throws in his get the dark brown—almost black—eyes, coal black gums, flews and dark gray skin color.

Fewer than ten dogs listed, observes Mrs. Becker, indicates fewer than ten dogs with group placements.

Ever since the Puli appeared in American dog circles, fanciers have been fascinated by his incredible combination of brains and feet held together by a mop of long hair. As a result, there have been many phrases used to describe him. Ruth Appel of the *San Francisco Chronicle* refers to Pulis as "the eggheads from Hungary." He has also been called a "Beatle Bow-Wow," a rag mop, a trained mop, and even an animated haystack. Canadian cartoonist George Feyer says that he knitted his Puli Molly out of reclaimed wool. To his friend, writer Pierre Berton, Molly is perhaps an incredibly clever canine that has learned to walk backwards. She once disappeared while George was in the rug

Ch. Hunnia's Betyar Macko (Ch. Erdalsoi Adu Betyar Matyi X Pioi Star of Hunnia Aniko). This fine son of "Matyi" is owned by Ray and Lois Powers of Orange, California. Photograph: J. Ludwig.

department of Eaton's, so he asserts, and a customer tried to buy her as an occasional rug for his bedroom until she stuck her tongue out at him. The suggestion has even been made that perhaps the reason for the Puli's herding success is because he looks the same in the front and the back and the sheep can't tell whether he is coming or going. The picture that comes to Robert Ward's mind when he thinks of a Puli is "a small, narrow-gauge railway locomotive flying around a mountain track, wearing a raincoat and hat and bouncing ready for the next turn." One wonders if even Mr. Ward realized to what extend he had captured the essence of the Puli—here is the size, agility, resourcefulness, the sense of motion, and above all, the humor which makes owning a Puli such a delight.

Howard Trautwein's description of a Puli has become a classic. It has been used from coast to coast in Puli publicity since it first appeared in the *AKGazette* of October, 1961, in the Puli column written by Lois McManus. He begins by calling the Puli "a ridiculous mop of hair that goes about pretending he is a dog." He ends by admitting (in view of the fact that his two were reading over his shoulder) "that if you are the type that wants to laugh your life away and have a dog look at you as though you were God, buy a Puli! Buy two Pulik! Raise Pulik! Some day they will rule the world anyway."

Be that as it may, there now seems to be greater emphasis on the individual breeder-owners than in the past, especially if they do not live in an area where a kennel license may be obtained. By selective breeding, these owners are showing superior stock in the show ring today.

But civilization inexorably moves on. It was inevitable that urbanization would swallow up the vast grasslands where once sheep and cattle grazed. Many young people left the farms for work and life in the cities. Many of the older rural people retired to a less strenuous life in nearby towns. But now the trend seems to have reversed itself. Young people are rediscovering the good earth. Young parents are moving out of the huge metropolitan areas, looking for clean air, clear skies, and a healthful, wholesome way of life for their children. Perhaps the days of the small farms and ranches will come again, and out in the open spaces the Puli

Hunnia's Akaratos Lurko (Ch. Erdalsoi Adu Betyar Matyi **X** Ch. Hunnia's Pride O'Misty Tunde). Matyi's other son is the finest example of the laws of genetics. He is a carbon copy of his father to the smallest details in structural make-up as well as in behavior. Owner: Mrs. Toni McLaughlin. Photo: R. Klein.

Ch. Thunder Mount Arpad (Acsi of PuliKountry **X** Star of Hunnia Furtos) is building fame for this relatively new Puli kennel. He is shown here handled by owner-breeder Miss Augusta Planck, going BOB at a Kennel Club of Beverly Hills Show. Judge is the author.

may again be the "little king of the sheepherders." Stranger things than that have happened.

This great little dog has a heritage so rich we are just becoming aware of hitherto untapped sources of information about him. A study of the Puli as it is presented in these chapters cannot help but add greatly to the knowledge and understanding of how and why a Puli is "not a dog—he is a Puli."

Chapter 2

THE STANDARD OF THE PULI

THE STANDARD OF THE PULI

The following is a partial quote from the "Breed Histories" section of the *Complete Dog Book*, the official publication of the American Kennel Club. The description of the Puli is so perfect in this section that it should be considered the foreword to the Official Standard.

"The Puli (plural Pulik), or driver, has been an integral part of the lives of Hungarian shepherds for more than 1000 years. When the Magyars came into Hungary they brought their sheepdogs with them. . . . Color and size both played a part in the development of Hungary's sheepdogs, each for its particular type of work. The more easily seen, lighter-colored kinds guarded herds and flocks from robbers and wild animals at night, while the smaller, darker-colored Puli was used to drive and herd the sheep during the day. There was ample reason for this, since sheep take direction more certainly from dark dogs then from light-colored ones. Moreover the dark dog was more distinctive to the shepherd's eye, as it worked among the flocks rounding them up and even so, it is claimed, jumping on them or running over their backs to cut off or turn back a runaway.

"The dark color has always been recognized as truly characteristic of the Puli. Ordinarily it is called black, but it is a black so unlike that of any other breed as to warrant explanation. It is dull; in some cases bronze-tinged, in others just barely grayed like a weather-worn old coat faded by the sun. An out-of-door life on the hillside, in all weathers but particularly under a constant and glaring sun, robbed the black of its intensity and its sheen. This was the black prized as typical of the breed in its homeland. There are, in addition, Pulik both gray and white. Any shade of gray is allowed so long as it is solid gray. The Puli is first and last a solid-colored dog. There may be some intermixture of hair of different colors usually present in the grays, and this is acceptable if the general appearance of solid color is maintained.

"The Puli coat, too, is unique. There is nothing exactly like it in all dogdom. The undercoat is soft, wooly, very dense; the outer coat long and profuse. The puppy coat is tufted, but with growth the undercoat tangles with the top coat in such a manner as to form long cords. . . .

". . . He is a medium-sized dog averaging seventeen inches height and thirty pounds or so weight, and so striking in appearance that it would be impossible to confuse him with any other kind of dog. His shaggy hair covers his head like an umbrella, and falls all over his body to the very tip of his up-curled tail in such profusion that he seems larger than he actually is. He is keen and quick, and he moves with a gait as springy, almost, as a bouncing ball, this trait a hand-me-down, perhaps, from those dogs of long ago whose dazzling footwork was the admiration of the shepherd boy with his sheep."

NOTE:
The portions of the following discussion appearing in regular type are the American standard; the portions set in italic type are the Hungarian standard.

GENERAL APPEARANCE

A dog of medium size, vigorous, alert, and extremely active. By nature affectionate, he is a devoted and home-loving companion, sensibly suspicious of strangers and therefore an excellent guard. Striking and highly characteristic is the shaggy coat which centuries ago fitted him for the strenuous work of herding the flocks on the plains of Hungary.

The Puli is medium sized. Lively, nimble, intelligent, undemanding, of sturdy constitution, fine boned, wiry. The whole body is quite sinewy. Its trunk and limbs form a square figure. It is difficult to observe the individual parts of its body, for the whole body is covered with long, profuse, wavy hair that is inclined to get matted and felty. Its long hair overshadows the eye like an umbrella, and so the head seems to be round. The rump may give an appearance of being higher, due to the heavily coated tail curling over the back. It is not possible to trace closely the outlines of the rump, nor the single parts of the limbs by visual inspection. It is an ancient species of Hungarian sheepdog of Asiatic origin, that serves excellently as a herding dog, as well as a watchdog. In fact, some individuals are even used for guarding and police work.

THE HEAD

Head—of medium size, in proportion to the body. The skull is slightly domed and not too broad. Stop clearly defined but not abrupt, neither dished nor downfaced, with a strong muzzle of medium length ending in a nose of good size.

Disregarding hair, it is on the whole rather small and fine. From the front it appears round; from the side almost elliptical. The skull is domed. The muzzle is not snipy, but bluntly rounded. The nose relatively large, black in color as are the eyelids and flews. Its upper and lower jaws are equally fully developed.

TEETH

Teeth—are strong and comparatively large, and the bite may be either level or scissors. Flews tight.

Its teeth are regular and strong. Its incisors close like scissors. The lower canine teeth are disposed more forward; the upper canine immediately behind them. The remaining teeth cover each other. The flews fit tight to the set of teeth.

EARS

Ears—hanging and set fairly high, medium sized, and V-shaped.

Its ears are medium set and take up at once a hanging posture. These do not move upwards, even when alerted: they are V-shaped.

EYES

Eyes—Deep-set and rather large, should be dark brown, but lighter color is not a serious fault.

Its eyes are of dark coffee brown color. The expression is lively, sensible, and intelligent.

NECK AND SHOULDERS

Neck, strong and muscular, of medium length, and free of throatiness. Shoulders clean-cut and sloping, with elbows close.

The Puli's neck forms an angle of forty-five degrees to the horizontal. It is of medium length, tight and muscular. As a consequence of the profuse coat, the neck is not noticeably separate from the body. If the neck does appear noticeably separated from the body, it is indicative of some fault.

BODY

The chest is deep and fairly broad with ribs well sprung. Back of medium length, straight and level, the rump sloping moderately. Fairly broad across the loins and well tucked up.

The withers are elevated just slightly over the level of the back. The back is tight and straight. Its back is of medium length, and the loin is short. The ribs are slightly stave-like. The rump is short and slightly sloped (but does not strike the eye because of the tail curling over the rump). . . The chest is medium broad, deep, and long. The forelimb fits tightly to the foreparts of the chest. The stomach is slightly tucked up. The brisket is the lowest point of the body. A wide pelvis is desirable, especially with bitches.

TAIL

Occasionally born bobtail, which is acceptable, but never cut. The tail is carried curled over the back when alert, carried low with the end curled up when at rest.

There are eighteen to twenty tail vertebrae. The tail is curled over the rump-loin area.

The long hair of the tail mixes indistinguishably with the similar hair of the rump so that the tail does not appear separate.

LEGS AND FEET

Forelegs straight, strong, and well boned. Feet round and compact with thick-cushioned pads and strong nails. Hindquarters well developed, moderately broad through the stifle which is well bent and muscular. Dewclaws, if any, may be removed from both forelegs and hind legs.

The shoulder blade is tightly attached to the chest. (The point of shoulder should be in line with the forepart of the chest). The shoulder blade forms an angle of ninety degrees with the upper limb. The upper limb should be of medium length, strong-muscles, elbowed neither out nor in. The forearm and the upper limb enclose an angle of 120 to 130 degrees. The forearm is long and straight, and vertical in direction. Its musculature is lank. All parts underneath the forelimb should be short and dry. The metacarpus is vertical. The second digital bone is forty five degrees to the horizontal, with a short third digital bone. The paws are short, roundish, and tight. The nails are black or slate-grey colored. The pad is full, springy, dark grey in color. The stand is medium broad. . .

The lower thighbone and upper thighbone are long and richly muscles. The pelvis forms an angle of ninety degrees with the upper thighbone. The upper and lower thighbone enclose an angle of 100 to 110 degrees. Deviation from this angulation in either direction is undesirable. The hock is gaunt, and the parts beneath it are short and dry. The metatarsus is vertical. The third digital bone somewhat longer. The second digital bone forms a smaller angle to the horizontal than the fore one; the hind paws are therefore a bit longer. The nails are stronger, black or slate-grey. The pads are strong, resilient, and dark grey in color.

COAT

Characteristic of the breed is the dense, weather-resisting double coat. The outer coat, long and of medium texture, is never silky, it may be straight, wavy or slightly curly, the more curly coat appearing to be somewhat shorter. The undercoat is soft, woolly, and dense. The coat mats easily, the hair tending to cling together in bunches, giving a somewhat corded appearance even when groomed. The hair is profuse on the head, ears, face, stifles, and tail, and the feet are well haired between the toes. Usually shown combed, but may also be shown uncombed with the coat hanging in tight, even cords.

Its coat consists of rougher upper hair and finer undercoat. The proportion of these determines the quality of the coat. Much upper hair and sparse undercoat results in an open coat. Too much undercoat and not enough of the upper hair creates excessive matting and felting. The correct proportion of these two kinds of hair creates the desired narrow felted form. This corded form consists of uniform, but tightly wavy hair. This type of hair readily forms long cords which are less inclined to become matted. The coat is longest on the rump, loin, and thigh 8 to 18 cm (3¼" to 7"); shortest on the head and paws 4 to 6 cm (1½" to 2½"). But there are also some individual examples where the coat may even reach the ground. After bringing forth offspring, in work, due to illness, or insufficient foraging, the Puli may lose part or, in exceptional cases, all of its coat. Partial loss of coat generally occurs on the fore part of the trunk and chest, the forelimbs and the stomach. It is difficult to make an accurate judgment of such an example. A combed coat is undesirable, as is a completely neglected one.

COLOR

Solid colors, black, rusty

black, various shades of grey, and white. The black usually appears weathered and rusty or slightly grey. The inter-mixture of hair of different colors is acceptable and is usually present in the grays, but must be uniform throughout the coat so that the over-all appearance of a solid color is maintained.

Nose, flews and eyelids are black.

The Puli may be found in different colors. Presently acceptable are: black (rusty black), various shades of grey, and white . . . On the chest you can tolerate a lack of pigment (white spot) of not more than five cm (2.5 inches) in diameter. A few scattered white hairs in the pad may also be tolerated. Any other markings are undesirable.

Its skin is slate-grey colored, thus it contains much pigment. Regardless of coat color, the skin has a uniformly deep pigmentation. The skin's free surfaces (nose, flews, eyelids) are black. The roof of the mouth is uniformly dark or variegated with deep pigmented spots on dark base. The tongue is bright red. The nails and pads are black or slate grey.

HEIGHT

Males about 17 inches and should not exceed 19 inches. Females about 16 inches and should not exceed 18 inches.

Height at the withers as measured with a stick:

MALES:

Desirable height: 40 to 44 cm (15¾ to 17 3/8 inches). Permissible height: 37 to 39 cm or 45 to 47 cm (14 ½ to 15 3/8 or 17¾ to 18½ inches).

BITCHES:

Desirable height: 37 to 41 cm (14½ to 16 1/8 inches). Permissible height: 34 to 36 cm or 42 to 44 cm (13 3/8 to 14 1/8 or 16½ to 17 3/8 inches).

The comparative sizes of single proportions of the body expressed in percentage of the height at the withers are:

Length of trunk:	100%
Depth of the chest:	45%
Width of chest:	33%
Belt measurement:	125%
Length of the head:	45%

The length of the muzzle is 35% of the length of the head. The length of the ears is 50% of the length of the head.

Body weight:
Males:
13 to 15 kg (28 to 33 lbs)
Bitches:
10 to 13 kg (22 to 28 lbs)

MOVEMENT

Its stride is not far reaching. Its gallop is short. The movement is short-stepping, very quick and typical, in harmony with its lively disposition. The movement is never heavy, lethargic, or lumbering.

SERIOUS FAULTS

Overshot or undershot. Lack of undercoat, short or sparse coat. White markings such as white paws or spot on chest. Flesh color on nose, flews, or eyelids. Coat with areas of two or more colors at the skin.

Long muzzle, steep carriage of the neck, long body, which is not square, horizontal rump, loose tail carriage. Straight or open coat (lack of undercoat), excessive matting and felting as a result of too much undercoat. Light brown eyes. With males a height between 34 to 37 cm (13 3/8 to 14½ inches) or 47 to 50 cm (18½ to 19.5 inches); with bitches a height of 31-34 cm (12¼ to 13 3/8 inches) or 44 to 47 cm (17 3/8 to 18½ inches).

DISQUALIFICATIONS

None.

Large degree of overshot or any degree of undershot bite.

Erect ears. Straight tail carriage, bobtail, particolor or large marks. Short, straight, open coat. Lack of pigmentation. Chocolate-brown color, showing in the pigment of the skin also. Males under 34 cm (13 3/8 inches) or over 50 cm (19.5 inches). Bitches under 31 cm (12¼ inches) or over 47 cm (18½ inches).

Chapter 3

THE STANDARD IN MORE DETAIL
AND ILLUSTRATED

The average Puli owner today is so enthusiastic over the coat, general appearance, beauty, and the cuteness of his own dog that he sees his dog as the best representative example of the breed, regardless of the dog's structure under its coat and skin. Enthusiasm is a good thing and very necessary, for without it the breed would not be where it is in the United States today. On the other hand, blind loyalty to a certain dog or even to a certain bloodline has yet to advance any breed. There is no advantage for the breed if a good looking but "bad-bited" son of a great winner of the past is advertised, campaigned, and offered at stud. Could the name of any of the great dogs of the past mean that much to anyone? Is it sentiment, or lack of knowledge? Or do we have some breeders who not only do not look under the skin of their dog, but do not look even in the mouth of their own dog? You might ask if this has really happened, that breeders can be so "kennel blind." But, dozens of dogs in various breeds are being advertised for stud, that have faults just as serious or worse than a bad bite, but the faults are hidden under their skin, or in the case of the Puli, under their coat. And we in the breed all realize how much that coat can really hide!

In this respect there are two kinds of dog people. To prove this to yourself, at any dog show or any place where reasonably experienced dog people gather, walk up to one and ask his opinion of your Puli. The first type will step back a couple of steps, take a good look at your dog, walk around it, and if you are lucky, he might ask you to move the dog for him. Then he is ready to give an opinion. The second type of dog person, first will go down on his knees and probably, even without looking at the dog, his fingers will measure every bone in the body of your Puli in just a few seconds. He will try to feel the angulation of the shoulder blade, the angulation of the stifle, and no doubt the height of the hocks. When he has a mental picture of your dog's skeleton he will then ask you to walk your dog. Which person's opinion would you value more? Once we understand the physical requirements needed for a structurally sound dog, such as: mechanical balance, the reasons for certain features, and actions and their causes, we can more truly weigh which is more important, appearance or the mechanics underneath. Then we will be able to separate the important from the fashion trends of the fancy. I do not mean to imply that the Puli's coat and appearance is not important. It is important, but unfortunately in the last few years I have seen the danger signs in this breed, of paying too much attention to coat, creating new colors and size, while completely neglecting what should be underneath that coat structurally. On the other hand, it can be just as bad to see a structurally sound dog in the ring with an inherited silky or thin, sparse, or multicolored coat, or lack of the real Puli "type."

The standard for the Puli was originally written by men who had a thorough knowledge of horses and dogs, and who collected information from hundreds of shepherds who used the Puli. They combined their knowledge of structure and the functional requirements for the breed and recorded it. Unfortunately, few of the Puli breeders today have a knowledge that comes from actual field experience. Even if they are familiar with certain characteristics of the breed that the standard calls for, they are not certain of what these words express, because the connotation of the words themselves do not create a mental picture for them. Even smaller is the number of breeders who know why these characteristics are desired, and called for by the standard. A complete knowledge of dogs in general is necessary to interpret the standard. Everyone who ever plans to produce a single litter or just own a show-quality house pet should be completely familiar with the background of the Puli, his functional requirements, and the basic mechanics of canine anatomy. Why is this knowledge of almost academic level desired? Because it is necessary to avoid the formation of a false mental picture of the breed that can be easily created if someone is not familiar with what is sound or unsound in a dog. When someone decides to become a Puli breeder, he should be careful and conscientious and study the standard and visit several dog shows before making the commitment to breed. But he has no general knowledge of why certain features are required in the standard. The mental picture he has formed is not what the standard describes, but the picture of that champion he has just seen win the last two shows he visited. However, this champion can possess a serious structural fault and still win because the others in competition were just as bad or worse, or because breeders in that certain geographical area were placing too much emphasis on a special feature. If he then goes out with his faulty mental picture and buys a dog for his breeding program, he is liable to buy an unsound dog that happens to have the same eye-appealing exterior features as the champion he has seen. Time passes and this unsoundness can become the trademark of his line or entire kennel.

The standard describes the Puli both by specific characteristics and by overall physical appearance. It does not deal with the question of how to breed these desired characteristics into the Puli. In the show ring we judge the described characteristics one by one, and in comparison to other dogs in the ring. But breeders must be much more demanding than just breeding a dog better than the one he happened to stand next to in the ring. The real judge of our dogs is the one who has the opportunity and knowledge to judge them on performance, and on the ability to function; that is the open minded and knowledgeable breeder who can observe them on long walks, in the back yard, on hikes or during exercise. To do this one has to have a basic understanding of the mechanics of the dog; to know what makes them move with less effort, and to endure better than other specimens. The breeder must understand the reason for such a statement in the standard as ". . . forelegs straight . . . feet round and compact . . . " He must realize that these are not just beauty requirements, but serious parts of a complex structural description that enable the dog to move with good speed for hours and days if he has to (See Figure A). The person who knows that "sloping shoulders" refers to a 45-degree shoulder angulation, and who knows that this saves as much as 25 percent of the energy used while walking, compared to a steep (less angulated) shoulder,

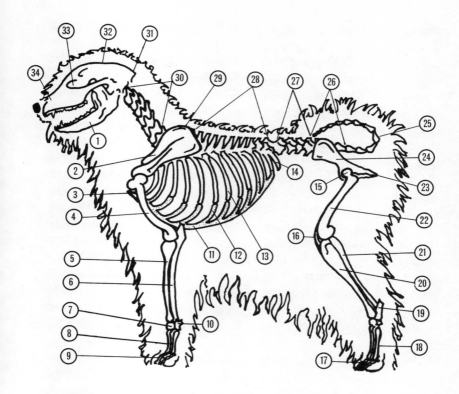

Figure A. Skeleton of the Puli

1. Lower jaw, Mandible. 2. Shoulder blade, Scapula. 3. Front end of sternum, Prosternum. 4. Upper arm, Humerus. 5. Front forearm bone, Radius. 6. Ulna. 7. Pastern joint, Carpus. 8. Pastern, Metacarpus. 9. Toes, Phalanges. 10. Pisiform. 11. Sternum. 12. Costal cartilage. 13. Ribs. 14. Floating rib. 15. Head of femur. 16. Knee joint or stifle, Patella. 17. Phalanges. 18. Metatarsus. 19. Point of hock, Os calcis. 20. Tibia. 21. Fibula. 22. Thigh bone, Femur. 23. Pubis. 24. Pelvic bone, Pelvis. 25. Tail bones, Coccygeal vertebrae. 26. Sacral vertebrae. 27. Lumbar vertebrae. 28. Thoracic vertebrae. 29. Top of shoulder (withers), Scapula. 30. Neck bones, Cervical vertebrae. 31. Occiput. 32. Skull, Cranium. 33. Orbital cavity. 34. Nasal bone.

will be less forgiving of these faults when it comes to comparing them.

This brings us to the excuse most frequently used by those who base their breeding purposes more on the sentiment they feel toward their dogs than on real knowledge: "Our dogs don't work any more!" It is true that they do not run around a flock for sixteen to twenty hours daily. But would any of us mind if they could, if given the opportunity? There is nothing shameful about breeding the capability for tireless performance into our dogs, as they have had it for thousands of years. Working ability is not going to take away from their appearance. "Times have changed" . . . "Dogs are better fed and they tend to grow bigger in America" . . . "We are breeding dogs under modern conditions" . . . excuses, excuses! If we want to change anything in the Puli breed, we should have a purpose for it. If I knew that any of the changes were intentional, or if the persons who breed Pulis with straight shoulders, long bodies, heavy bones, coarser heads, sloping pasterns, straight stifles, or silky coats, can draw a picture and explain to me the mechanical advantage of these changes, I would not discredit their purposes.

Cliques come into existence among fanciers, sometimes without intention. These cliques inadvertently have the power to change certain characteristics in the dogs they are breeding. The dog that wins a big show is the "type of the day."

Some newcomers may drift toward the clique by association with the winning dog. The problem is that the pattern for breeding dogs is not like that for a skirt that can be changed in style from mini in spring to midi in the fall. Popular demand is a false convention to follow in dog breeding. It is usually the result of propaganda. The general public in a locality accepts this because they are not knowledgeable. But we should not forget the fact that part of this general public will be breeders of the next generations of our Pulis. The responsibility is the breeders' and since a large percentage of the Puli puppies come from occasional breeding, I am not talking about the large scale kennel owners only. Every single person, who chooses a mate for his bitch, should have a basic knowledge of what to look for in a sound dog, and why. The shepherds who kept this breed for us through thousands of years walked or rode for days to find the proper mates for their bitches. The

This head study illustrates the most obvious faults in a Puli: silky straight coat, high ear set, long muzzle, and light gray nose.

least we can do is to have a better reason to breed than just to produce cute, shaggy dogs to impress prospective purchasers who are not sufficiently informed to be discriminating.

Judging or evaluating the Puli can not strictly be called a science. We would be closer to the truth if we called it an art. No matter how technically correct the conformation of a dog may be, or how close it nears the standard in the smallest details, the final selection will still be influenced by the overall impression and the dog's picturesque appearance. No matter how objective a judge is, his personal attitudes and preconceived ideas will influence his decisions.

Whether a judge realizes it or not, he may have an antipathy for a certain fault. This is usually true of one who becomes a Specialty judge for his own breed and is keenly aware of the most common faults of that breed. Years after he starts judging other breeds, his eyes are still trained to pick out these faults immediately in other breeds of dogs. As a result, he may attach a greater penalty to a fault in another breed than the fault deserves. For example, a certain judge was making his final decision between two Pulis. The two appeared very close in merit, both were impressive. In his mind, the judge picked out the slight faults in each of the dogs: one was slightly weaker in topline, was heavier-boned, and was a more massively constructed Puli (with a deep chest and a certain softness of spine, contributing to this heaviness); the other, although possessing an excellent topline and good shoulders, was somewhat lighter in construction (possessed a shallower chest than that judge liked to see). The judge gave the win to the dog with the softer topline. Had he known at the time that the major concern of Puli breeders was the elimination of the heavy, coarse species from the show ring and breeding circles, he would have reversed his decision.

Faults are not absolute; they are to be found in degrees. There are: too deep chests, excellent depth, slightly shallow, and inadequately shallow chests, just as there are roach backs, strong sound backs, flexibility at the spine, and swayed backs. It is of utmost importance to determine the degree of the fault and to determine which faults are the most important to discourage. Judges should be concerned with merits and faults. Overall poor quality in a small geographical area should not be an excuse for a lack of

"East-west" front. Paws are pointing out.

Down in pasterns.

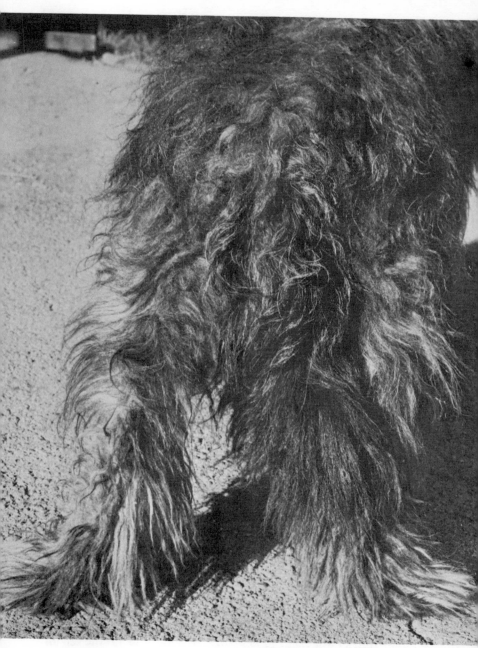

Cow hocked.

Lack of type: long in body, long muzzle, down in pasterns, silky straight coat on head, and silky slightly wavy coat on rear. This type of coat does not have the required tendency to cord.

interest or knowledge on the part of the judge or the Puli owner. It is very discouraging to have a judge put up a silky, open-coated Puli with weak sloping pasterns, and when asked why, to answer "because I am used to seeing them that way." It is the judge's duty to recognize and reward the outstandingly good qualities and penalize the bad ones. But it is the breeder's duty to develop those desired qualities in his dogs in the first place!

Varying with times and geographical locations, different faults come into focus, cause concern, and slowly disappear. For example, during the late 1950's, size became one of the major concerns in the United States. Later the breed got into the problem of the straight, silky, thin coats, multi-colored coats, and their many combinations. Today, the one-time threat of the 20- to 21-inch, 50- to 60-pound Puli is all but eliminated. Even dogs that are encroaching upon the 19-inch upper limit are now scarce in the ring. There are still a few breeders, and a small number of dog show judges, who do not know even now that the AKC spelled out in the breed's general description that the height of the Puli shall average 17 inches and should never go over 19 inches. The problem of the coat seems to be a more persistent one, and we still see multi-colored or silky-coated Pulis taking a win occasionally, but they are rapidly diminishing in numbers.

No single award can be considered an absolute determining factor as to which dog is best. It is only the reflection of the opinions of that one judge at the time and under the given circumstances and conditions in which he made his determination. Another judge, or even the same judge, on a different day and under different circumstances might reverse the placings. The most consistent winners, that win over a wide variety of competition in the breed, for a long period of time, and under many expert judges, may well be considered to be the top or the "approximate top" of their time. But it must be taken into consideration that the vast majority of pure-bred Pulis are not being exhibited. It could very well be that the really best Puli of its time is herding sheep somewhere on a tiny ranch and making its owner happy with its performance, rather than winning conformation awards.

For all of the reasons mentioned, it is clear that the Puli owner has no absolute measurement to follow in determining his dog's excellence. This chapter is not intended to make an "instant expert" out of the novice, nor a dog show judge out of a person with little experience in the breed. It is intended only as a guide for persons who are involved with the Puli, to aid in the evaluation of the Puli and to create a mental picture of the ideal specimen so as to show what basic qualities are to be sought and which should be eliminated. The intent here is to draw a line between excellent and mediocre, between mediocre and seriously faulty, to provide a guide toward how one may determine show quality and breeding quality, and, last but not least, to enable the reader to sit at ringside and watch the judging of Pulis with some idea of what is going on. Why and how certain undesired structural traits or

The ideal head. Istenhegyi Duda Pajtas, famed stud of the early 1950's in Hungary. Owner: Mr. Domotor. This photograph was used on the front cover of the book *A Puli*, by Dr. Imre Ocsag. Photograph courtesy of the late Mr. Domotor.

deviations from this ideal will affect a dog will be discussed at length elsewhere in this book.

All the available "official standards" from around the world were extensively used in preparing this chapter. Nothing in this chapter is intended as an objection to any of the official standards of the Puli, or as an attempt to contradict or change them. Breed standards are written by committees and modified by other committees; this generally reduces personal influences, but it also tends to reduce the clarity of the Standard. The AKC Standard of the Puli is an almost direct translation of the Hungarian Puli Standard, which in turn is the same as the internationally accepted Standard of the breed. The Standard has gone through many translations from its original Hungarian. Any translator, no matter how good he may be, encounters the problem of decision between literal accuracy and the exactness of the concept to be conveyed. My own ideas have been inter-mixed as well, to bring out points I consider important and necessary, because any technical presenta-

Champion Gyali Csopi (Csutora X Pajti). Bred by Nandor Mincer.

tion prepared by man and read by other men is subject
to interpretation.

THE HEAD

A fully-developed, well-coated Puli's head should appear round
when looking at it from any direction. The muzzle is short,
approximately 30 per cent of the length of the head. Although
muzzle length is allowable up to 50 per cent of the length of the
head, a dog that has a muzzle longer than half the length of its
head, no matter how heavy his coat, will not give the true impression
of the Puli.

115

Champion Csardas' Bandit of Sczyr (Ch. Matyasfoldi Kapuore Bi-tang **X** Sczyr's Grey Babe) at the age of 3½ years already exhibits well formed cords on the head, covering the muzzle completely, thus making the head look round from all directions. Photograph: Robert Kline.

The head of a hard-working herding Puli, photographed in Hungary by the author. The coat is not as neat as his show-going relatives, but the head still appears well rounded with superfluous coat and the properly proportioned muzzle (the light spot on the nose is mud, not a lack of pigment).

Champion Sasvolgyi Pici Pamacs (Int. Ch. Pusztai Furtos Ficko **X** Dorozsmai Fruzsi) at the age of 18 months. Seldom can one find such fully blossoming head coat at this age. This breeding combination provided a uniformly heavy coat on all puppies.

Borgvaale Pusztai Marok Marcsa, owned by Mrs. Pat Lanz of England, exhibits the beginning of correct cording. "Marcsa" is a true asset to the breed's future in England. Photograph courtesy of Borgvaale Kennels.

Figure B. Eye Characteristics of the Puli

1. Preferred. 2. Eyes are set too far apart, an indication of a coarse head. 3. Eyes are too close, usually the result of a narrow long head.

EYES

Horizontally placed eyes are not ideal; they should be slightly slanted, with eyelids tight (Figure B); color should be a dark, coffee-brown although eyes of somewhat lighter color are not considered a serious fault. (Many veterinarians agree that canine eyes of lemon-yellow, blue, white, or of disparate coloration are indicative of inherited pigmentation irregularities, even if such variants are not shown on the skin.)

BITE

Since the bite of the dog is a very strongly inherited trait, serious consideration should be given to it. There are some breeds wherein the bite is not considered important, but it is of major importance in any working breed. The teeth should be even and closely spaced in both the upper and lower jaws. The drawings (Figure C) illustrate the various types of bites as revealed with the mouth in a slightly open position.

Figure C. Teeth of the Puli

1. The ideal scissor bite, with the lower front (incisors) teeth touching the upper ones from the rear. 2. The less-perfect but acceptable level bite. 3. Overshot bite. 4. Undershot bite. 5. A bite that is unsatisfactory because teeth are too forward-leaning. The angle between the upper and lower incisors should not be less than 135 degrees from the vertical. Bites such as illustrated in 3, 4, and 5 are considered as serious faults and dogs possessing the like should not be used for breeding or showing.

Figure D. Ear Set of the Puli

1. The ideal ear setting. Notice that the head gives the desired appearance of roundness, that the line of the ears is slightly over the eyes, and that the correct ear length allows touching the inner corner of the eye when the ear is pulled forward. 2. Ears that are set too high. 3. Ears that are set too low. 4. Ears that are too light. 5. Ears that are too heavy and long. (Note spaniel-like look.) 6. Ears that are too small and light and move upward. (Note the fox terrier-like appearance.)

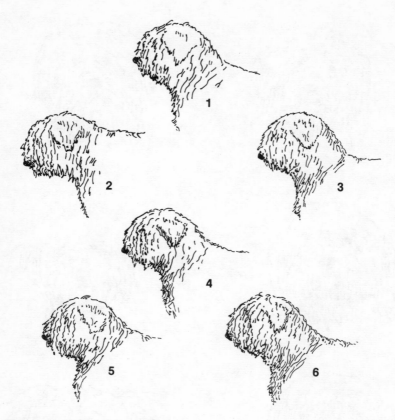

Figure E. Neck of the Puli

1. The ideal angulation of the Puli neck. 2. A neck that is too low. 3. A neck that is too high. 4. A Puli neck of ideal length. 5. A neck that is too short. 6. A neck that is too long.

NECK

When evaluating the neck of the Puli (Figure E), it is important to avoid any unnatural position. Take the time to observe the dog when it is completely relaxed, paying attention to the length of the coat, while evaluating either the angle or the length of the neck. If the dog has lost some coat on its head and neck, but not on the rest of the body, you might not get a true picture of the dog's neck. The most reliable way to judge your Puli's structure is to do so when the dog is dripping wet. When evaluating a dog's neck do not stack the dog; observe the animal in a natural pose.

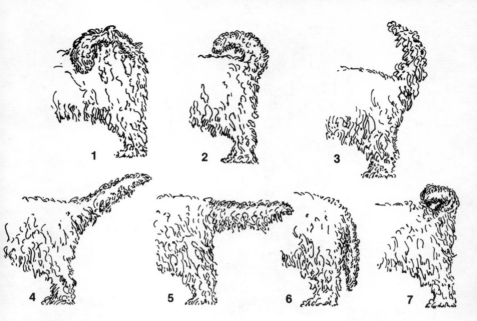

Figure F. Tail Set of the Puli

1. The ideal tail set: curled over the back, flat against the body. 2. The tightly-curled "corkscrew" tail. (This type of tail is also very good, but it should be in position over the back most of the time, not just when the dog is overly excited.) 3. The "sickle-tail" is undesirable. 4. The "flag-tail," also undesirable. 5. The straight tail. 6. The always-hanging tail. 7. The too short (or docked) tail. Tails as illustrated in 5, 6, and 7 should be considered serious faults.

TAIL

Probably the most dominating and noticeable feature of the Puli is his tail. When the Puli tail, the umbrella-like coat formation on the head, and the unmatched coat texture are considered, the uniqueness of the breed emerges. The tail (Figure F) is also described as a "barometer" of the Puli's current mood. For example, if it is tightly curled over the back, the dog is alert and ready for action. Aside from indicating moods, the tail is often an indication of a degree of excellence. The condition and the length of the coat on the tail is also very important. A short coat on the tail is just as bad as on any other part of the body. It has been said of the Puli that "One cannot tell which end is which," and such is the case when tail carriage is excellent.

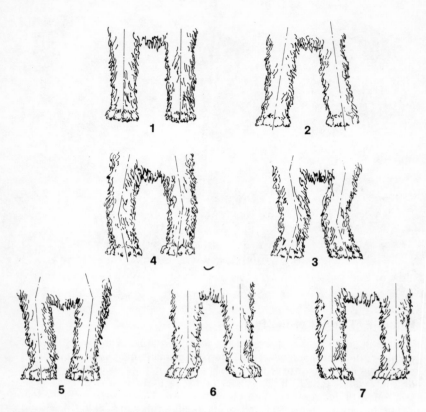

Figure G. Front Assembly of the Puli

1. Correct appearance of forelegs. 2. The wide stance, usually an indication of a narrow chest. 3. Close stance, usually as a result of a barrel chest or being out at the elbows. 4. A front stance that is out at the pasterns, or the bow-legged front. This front is seldom found among Pulis growing up on well-balanced diets. It is almost always an indication of a rickety, weak structure resulting from malnutrition during the growing stage. 5. The fiddle front, more common in fast-developing, heavy puppies, as are: 6. (paws pointing out or east-west) and 7. (paws pointing in).

FRONT ASSEMBLY

The ideal forelegs are straight when viewed from any direction. In a front view, Figure G, the center line of the leg bone is vertical and goes through the center line of the paws. Viewing the leg from the side, Figure H, the center line of the leg bone is vertical and falls right above the heel of the pad.

Figure H. Front Assembly of the Puli, Side View

1. Ideal foreleg, straight when viewed at any angle. 2. Leg of a dog down on its pasterns. 3. Leg of a dog that is knuckled over.

REAR ASSEMBLY

The hindquarters are a very important part of a working dog. This is the part of the dog that moves the whole body, keeps it in good balance, and can be the cause of unnatural movement. From good rear movement comes soundness and power. It is almost impossible to find a dog perfectly constructed in other parts of the body if the rear is malformed. For example, if the rear legs lack angulation, it is natural that the front assembly will have to keep the body in balance; consequently, the front legs cannot be vertical. If the fore and rear legs are not in the correct angulation, the spine and the neck must be deformed as well. From one unbalanced condition, a chain reaction takes place. (See Figures I and J.)

BODY

Unfortunately, many people pay less attention to the overall proportions of their dogs than to the many less-important details. A serious effort by Puli people should be made to examine their dogs to obtain a true picture of what is under the heavy coat.

The only way to gain a correct evaluation of a dog's proportions is to get a measuring stick and measure. The points at which the correct measurements should be taken are indicated by small circles on the drawings of Figure K. Slight variations should not be considered as serious faults, especially in females; but a dog with a long body cannot look like a good Puli, and should not be considered as such, regardless of his other qualities.

Under the Hungarian Standard, it is considered a serious fault if a dog's length is over 110 percent of its height in males, or over

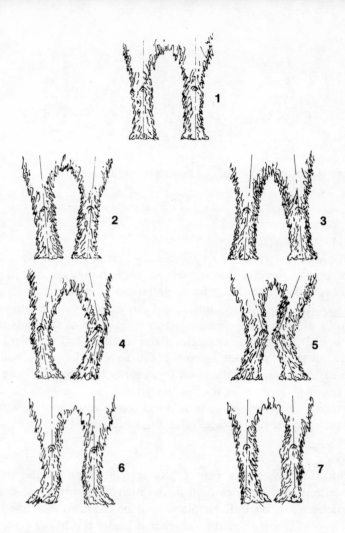

Figure I. Rear Assembly of the Puli

1. The ideal rear leg and the ideal stance. In the rear view of the dog, the centerlines of the legbones go through the centerlines of the paws, which are pointing straight forward. 2. Rear legs that are too close. 3. Rear legs that are too broadspread. 4. Bowlegged (hocks pointing out). 5. Cow-hocked (hocks pointing in). 6. Toeing out (paws pointing out). 7. Toeing in (paws pointing in).

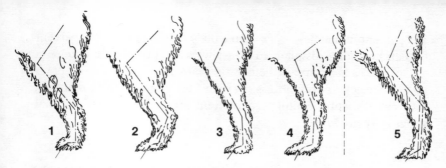

Figure J. Rear Assembly of the Puli, Side View

1. The rear assembly viewed from the side: ideally the centerline of the third digit is close to the horizontal and the heel is firmly on the ground, not in the air as in faulty stances. 2. Sickle-hocked legs. 3. Straight-stifled legs. 4. An over-angulated stifle (usually from long hocks). 5. A hock that is too long (not enough angulation between the pelvis and upper thigh).

Figure K. Body of the Puli

1. Ideal "square" appearance. 2. A dog with body that is too long. 3. Though appearing perfectly square, the illustrated dog might actually be too short.

112 percent in females. Dogs with a body length of over 125 percent of their height are disqualified from shows and breeding in Hungary.

Do not judge puppies before they are fully matured. Puppies do not develop in even phases. In their "teen-age" (6 to 12 months), they can present a completely different picture from that revealed when fully grown.

SIZE

The ideal male Puli is 17 inches at the shoulders; the ideal female is 16 inches. Slight variations are allowed in both directions, but males should not be over 19 inches nor the females over 18 inches. In the chapter wherein are compared the AKC Puli standard and the FCI approved International Puli standard, one can see how carefully they both regulate the size requirements. The AKC standard seems to be more concerned with *oversize* than undersize, by spelling out in two different sections of the *Complete Dog Book*: In the general description ". . . He is a medium sized dog averaging seventeen inches in height . . ." while under height, in the official standard; ". . . males about 17 inches, and should not exceed 19 inches . . .," without giving a lower limit in either paragraph.

COAT

The quality, color, and care of the Puli coat fills an entire chapter elsewhere in this book, but to create the desired mental picture of our ideal specimen of the breed, I wish to quote from the AKC's Complete Dog Book: ". . . The Puli coat too, is unique. There is nothing exactly like it in all dogdom. The undercoat is soft, wooly, very dense; the outer coat long and profuse. The puppy coat is tufted, but with growth the undercoat tangles with the top coat in such a manner as to form long cords . . ."

The coat of a fully matured Puli can reach the ground on its sides and cover the entire body evenly in an eye-appealing manner.

●

I am confident it is possible for Puli owners to evaluate their own dogs as well as any licensed judge can, by performing the following:

1. Study the Puli Breed Standard and the illustrations presented in this book.

2. Read the available general dog publications on movement, structure, and behavior.

3. Take an active part in dog shows, matches and, other events that formally evaluate dogs.

But most importantly, after performing all of the above, you, the Puli owner, must perform the evaluation of your dog with an open mind, using facts alone, and leaving out the personal element (sentiment and emotion) as much as possible.

My intent with this chapter is to shake *ALL* Puli owners into the realization that NOT ALL Pulis were born to be bred!! Dogs with serious faults can be wonderful pets and outstanding lifelong companions. Their faults certainly do not have to influence the sentiment one feels toward them, but they do not have to be reproduced. Through the love and attachment one feels toward his own dog, a much more important feeling should develop in every Puli owner, that being the feeling of responsibility we tacitly accepted when we bought our first Puli. That responsiblity is: TO KEEP THIS BREED UNCHANGED! to keep it exactly as it was handed down to us, with its history of thousands of years, from its Sumerian origin, through the Hungarian Shepherd, to today's pet lover or dog show exhibitor all over the world.

MOVEMENT

I was only a few years old when I went to my first dog show, but I remember it as if it were yesterday. At the show I noticed a Puli left alone on the bench. Occasionally he would jump straight up in the air as though he were trying to see somebody on the other side of the bench. When I asked what was wrong with him, someone explained that there was nothing wrong with him, that he was just a Puli! Pulis are much the same as Arabian horses. They are very active and must find a way to use their energy by dancing in one place or by jumping if confined. Ever since then, each time I see a painting or photograph of an Arabian horse, it reminds me of that Puli.

Have you ever encountered a neighbor while walking your Puli? If you stop to talk, your Puli will wait patiently next to you, but all of a sudden, without seeming to move a muscle, he jumps off the ground in a very peculiar manner—all four legs leave the ground at the same time. His top line is straight and level as if he were standing still. He can come up enough to look you straight in the eye, as if to say "Hey! Didn't you forget the real purpose of this walk!" For a split second he seems to float at this level before dropping back on all fours.

I have seen Ch. Nagykunsagi Csorgo C.D. in his younger days clear a four foot fence from a stand-still position by just the flexing of his muscles. This effortless movement is the real trademark of the breed. Terriers are known to be restless, bouncy, active, and feisty, but this is a distinctly different trait from that of the Puli. The Puli's effortless movement is evident when watching one perform his ancient duty of herding sheep. He will run as if he is floating through the air. Suddenly, he will notice a sheep running in a different direction. Without even slowing down, the Puli changes direction as a rabbit would, and takes after the runaway.

There is nothing visibly special to warrant the Puli's high degree of agility. Even examining both the front assembly and the hind quarters of the Puli, we can not find any significant difference from other breeds. The shoulder blade is roughly 45 degrees to the horizontal, and the shoulder blade and upper arm create a 90 degree angle. The pelvic bone slopes about 30 degrees to the horizontal, with well-built stifles. This could describe almost any dog. What then is the difference? The secret of the Puli's ability to turn on a dime and change direction quickly is in the shortness of his body. The equal length of the shoulder blade and upper arm, taken in conjunction with the short level back, accounts for the fact that the Puli does not have a far-reaching gait.

The very first written standard of the Puli in his native land described his length to be 93 percent of his height at the withers. Today, the standard is somewhat more lenient, and describes him as being perfectly square. The Hungarian standard says that the body length for males is considered a serious fault when it is 110 percent or more of its body height, and such a faulty dog should definitely not be used for breeding. Translated into inches, that would mean a Puli 17 inches high and 18¾ inches long should be considered seriously faulty. I can not emphasize enough that even if the AKC standard does not list disqualifications for the Puli breed, we must draw a strict line for ourselves somewhere if we want to retain the qualities the Puli has had for thousands of years.

The short body, combined with the wiry, lean, well-muscled

build is the real secret of the Puli's performance that he has brought with him down through the last 8,000 years.

Within the limits of this book, I cannot go into great detail on how the smallest parts of its body can influence movement of a Puli, or that of any dog. In this book, I am trying to limit the discussion to the most important factors and their related parts of the body. There are books on the market that are devoted entirely to the movement of the dog, and if that is not enough, many books on the movement of the horse are available. Since the laws of physics apply equally to horses and dogs, these books are excellent references for dog breeders.

The question of movement must be approached in terms of function. The build of a dog that was created to pull carts will be entirely different from that of a short-distance racing dog. The Puli is a working dog. The function of his body is to enable him to run for many hours without tiring. In any evaluation of this breed, this function must be remembered. Anything that adds to his ability to endure is good, whereas anything that detracts from it is a fault.

First we will take a look at the Puli's balance. Let us assume that we have placed our Puli on a heavy glass slab on two saw horses and we are beneath and looking up under the dog. What we will see, are the four paw prints and the chin of the dog somewhere ahead of the front legs, as represented in Figure L. The relationship of these five points to each other is of great importance.

In the course of a recent discussion with a relative newcomer to our breed, the talk revolved about what is ideal in a Puli. He used terms such as "well boned, well put down Puli." When I asked him to define these expressions he said "well boned to me means heavier than medium boned." (The same term, "well boned," appears in the St. Bernard standard.) "Well put down means that he is a stocky little fellow in the ring, relatively wide standing when he is stacked," the novice continued. When I tried to explain to him why he was wrong, he cut me off half way through my first sentence. "Oh, you are just prejudiced against heavier dogs!"

In 1959 when our present AKC standard was published in the form of a proposal, a weight limit for Pulis was included. After the proposal was published, a few of the sentimentally inclined breeders wrote protesting the weight limitation. "We like to keep

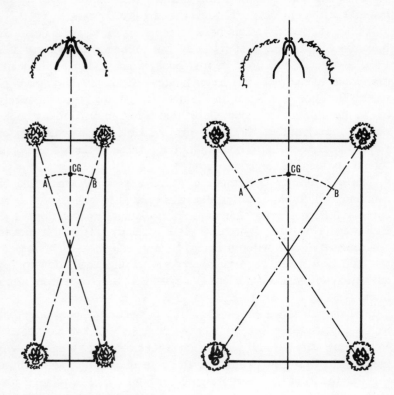

Figure L. Balance Points

our dogs on the heavier side," they said. "It should be a matter of personal preference . . ." As a result the AKC removed the weight limitation. Ten years later, half the Puli breeders are still convinced that weight really is a matter of personal preference! Some bloodlines are constantly producing the ideal 17 inch Puli with a 25 to 30 pound average weight. Other bloodlines are producing Pulis of the same height but with an average weight of from 40 to 43 pounds. Anyone who claims that a 17 inch, 43 pound Puli can move with the speed and agility of a 25 pound Puli cannot logically defend his argument. This fact has no relationship to personal preference, but relates solely to the laws of physics, and of weight and balance.

Let us again go back and look at our Puli through the glass while visualizing lines of reference as drawn in Figure L. We know that a dog's center of gravity is not in the intersection of the diagonals drawn between the four paw marks, because the head and neck are ahead of the front paws, and most of the inner parts of the body are closer to the front assembly of the dog. The center of gravity falls somewhere between the intersection of these diagonals, and the line drawn between the two front paws. It can not be forward of this line, or the dog would not be able to balance himself. If it were outside of this line, the dog's hind legs would leave the ground and he would have to use his nose for a third point to stabilize himself. The 43 pound Puli of the same height (17 inches) must carry this extra weight somewhere. As a result, this heavier dog will have heavier bones, a wider chest (possibly even to the point of being barrel chested), and a much wider stance with all four paws.

What happens when a dog starts moving? He lifts up one of his fore legs and the weight from the diagonally opposite hind leg comes up at the same time. This is assuming that the dog is moving at the normal trotting gait, and is not pacing. In order to stay in balance, the dog will lean towards the front leg that is firmly down. While he is leaning, in mechanical terms, he is moving his center of gravity to the imaginary diagonal line of the two legs still on the ground. His moving front leg will come down, and the same motion will start toward the other side. This time the center of gravity is shifting to line up with the diagonals of the other two legs.

It is easy to see on the two drawings that the arc on which the center of gravity travels (between point A and B) is greater on the widely built dog. Thus, the dog with the wider stance must lean more at each step to keep himself in balance. Since this leaning motion is not in the direction of the dog's travel, it is a hindrance to the dog at every step, results in a loss of useful energy and saps the dog's endurance. This movement of the center of gravity is technically called "lateral displacement." Racing dog breeders and racing horse breeders are very much aware of its existence. The Puli must have a chest wide enough to comfortably accommodate its lungs, heart, and other important organs, but it does not have to have a heavy build and broad stance. The Puli evolved through the centuries to become a speedy long distance runner. Have you ever compared the build of a long distance runner to that of a wrestler? They are two entirely different types, and cannot be expected to perform with full efficiency if exchanging roles; the same is, of course, the case with dogs of different conformation.

The same lateral displacement is responsible for the characteristic "rolling gait" that is a required part of the Old English Sheepdog's movement. However, it is a serious fault in our breed. The longer the neck of a dog the further forward the center of gravity will be, and the longer the radius of the A-B arc will be. For this reason we are not looking for Pulis with necks set low, nor for those that carry their heads a-foot-and-a-half in front of their bodies, no matter how impressively that neck is arched when standing.

Nature has ways of trying to correct a fault that breeders have introduced in a dog. Dogs that are too wide tend to move in close (coming and going) to get the paws closer to the center of gravity and to cut down the travel of the moving center of gravity. Or, they may develop a stance referred to as "out at the elbows." If the elbows are out, the paws frequently turn inward in trying to get closer to the center of gravity. In the most extreme case of the problem, as in the English Bulldog's front, the upper arms of the front legs are bent on a curve to get further under the dog's wide chest, and the lower arm is even twisted to get the paws close to the center line of the body. If we let it, nature will correct the faults we build into our dogs, or rather will counter-balance them. But if this happens, we have a dog that is not only too wide, but may also be out at the elbows or have a rolling gait. Any of these problems will be a detriment to the original function of the breed.

After looking at the Puli from above and below we have to examine the skeleton from a side view (Figure M) before we can go into detail on movement. (Reference to Figure A for skeletal nomenclature may be helpful here also.)

Reference to the standard reveals that "shoulders clean cut and sloping." In dog show terminology, sloping means roughly 45 degrees to the horizontal. The upper arm is joined at the point of the shoulder, creating a 90 degree angle between the two. The ratio of the length of the shoulder blade to the length of the upper arm is 1:1. Then the upper arm and the forearm must form an angle of about 135 degrees to comply with the standard's description of straight forelegs.

To keep the dog in balance, the pelvic bone is about 30 degrees

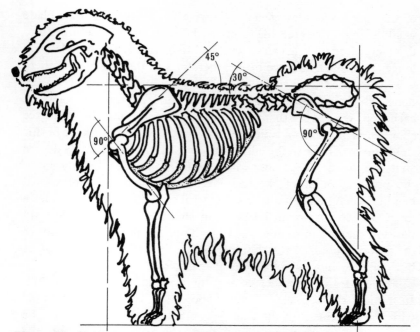

Figure M. Skeleton, Viewed to Show Balance Points

from the horizontal. In a stacked, natural position, the upper thigh bone will create a 90 degree angle with the pelvic bone. The hocks are vertical and short, with the center line of the paws falling roughly under the protruding rearmost portion of the pelvic bone.

The area between the last rib and the foremost portion of the pelvic bone is called "Coupling". The length of the coupling greatly affects movement. The ideal Puli possesses a long rib cage and a relatively short coupling.

In discussing the front in more detail, I will show that these angles were not born in the mind of a mechanical engineer with a computer complex, but were derived from function and such common sense as the shepherd used in choosing his lifetime helpers. He did not have instruments to measure these angles, but he knew from experience which qualities made a dog move more smoothly and therefore with more endurance. The 45 degree shoulder blade is ideal for more than one reason. First, we must assume that a 45 degree shoulder blade reaches the same height from the point of the dog's shoulder as, let us say, a 65 degree shoulder blade would. The 45 degree blade gives the dog more bone area, and therefore more muscle can be attached to it. It will also be relatively longer than the 65 degree blade; therefore, as the dog moves, there is a longer arc traversed around its pivot point at the center of the bone, which is closely related to the front leg's travel distance in each step. We can see that in all of these comparisons, the 45 degree shoulder is of greater advantage, and it shows the importance of this single piece of bone in the entire structure of the dog. This 45 degree angle can be measured only when the front pads are directly under the pivoting point of the shoulder blade. Watch a professional handler when he is handling a dog with straight shoulders under a judge who is known to be keen on shoulders. This handler will position the dog in such a way that the paws are placed in front of the pivoting point of the shoulder blade, thus making the shoulder blade appear more sloping than it really is.

The 45 degree shoulder creates the most ideal reach for a Puli. In motion, the dog has a forward speed, and this speed combined with the movement of the front legs gives travel, momentum. The momentum arc that is derived from the speed should hit the ground exactly where the extended front leg is touching the ground. If the shoulder is considerably steeper, we run into two faults that can be easily observed, even by the novice eye. If the dog keeps his straight front in tension, his paws will hit the ground before the forward speed would call for it. In dog show terms this is called pounding. The dog's head will bounce each time his front paw hits the ground, from the energy absorption of the extra forward momentum.

A pounding dog may break the tension in his front leg by lifting it higher, which is nature's way of protecting him from a concussion. When a dog exhibits this, it is called padding (not to be confused with paddling). His front paw will be still up in the air when his forward speed terminates for that particular step; therefore, the dog's front will practically fall down from this suspended position. Race horses born with this fault usually end up in front of a carriage or wagon instead of under a jockey. These are the dogs that the novice visitor to a dog show will pick out . . . "Look at that dog gaiting like a high-stepping horse" . . . "Isn't that beautiful." It may seem to some to be beautiful, but it reminds me of the goose-step of the German Army, and not a natural walk of a working dog.

If the forelegs are as straight as a shotgun barrel, as the shepherds used to say, with the desired angles, the paws will be right underneath the suspension point of the shoulder blades and the dog will be in static balance. If the paws fall behind this point, the dog's front weight will be carried on his toes. In such case, the paws will be in front of this position and the dog will need constant use of muscle power to keep himself in balance, creating a constant strain on his front assembly.

Nature will try to counter-balance this with sloping or, in extreme cases, broken-down pasterns. Even the requirement of the compact, round foot, as unreasonable as it may sound, also comes from a weight and balance problem. We know by now that the weight coming down through the pastern is vertical and, ideally, through the center line of the bone. A hare-footed dog (with a long third digital bone in the paw) will have a longer leverage from the weight line, and will tire faster.

The normal front shoulder blade is at a 45 degree angle to the horizontal, the upper arm forming a 90–110 degree angle with the shoulder (90 degree is preferred). The lower arm is completely vertical. The imaginary vertical line through the rotating point of the shoulder blade falls in the center line of the leg, passing through the ground in the centerline of the nice round and firm paws as illustrated in Figure N. This type of front is an important requirement for proper movement and an asset which is relatively easy to visualize. If we extend the imaginary center line of the shoulder blade to the ground, this will give us the dog's maximum forward reach with the leg in fully extended position. Assuming that the dog's body is square and has the proper rear assembly to go with it, this front will provide the ideal reach. There is nothing new in this requirement and all squarely-built dogs (Doberman, Great Dane, Boxer, to mention a few) show similar fronts. This front is not to be confused with the "Terrier front." Terriers have a considerably shorter upper arm and a longer lower arm, which is an important feature for the underground digging for which they were originally bred.

Another 45 degree shoulder blade is illustrated in Figure O. The upper arm is forming the same 90–110 degree angle with

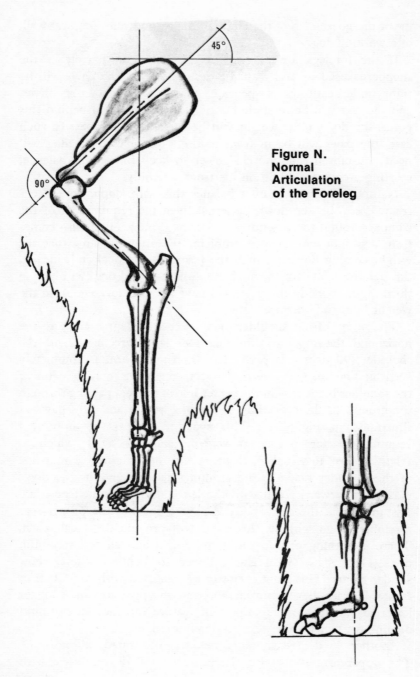

**Figure N.
Normal
Articulation
of the Foreleg**

45°

90°

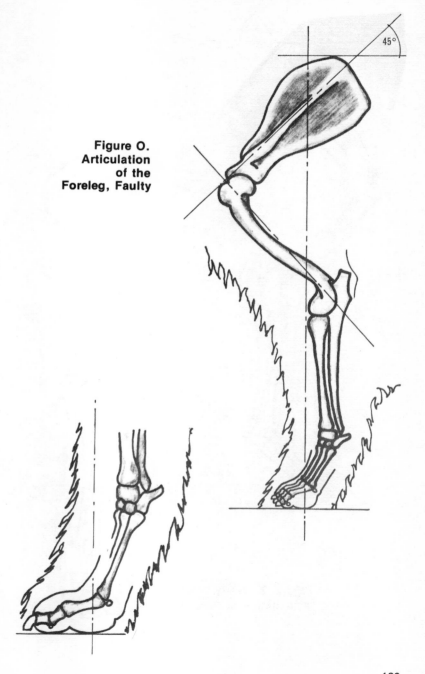

**Figure O.
Articulation
of the
Foreleg, Faulty**

45°

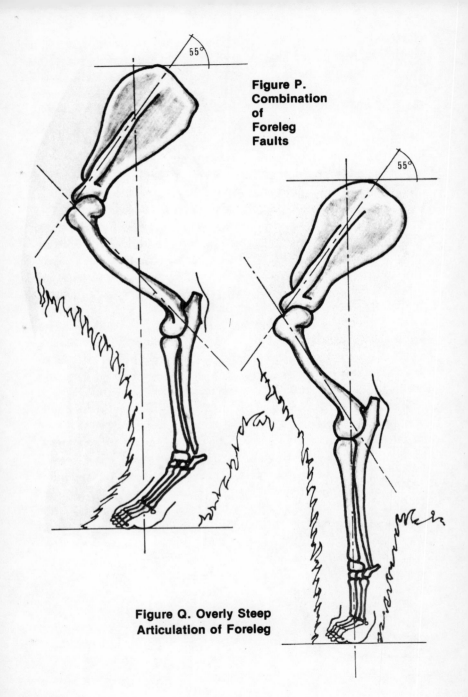

55°

**Figure P.
Combination
of
Foreleg
Faults**

55°

**Figure Q. Overly Steep
Articulation of Foreleg**

the shoulder. The only difference is the slightly longer upper arm and slightly shorter lower arm. But these slight differences place the front leg behind the imaginary vertical line passing through the rotating point of the shoulder blade. Since this line also represents the line where the weight carried by the front assembly is transmitted to the ground, it has to go through the paws. To fulfill this requirement, nature had to create a sloping pastern to put the paw under the weight line. In many cases this type of front also causes one of the most frequent faults in general appearance, the low front. Pulis with this fault are easy to spot from a far distance. They are lower at the withers than at the croup and have a forward sloping top line, creating the appearance of going down hill all the time. When a front with a sloping pastern is combined with an elongated body and an over-angulated rear assembly, we can have a very impressive but a too-far-reaching German Shepherd type mover. While this movement can be very eye-appealing, it is not compatible with the type of function for which the Puli was created. Have you ever watched a German Shepherd taking a turn at a fast gaited speed? It requires about a 50-foot turning radius. Pulis are supposed to turn on a dime! And never forget that this quick-turning ability, to change direction at full forward speed, kept the Puli in the herding business for thousands of years.

Illustrated in Figure P is an exaggerated form of one of the most common combinations of possible faults. The shoulder blade is steeper than the ideal 45 degrees; the ratio of upper arm to lower arm about the same as shown in Figure O, but because the steeper shoulder blade brings the imaginary line of weight transmission even further forward, the pastern has to slope more. In such a case we are talking about "down in pastern" or in more extreme cases "broken down pastern." Although the upper arm, lower arm, pastern, and the elongated paw create a visible curve forward due to the steeper shoulder blade, this dog will not have a good reach.

Figure Q shows that a steep shoulder and steep upper arm are totally limiting the reach of a dog with this type of front. The straight front legs are easy to achieve with a shoulder like this, but the fault becomes quite apparent as soon as the dog starts moving. Such a dog is very limited in forward reach, and, if it has any kind of balance at all, it will lack in rear assembly angulation as in correcting for a bad front. The illustration is exaggerated for easier

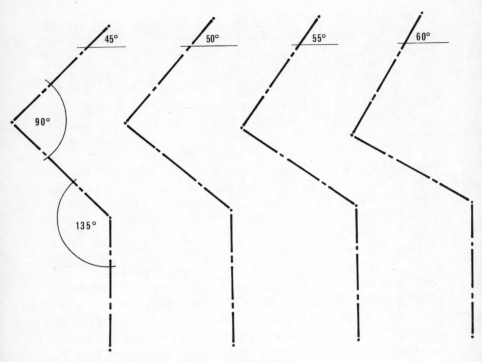

Figure R. Deformities of Front Assembly

understanding. Slighter faults of this sort are harder to recognize. Dogs should be stacked properly and examined carefully under their heavy coat if one is determined to get the true picture of the skeleton underneath.

Figure R illustrates some of the many possible deformations of the front assembly. Here we assume that the 90 degree angle is constant between the shoulder blade and upper arm. Only the angle of the shoulder blades varies. The dotted lines denote the imaginary centerlines of the respective bones.

Figure S depicts the most common fault found in front assemblies of today's show dogs. The straight lower arm is the only constant in this case, and the angle between shoulder blade and upper arm varies as much as the angle of the shoulder blade to the top line. It is interesting to note that (assuming that the drawing with 45 degree shoulder blade is showing a 17-inch high Puli) keeping the same relative bone lengths for all three components of

142

the front assembly, the dog with 60 degree shoulder blades can be almost 2 inches higher (or 19 inches) at the withers. This indicates that without changing the dog's relative bone size, its height can vary 2 inches just by changing the angles from excellent to seriously faulty.

The function of the rear assembly is entirely different. When the dog is not in motion, it is merely carrying the body weight, and the acting forces are vertical to the spinal column. If this were its entire function, a 45 degree pelvic bone direction would be ideal, but that is not the purpose of the rear.

While a dog is taking a step, the rear leg is being moved forward, contacting the ground at a point where the forward energy takes it. Preferably this point is where the motivating energy is exhausted. (This is similar, as we noted, to the functioning of the front leg.) At this moment, the leg is extended, the pad touches the ground

Figure S. Most Common Fault of Front Assembly

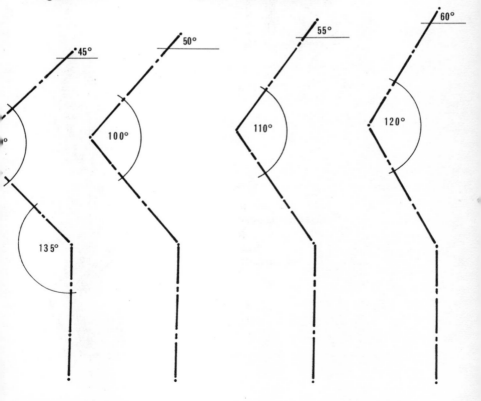

Figure T. Ideal Rear Assembly

**Figure U.
Over-angulation
in
Rear
Assembly**

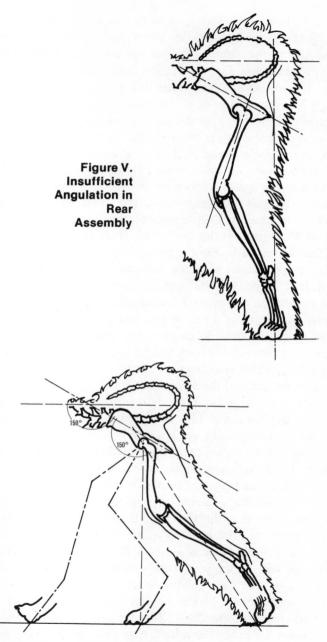

**Figure V.
Insufficient
Angulation in
Rear
Assembly**

150°

150°

Figure W. Rear Leg Action in Walking

first and absorbs the shock, as shown in Figure W. The toes are still off the ground; from this point, the leg starts the backward action and at the same time starts to contract by bending at the stifle and the hock. The contraction ceases when the paw is exactly under the hip socket, and from this position the toes come into play. The transmission of power from the pelvic bone through an imaginary vertical line to the point of complete extension of this leg, where all the forces (that is, the push) and the power come from, to the dog's spinal cord, is what causes the dog to move. It is a mechanical law again, that two equal angles can carry this power into the spinal cord easier than two unequal angles. At the peak of the power transmission, the angle of the entire back assembly is roughly 120 degrees to the horizontal. If the pelvic bone is 30 degrees to the horizontal, there is created a 150 degree angle at the center line of the pelvic bone. There is created in turn a 150 degree angle with the horizontal line of the spine. The 30 degree slope of the pelvic bone has been proved most advantageous in achieving a useful relationship between the stifle angulation, length of lower thigh, and the height of the hock. If the angle is less than 30 degrees, the stifle will be straighter; to compensate for this, the hock will be higher. If the angle is greater, the pushing action is shortened.

The importance of the short hock is also mechanical. The closer this joint is to the ground, the less amount of power is needed to move the dog's weight. This is advantageous for breeds that were bred for endurance. Higher hocks are required on short-distance racing dogs. Even today, breeders of field hounds (where endurance is most important) sometimes select their puppies just by the comparison of the length of hock. Short-hocked dogs will tire less-swiftly than will high-hocked dogs of similar size and quality.

In the show ring, the Puli is judged like all other breeds, at a gaiting speed, or brisk walking speed. However, this is the type of movement that the Puli is least likely to use when working with sheep. He will either walk slowly behind the flock, next to the shepherd, or will trot, gallop, or use suspended gallop, running after the stray sheep. Never-the-less, gaiting speed is sufficient to detect structural unsoundness. It is far better than judging stacked dogs, where the judge has a hard time determining what is natural for the dog and what is the result of ring training.

COAT AND COAT COLOR
Coat

The Puli coat is as unique as the breed itself, to say the least. It is composed of a fine, very woolly, dense undercoat and a somewhat coarser, long, wavy or curly outer coat. The texture and the proportions of the outer coat and the undercoat make it the distinctive Puli coat. There is nothing exactly like it among other dog breeds. The coat of the Komondor, also a Hungarian Sheepdog, is nearest like that of the Puli, but it is still somewhat coarser in texture. The texture of the outer coat can vary from slightly wavy,

American, Mexican, F.C.I. International Champion Cinkotai Csibesz, shown here winning his third Specialty Show at the age of 8 years, at the Beverly Hills Kennel Club in 1968 under the late judge Major Godsol. "Csibesz" was top-winning Puli in the U.S. during 1965, 1966 and 1967 (Phillips rating system). Exhibited in seven countries of two continents, he won over more of his own breed than any other Puli in the breed's history. He is also the all-time top-producing sire in the U.S. Photograph: J. Ludwig.

Champion Pride O'Misty Tobi (Ch. Cinkotai Csibesz **X** Ch. Star of Hunnia Misty Baba), owned and bred by Mr. J. Heiden of Van Nuys, California, pictured here finishing his title under judge Dr. Malcolm Phelphs. Photograph: J. Ludwig.

Tobi's litter sister, Champion Hunnia's Pride O'Misty Tunde. Owner-handled by Klara Benis. She is shown here finishing her title under judge Glen Fancy. Photograph: J. Ludwig.

to wavy, to curly. Nature tends to interweave this outer coat with the undercoat to form long uniform cords. The degree of waviness and the amount of the undercoat will determine the width of the cords, or, in the case of the combed Puli coat, the ability to cord. For the purposes of this book, it is technical enough for all practical purposes to say that the texture of the Puli coat is correct if it has a tendency to cling together and form cords.

Dr. Ocsag, a research scientist and a scholar regarding the Hungarian breeds, presented a technical paper at the World Kynologic Congress in 1966. In this study he scientifically researched the Puli coat. For his purposes, he graded the coat by texture into seven categories. These categories ranged from the

Champion Hunnia's Suba (Ch. Cinkotai Csibesz **X** Ch. Tatarhegyi Borka Panna), owner-handled to his title by Mrs. Barbara Pohlmann, winning a major at a Santa Barbara Kennel Club Show under judge Mrs. Eileen Pinlott.

small, shoe lace-like, narrow cords, through the ideal, half-inch, ribbon-like, flat cords, to the very wide, heavy, mat-like cords. All seven of these categories are within the requirements of the coat as described in the standard. All the non-cording, silky, open coats were placed in the eighth category and labeled "non standard" for the Puli.

Without the help of the microscope and all the electronic measuring devices of the modern age, Puli breeders have been aware for a long time that all Puli coats are not created equal. The curlier type coat tends to cord in narrow cords and is very hard to keep combed (as it twists into cords minutes after it is combed). The ideal Puli coat has the proper proportions of undercoat and

Hunnia's Mazsola (Ch. Cinkotai Csibesz X Ch. Belzebub Gezenguz) collecting points toward his championship. Owners: Mr. and Mrs. Frank Pataki of Canada. Photograph: Missy Yuhl.

Imrei Ficsur Bogancs. This outstanding son of "Csibesz" collected a wide variety of titles in Hungary before being imported to the U.S. by Joseph DeLengyel Kennels of Englishtown, New Jersey.

Imrei Fruska (Ch. Cinkotai Csibesz **X** Dorozsmai Csitri). Owner: Mrs. Grossz of Budapest, Hungary.

outercoat with enough wave or curl to allow either method of grooming, without losing the tendency to cord. Some Puli coats do not have the tendency to cord at all, because of an improper balance between the undercoat and outercoat, or because they completely lack the necessary wave or curl. This coat is generally faulty and should be eliminated from the breed completely.

The quality and amount of coat as a basic measurement for the Puli's required appearance has developed through thousands of years of function. The standard describes it thoroughly, but it cannot be emphasized enough that the Puli's coat should never be silky, regardless of the amount of care he receives or the method of grooming. A coat that approaches the straightness and silkiness of that of the Afghan, Maltese, or Silky Terrier cannot be considered a Puli characteristic, and having such a coat is a very serious fault. In most instances, the appearance of a silky coat is either an indication of an "unfaithful" Puli bitch somewhere in the background, or the sign of a long line of wrongly selected or overly inbred breeding stock.

For years there was much debate among American breeders and owners on whether to comb or to cord the Puli's coat. This should never have been the issue at all. The issue should have been that the Puli's coat HAS TO HAVE the tendency to cord by itself. This is the characteristic that he brought with him from ancient times. The AKC Standard spells it out ". . . the hair tending to

Champion Hunnia's Cinkos Cuki (Ch. Cinkotai Csibesz X Karpathi Magda's Erzsi), owned by Mr. and Mrs. W. Pohlmann of Palos Verdes Estates, California, shown here handled by Barry Becker under judge Nicholas Kay.

Champion Star O'Natasha Shamu (Ch. Cinkotai Csibesz X Shagra Narasha). Owner-breeder Mr. Quiseng handled "Sam" to BOB at a Del Monte Kennel Club Show. Judge is the author.

Shamu's litter brother, Champion Shagra Piperkoc, owned by Mrs. Luella Gray of the Shagra Kennels, California.

"Cuki's" litter brother, American Hungarian Champion Hunnia's Cinkos Cifra, being owner-handled by Mrs. Judy Mishka to BOB under breeder judge Robert Kennedy. "Cifra" is the first, and to date the only, American-born Puli ever to finish championship in the breed's native country.

cling together in bunches, giving a somewhat corded appearance even when groomed. . . ."

In the early sixties, at the height of the "to comb or to cord" controversy, advocates of both sides ventured into extremes. Friends of the comb maintained that the cords are held together by dirt as a glueing agent and that clean Pulis could not be corded even if one wanted to cord them. Meanwhile the other side asserted that the combing of Pulis changes even their biochemical balance. One does not require an academic level of knowledge to disprove both of the above views. It seems to this writer that the cording controversy was perpetuated by several breeders who at the time were breeding

Champion Hunnia's Belzebub Bordros (Ch. Cinkotai Csibesz X Ch. Belzebub Gezenguz), owned by Gloria Humphlett, was handled to a 5-point major at the 1972 P.C.S.C. Specialty by Barry Becker under judge Charles Hamilton.

Hunnia's Gezenguz Gondor (Ch. Cinkotai Csibesz X Ch. Belzebub Gezenguz). Owner: Mrs. Sarah Millard.

Pulis with coats that could not be corded because they were faulty in being short, straight, silky, or sparse.

Owners of Puli puppies would do well if they would base their decision of the care of their dog's coat on nature, rather than their personal likes and dislikes. If the young Puli is developing a heavy, wavy, thick coat, it can be kept either combed or corded. If the Puli puppy is showing a very dense and strongly curling coat, it more or less has to be left corded if the owner wants to have any coat on the dog at all. When kept combed, this type of coat will always be shorter and require constant care. However, if it is left to cord, it will develop nice even-sized cords and have the impressive unique Puli appearance.

Hunnia's Miklos (Int. Ch. Cinkotai Csibesz X Ch. Belzebub Gezenguz).

It is well to mention here that only in America can the question
of how to keep a Puli's coat be made into an issue. In any other
country where Pulis are known and shown, they have to be shown
corded, and Pulis with combed coats are excused from the show
rings.

Dr. Kubinszky is a well-known veterinarian from Budapest,
Hungary, the author of numerous books on dogs, and a dog show
judge of international reputation. While touring the United States,
he saw his first combed Puli and exclaimed: "To comb a Puli is
like fighting nature itself. You can temporarily change his
appearance to fit your own preference, but if they have the proper
coat texture it must be real work to keep them that way."

Color

Even a small amount of experience with different breeds of dogs makes it obvious that the range and variations of colors in dogs is unlimited, and more or less a matter of taste. Some breed standards completely disregard color, while other breeds are very strict, and the smallest color deviation is considered a disqualification. The Puli falls somewhere in the middle, offering a relatively wide choice of colors, but within definite limits set by the standard.

Since individual preferences vary, one could argue that a wider range of permissible colors would help sales by appealing to a wider market. There are those seriously involved in the breed who claim that the limited color range long ago became one of the important "trade marks" of the breed, and the customer to whom the breed appeals will desire the color that he mentally associates with it. Color may become a matter of fashion. For example, in a large class of black Pulis a white dog may appear flashy, thereby catching the eye of the judge and the people at ringside. If the white Puli should start winning, perhaps on his merits, the novice at ringside may contribute his success to the flashy "standout" color. This could result in the whites becoming more desirable, based on the record of one winning dog. Color does, and always will, play an important part in the popularity of a breed. To the experienced breeder it is part of the breed's history and he will always place structural perfection, working capability, and intelligence above color. Any radical change in the accepted colors would mean breaking with the Puli's thousands of years of tradition. Perhaps, as in the case of the multi-colored Puli, it would even mean an infusion of foreign blood.

The Puli standard specifies three basic colors: black, gray, and white. The black can vary from jet black to rusty black or a sun-beaten dull black color, referred to in Hungarian literature as "Avet." The latter shade is considered by Hungarian experts of the breed to be the ancient "original" color of the Puli. In their point system of judging, Hungarian judges give maximum preference to this color. The gray can vary from black with some "salt and pepper" effect evenly intermixed, through various shades of gray to the very light, almost white color. The white should be snow white, sometimes giving the impression of blue white because

Littermates (Ch. Cinkotai Csibesz X Arpadligeti Merges): Frosty Star of Hunnia, Star of Hunnia Furtos.

of the required black or dark pigmentation showing through, around the mouth and eyes and in areas where the coat is thinner and shorter.

The most important fact in assessing the Puli's color is that regardless of which of the three basic colors you look at, the color has to appear solid throughout the entire dog, including the head, tail, and extremities. Also the black nose and flews, black or slate gray pads, dark brown eyes, and dark bluish-gray skin pigmentation must be present in all colors, *including whites.* The geographical distribution of colors today is difficult to determine. In Europe, basing the ratio on the Puli entries in the larger international shows, the shepherd's historical preference for the black color is still highly evident. Blacks outnumber the grays about 40 to 1, and they outnumber the whites about 85 to 1. The white color is practically non-existent in Germany, Switzerland, and Israel. Although the three colors are judged separately in Europe, the number of grays and whites is increasing very slowly. In America, the influence of fashion is more evident; the ratio of blacks to grays can be considered 2 to 1. The blacks still outnumber the whites about 100 to 1 in show quality Pulis, but the overall number of whites is increasing.

In May, 1971, I judged Pulis in Hungary, at the largest International Dog Show to date in Central Europe, and I noticed that the number and quality of whites exhibited there had not changed considerably in the past few years. However, in the same period, both the number and the quality of the blacks advanced tremendously. An answer to my inquiries concerning the whites came from a colleague judging another breed in the next ring. He leaned over the ropes and whispered into my ear "you see, white Pulis are like the striptease in Paris. It is strictly for the American tourists. . . ."

Let us examine the inheritance of color in the Puli. Every breed has dominant and recessive traits. Some of the dominant traits of the Puli are alertness, quickness, long coat, dark pigmentation, scissors bite, square compact body, and solid coat color. The darker colors are dominant over the lighter colors. The black and gray colors are dominant, whereas the white and other colors are recessive. The only way a recessive quality is brought to the surface is by mating a dog and a bitch that both carry the particular recessive gene which produces the characteristic when paired. The only way a white Puli will be born is when both parents carry the genes for white. This does not mean that they have to be white themselves, but that somewhere in their background (it can be as far back as 10 to 20 generations) there were some white ancestors, and the recessive white gene is present in their genetic makeup. (Exactly the same holds true for other recessive traits, such as bad bite or light eye color. The only way an overshot or undershot mouth will be produced is by both parents carrying the recessive gene for "deformed jaw" production. Naturally, when two dogs of a family wherein bad bites appear are mated, the possibility of offspring with bad bites is greatly increased.)

What is the case with the faulty or "non standard" colors (those not listed under permitted colors in either the AKC or Hungarian Puli Standards) such as the black and tan, white and tan, beige, blonde, fawn, champagne, or brown that occasionally appear in a litter? If one checks the pedigrees it will be found that such colors occur most often in lines where there is evidence of an excessive amount of non-selective inbreeding. Pulis with these colors often run into pigmentation problems; the browns will have brown noses and pads, the blondes will have either pink noses or what is often referred to as "seasonal pigmentation," but they seldom have the desired solid black nose, flews, and dark gray pads. Their skin will not be the well-pigmented blue-gray, but will be a pinkish flesh color. True, there might be an occasional puppy that shows good pigmentation, but what will it produce in turn if used in breeding? These colors are recessive and will appear "accidentally." With proper elimination from breeding stock, the recessive genes can be kept well-suppressed genetically. The wisdom of cultivating for new colors within this breed is questionable in my opinion. Unfortunately, however, as long as there are fashion-hunters there will always be those who cater to them.

I would like to point it out here that although the written modern day history of the breed dates back to the early fifteenth century, prior to the beginning of the appearance of Pulis in the cities, I have not been able to find any written reference to colored Pulis whatsoever. The "shepherd's little black Puli" is mentioned in history books and in travelogs as far back as Hungarian history can be traced in modern literature.

Since the AKC Puli Standard contains no written disqualifications at this time, the conscientious breeder must feel morally obligated to maintain the unwritten but historically established standard even when it means considerable sacrifice on his part. It is this moral obligation or "code of ethics" that should keep every Puli owner from breeding or showing Pulis that are non-standard in any way, whether the fault be structural or limited to non-standard coloration.

Chapter 4

WHO SHOULD HAVE A PULI

Unless there is a natural love of animals, the person or family with a Puli will never make a success of keeping it.

When you acquire a Puli, you acquire responsibility and delight. Over its lifespan it will cost you a good deal more than its initial purchase price. And it will cost more work than money. The owners of Pulis have to joyfully sacrifice part of their comfort and leisure time for the training, exercise, and care of their Puli.

Besides his original herding work, there is practically no activity applicable to any canine that cannot be taught to a Puli. In his modern history he has proved himself to be a worthy farm dog, hunting dog, guard dog, police dog, pet, or show dog. His extreme alertness and adaptability has even opened doors for him in the entertainment business. The Puli is excellent with children, provided he is not forced to take rough treatment or abuse from them. If he is intelligently trained for the purpose, he can be an excellent baby-sitter, gentle and careful while playing with small children, and energetic and spirited while playing with teenagers.

With untiring wit and energy, his character limits ownership. Prospective owners should be ready to devote plenty of time to him from his puppyhood to old age. His spirited dance when you go towards the door demands long walks and exercise, more than the average dog of the same size. The Puli is not a good kennel dog; he requires individual attention and needs companionship and home life. Extremely nervous persons should definitely not own a Puli. As with other intelligent breeds, Pulis are prone to pick up the temperament of their masters.

Kindness is probably as important for him as for human beings. Those people who are not sold on the breed before they go into it,

Champion-to-be Hunnia's Cinkos Cuki, at 12 weeks, keeping company with baby mistress Kristin Pohlmann.

or persons who do not like dogs in general, had better not attempt to keep a Puli at all. It is true that the Puli's natural enthusiasm will make the new owner's work lighter and his enjoyment more meaningful, but a beginner should also become familiar with what to do for his Puli's welfare. He should learn the general principle that the permanent improvement of his own breeding stock should be entirely founded upon animals that show unmistakable evidence of the Puli's world-famous vigor, speed, endurance, and structure that have complimented his thousands of years of function and beauty.

The author's son at the age of 9 months, being closely supervised by Ch. Belzebub Gezenguz.

Outstanding qualities are obvious at an early age. Hunnia's Garas (Ch. Cinkotai Csibesz X Ch. Belzebub Gezenguz) pictured here going BOB at a sanctioned match over an impressive entry of matured dogs. Owner handled by the author. Photograph: Missy Yuhl.

Kati Kossuth shares her watermelon with Ch. Erdalsoi Adu Betyar
Matyi and his son, Champion-to-be Hunnia's Betyar Macko.

All of the fanciers of the Puli and the clubs that promote its interests are naturally happy with its increasing popularity. However, we should make sure that the breed is not going to become suddenly fashionable. The slow gain in popularity, the steady increase in the overall number, are in the breed's best interest. In this way, new owners attracted to the breed can be educated and become familiar with the breed's real value while slowly extending their interest toward possible breeding experiments.

Education of the breeders, even if they are small-scale breeders, should be the main interest of the clubs and of all those who have the welfare of the Puli at heart. Education is important for more than one reason. More than likely if an uninformed novice should be lucky enough to acquire quality stock, his first breeding results are going to be disappointing because he does not have the knowledge and experience to choose a suitable mate with comparable qualities. This can result in either his losing interest in the breed completely, or, if he is a little "hard headed" and can afford to campaign his dogs, he can attempt to prove his point by doing everything possible to finish the championships of his mediocre specimens. This can result in a nerve-wracking pursuit of championship titles, Phillips System rating points, and whatever other rewards the dog sport can offer. In either case, the real loser is the breed itself, since no responsible breeder would like to see the breed flooded with inferior stock and "cheap" champions. This would hurt the reputation of the breed, and in the long run, would bring the price of puppies down below the cost of production while completely reversing the popularity of the breed. This, in turn, would leave only a few of the most dedicated breeders to face the ruin and long years of getting the breed back on its feet again. Such a going from a wave of popularity to quick decline has occurred in numerous breeds.

In recent years, the Puli in America has emerged from obscurity and made its name well-known. The Puli is one of the last breeds to enter the modern era of scientific dog breeding. It is not enough to base breeding theories on old wives' tales, personal sentiment towards one's own dog, casual examination of breeding stock, or hearsay concerning your dog's background.

Those who are entering the breed with the idea of occasionally breeding their Puli or of becoming full-fledged breeders of the

Nagykunsagi Hohanyo (Cegledi Fifi X Csillagkerti Aliz). Owner: E. Peter Munchheimer.

Hunnia's
Huncut Hajnal
(Hunnia's Kuszi
X Hunnia's
Ravasz) at the
age of 3 weeks
(above) and at
5 months (left).
Owners: Joe
and Barbara
Klein.

Puli have requirements that go beyond the above. Breeding success depends entirely on how much the breeder is willing to learn. Breeding dogs, or any other animal, requires a complex knowledge of genetics, structure, motion, the individualized requirements of the breed and its function, and above all, the faithful performance of selection for these qualities.

The beginner who decides to breed his Puli should first study, and adopt as his ideal and goal, the recognized standard of excellence of the breed. He should select his future breeding material from the bloodlines known to be most uniformly productive of the ideal as it is described in that standard. He should select the best available individuals from those bloodlines that are most likely to be blessed with the power to transmit their own quality to their progeny. He should learn the laws of breeding: how to mate like with like, generation after generation, in order to condense good qualities from many individuals, and to increase the reproduction capabilities of good qualities by selection.

HOW TO CHOOSE YOUR FIRST PUPPY

First, make certain that each member of the family is enthusiastic about having a Puli. The Puli is much too sensitive not to notice if anyone dislikes him, which could produce an unhappy, troublesome dog that easily becomes the "problem child" of the family. Also, be sure that the Puli is the right dog for you. The easiest way to find that out is to observe one in his home surroundings. Any Puli owner will be glad to show you his dog and to tell you all about him.

Once you decide to buy one, look at more than one Puli litter before reaching your final decision.

One of the most important factors, of course, is the temperament. The "Puli is sensibly suspicious of strangers," but this wariness, however, should never be confused with shyness. When looking at a litter of pups, try to spend plenty of time observing them. Puppies that hide in a corner minutes after their littermates have "made up" with strangers usually grow up to be shy and nervous. The most outgoing or even aggressive puppy is your best bet.

As for general appearance, the easiest to judge in a puppy is the coat texture. It is easy to separate the straight-coated puppies from

Pityerdombi Amor, "Kicsi". Kicsi was imported from Hungary after his Best Of Breed win at the 1973 International Show in Budapest. At this show he won over 180 Pulis, defeating several International Champions. He started his show record in the U.S. with two Best Of Breed awards and a Working Group placement out of the Open class. The first crop of puppies he sired in the U.S. took the top honors at both P.C.A. and P.C.S.C. Specialty Sweepstakes in the spring of 1975. Posed here with Mrs. Ruthlee Becker.

Star of Hunnia Hetyke (Ch. Star of Hunnia Attila X Ch. Nagykunsagi Apro) and kitten playmate. Owner: Geza Vass. Photograph: G. Vass.

the curly-coated ones. Usually, the ones that have a curly coat, or wavy coat, will later develop a heavier coat with a good undercoat. The coat will not necessarily stay curly as the dog grows up, but experience shows that wavy-coated pups are more likely to develop a heavy, unique "Puli coat" than are those born with a straight coat.

The pigmentation of the dog is just as important as the texture of the coat. The puppy has to have a strong, solid color: black, gray, or white. Any uneven shadings already evident in a young puppy will later develop into a light-colored area or spot, which is a serious fault. However, puppies are often born with a few white hairs on the chest which will disappear with the development of their adult coat.

The paws, nose, flews, and eyelids should be black or dark gray, and the nails black. Flesh colors on the nose or paws, and white or cream-colored nails, are indications of bad pigmentation. Good proportions of the body and the right angulation of the legs are part of good quality. Properly formed front legs are straight, and hind legs show well-bent stifle and short hocks. The body should be

Austrian import Champion Buksi Sajo von Funfhausen, (Jozsefvar-osi Ficko X Kisreti Bukfenc) pictured at 9 months of age. Owner: Mrs. Margaret Curran.

Champion Nagykunsagi Rojtos (Kisvattai Antal Ocsi X Nagykunsagi Ragyogo Ricsi) at the age of 5 months.

square, with the length of the body about the same as the height at the shoulders. This quality is usually evident at a very early puppy age, so when judging the proportions of a Puli, it should be taken into consideration. Sometimes there is quite a variation in size among puppies in the same litter. Since the Puli is a light-boned and very active dog, it would be a mistake to suppose that the biggest and heaviest puppy out of a litter will necessarily be the best one. Size is not an indication of degree of health, but of inheritance. Let other qualities determine your choice.

When examining the "bite" of a puppy, bear in mind the following: As a rule, the lower jaw develops more slowly than the upper jaw, so generally speaking it is safe to state that those pups that at 7 or 8 weeks of age appear slightly "overshot" will have the desired "scissors" bite when fully developed. Any pup that is already "undershot" at seven or eight weeks will definitely stay that way. Those that appear to have "level" bite at that age are more likely to be undershot when fully grown. Bad bite is definitely a hereditary fault. One can considerably lessen the risk by examining the bite of the parents, grandparents, and littermates.

You might not be able to find the right puppy on the first weekend you look for it. However, if you are really enthusiastic about the breed, you will appreciate breeders who are not rushing to produce puppies to meet the market, but are breeding only the best to meet the specifications of the "quality Puli," and you will be more than willing to spend the necessary time to find such a breeder and the quality puppy that satisfies your desires.

Chapter 5

SELECTION FOR BREEDING

Purposes in breeding a bitch can vary as widely as individual persons differ. I do not wish to argue the value of the education that can be derived through buying a bitch and breeding her for a youngster to see the entire life cycle developing in front of him. But I question its value for the particular breed employed for such instruction. Millions of pet animals are being put to death each year at various animal shelters and by the Humane Society. We like to refer to our dogs as "man's best friend," but unfortunately this friendship is more often than not proved to be a one-sided affair. In a society where we discourage unplanned parenthood for human beings, some persons seem to find it a fascinating pastime to produce an indiscriminate number of dogs without specific reason. Breeding dogs should, once and for all, be considered a serious activity. Just because purebred dogs are easier to obtain and cost less than thoroughbred horses, they should not be produced indiscriminately every time the opportunity presents itself.

Breeding dogs purposefully requires a thorough knowledge of a multitude of subjects, and it is not enough to own a less-than-average-quality bitch and to have the desire to keep puppies running round the house. In case the owner of the bitch does not have the required technical knowledge, he should engage the help of the most reliable, well-known, knowledgeable breeder in the area. An active breeder in a given locality is more likely than others to know the weaknesses and qualities of the parents and grandparents of the bitch, and more than likely also has some idea of what can be expected from the available stud dogs. If he is as honest as he should be, he is going to refer the novice "breeder-to-be" to the most suitable stud dog. Mates should be chosen in one respect

Ch. Hidegkuti Kocos, "Friend" (Jeddi Bikfic **X** Haraszti Bogar). Kelly and Friend proved to be a lucky combination as show competitors as well as breeding mates. Together they produced many outstanding puppies for the Kennedys' PuliKountry Kennels. Judge: Dr. W. Shute.

American, Mexican, Canadian Champion Nagykunsagi Csorgo, C.D. (Foldeaki Pajtas I Csibesz **X** Gyoztes Borcsa). To demonstrate the versatility of the Puli's coat "Kelly" was campaigned in American shows first with combed out coat for about a year and was later shown corded all the way through the rest of his continuing winning career. Photograph: J. Ludwig.

"Kelly," shown in the classical corded grooming, never retired from the show ring. He had been entered at the 1972 P.C.S.C. Specialty when he died at the age of 12. His outstanding show career was marked with a BIS in Canada. Owner-handled by Mr. Robert Kennedy.

to offset each other's weaknesses. Never choose a mate that has the same faults as your own dog. This is not to be construed that it is advisable to choose a mate with a fault that opposes a fault in your dog. For example, to correct for small ears, it is ill advised to choose a mate with oversized, meaty, or long, heavy, spaniel-like ears. Nor can one expect normally-built puppies from the mating of a narrow-chested bitch to a barrel-chested stud.

Before a breeding is attempted, the prospective breeder should honestly evaluate his motives by answering the following questions:

1. Is it your desire to produce puppies of better quality than either of the parents?
2. Is your bitch better than average, with unquestionable temperament, sound in body, and perfect in type?
3. Was the mating carefully studied and worked out in detail on paper after a thorough search of the available bloodlines data?
4. Will the prospective mates balance each other's possible weaknesses?
5. Have both been X-rayed and been declared by a qualified authority to be normal?
6. Did the bitch go through a complete health check by a qualified veterinarian?
7. Is she at least 18 months of age?
8. Are all her booster shots up-to-date?
9. Was she wormed not more than two months prior to the contemplated mating time?
10. Do you have prospective buyers lined up, or do you have certain knowledge that Puli puppies are easy to sell at a fair market price in your area?

If the answer is NO to any one of the above questions, one had better think over very carefully whether this is the right time to breed.

Novice breeders are often confused by statements like, "Oh, breed to so and so, he is carrying the features of this or that line, because he was line bred to do so." It is often felt that line breeding or inbreeding will place the branding stamp on the particular characteristic that is to be the desirable feature of the line. But, more often than not, it is not mentioned that at the same time that

Champion PuliKountry's Apro, C.D. (Ch. Nagykunsagi Csorgo X Ch. Hidegkuti Kocos). "Kelly's" best known son became top winning Puli in the U.S. for 1971 (Phillips rating system), as well as winning a BIS at the Catonsville K.C. Show, October, 1971. He is pictured here winning the Puli Club of America's Specialty, handled by Jane Forsyth under judge J. Trullinger. "Apro" is presently owned by Mrs. Lois McManus, Wisconsin. Photograph: Gilbert.

a desired feature is strengthened by inbreeding, one also will double up (or strengthen) the genes of bad characteristics. A typical one in our breed is the white bow on the tail of black and dark Pulis. Somewhere back in the history of the breed, a popular stud must have had this fault fixed, by line breeding or inbreeding, because it is just about inerasable in certain bloodlines. The same would hold true for cow hocks, broken-down pasterns, and hip dysplasia.

At the beginning of this breed, man did not cross-breed to arrive at the ultimate Puli. The Puli is one of the very few original breeds.

PuliKountry's Draga Masolat ("Barney") (Ch. Nagykunsagi Csorgo, C.D. X Zsuzsika) shown being owner-breeder handled to a 5-point major win under Major Godsol at the 1968 P.C.S.C. Specialty at K.C. of Beverly Hills, California. "Barney" died during air transit a few days later enroute to the East Coast.

As a result, the Puli breed has survived thousands of years in spite of modern breeding theories and man's "helping hand." The Puli's dominant characteristics breed through very strongly without line breeding.

Line breeding and inbreeding should be considered tools of the master artists of breeding, and should never be attempted by the novice. It is like a violin made by Stradivarius that can bring unprecedented pleasure when played by a Paganini, or it can sound like a squeaky toy in the hands of a gypsy. They both play the violin don't they?

While I do not attempt to discredit the value of books on genetics, most of them are based on highly sophisticated scientific methods

Champion Star of Hunnia Attila (Ch. Nagykunsagi Csorgo, C.D. **X** Ch. Gyali Csopi) shown completing his title under judge Mrs. Helen Writtrig, handled by Klara Benis for owner Mr. George S. DeBodnar. Photograph: J. Ludwig.

Champion PuliKountry's Arpad (Ch. Nagykunsagi Csorgo, C.D. X Ch. Hidekuti Kocos) pictured here taking a 5-point major under judge N. Kay, handled by Dorothy Williams for owners Mr. and Mrs. L. Lipka of Baltimore, Maryland. Photograph: Ludwig. ▶

Tengernagy's Macko (Ch. Nagykunsagi Csorgo, C.D. X Ch. PuliKountry's Csalfa Kocos), bred and owned by Sharron Dattilo, handled here to a 5-point win by co-owner Barbara Deremiah of Phoenix, Arizona. Photograph: H. Schley.

Champion PuliKountry's Feenix Pride (Ch. Nagykunsagi Csorgo, C.D. X Nagykunsagi Borka), owner-handled to her champion-ship by Mrs. Joyce Grief. Judge: Mr. G. Fancy. Photograph: J. Ludwig. ▶

of selection. Most of the researchers had the opportunity to keep all of the progeny of the experimental breeding, sometimes having at hand all the related animals for three or four generations and keeping them under constant observation. Today's average sport breeder does not have the facilities, money, or time to experiment with inbreeding on such a scale. To get a reliable picture of all the facts involved in inbreeding, such large-scale experimentation would be a must. Therefore, I heartily recommend outcrossing as normal practice for the less-experienced. Outcrossing based on the methods of selection discussed in this chapter can bring outstanding results even for the breeder with limited breeding experience. Most of the top producers and top-winning show dogs pictured in this book were so selected and bred.

This chapter is intended to try to help in the choosing of the "ideal" specimen for future breeding purposes. There are four major factors involved in the selection:

1. Selection by Working Capability,
2. Selection by General Impression,
3. Selection by Ancestry,
4. Selection by Offspring.

WORKING CAPABILITY

I have placed the working capability of the dog in first place because we cannot be reminded enough that the Puli is a WORKING BREED. Although very few of our Pulis are herding sheep today, their different environment and various "around-the-house" tasks that they attend to should not necessarily have a changing effect on them. This refers to both intelligence and physical appearance. If a Puli is given various duties to carry out regularly, and receives ample exercise, he will retain these qualities.

Naturally, working capability is closely related to the structural build of the Puli. The structural requirements that are discussed elsewhere in this book were derived from the functional requirements of the breed. Dogs bred for different purposes will reflect their function in their build. Dogs bred for pulling sleds have massive builds and masses of muscle for power. Dogs bred for digging animals from underground hideouts have shorter legs than their galloping hound relatives. The Puli's function requires speed

PuliKountry's Mischief Maker (Ch. Nagykunsagi Csorgo, C.D. **X** Zsuzsika), owned by Mrs. Robert Walker, Sudbury, Massachusetts. Photograph: Dianna Cooney.

combined with endurance, and his structural build has to reflect this, just as his coat reflects the ability to work under the most extreme climatic conditions.

I would like to point out the importance of size as related to working ability. The Puli is a fine-boned, quick-moving dog. He is not supposed to be large and sluggish under any circumstances. Reference is often made to the theory that a Puli can stop a runaway flock of sheep by jumping on the back of the lead-sheep and riding it until the flock slows down. Can you imagine a 45 to 50 pound Puli jumping on the back of a sheep? Surely the sheep would collapse! The question may arise: "Why such importance on the size? The Komondor and Kuvasz are big too." People forget the fact that these big dogs were used mainly to guard the flock when it was stationary. The Puli's duty was to drive it in the right direction and to bring back the runaways.

Temperament is another very important factor in working ability. Try to choose the most energetic, most intelligent dog, as the shy, slow-moving or phlegmatic dog is not Puli-like and should not be used as breeding stock. (The characteristic "wariness" should not be confused with timidity.)

Unfortunately, we don't have herding field-trials wherein the Puli's intelligence and ability could readily be shown. But obedience trials, and even the way they fulfill commands given them at home, can give us very good indications of the usefulness and willingness of the dogs that we plan to take into our breeding program.

GENERAL IMPRESSION

My personal preference would have been to leave the discussion of this guide for selection by general impression until last, but because many of the questions from the next two steps involving ancestry and offspring will be related to this one, and because this is the most common way of selecting, it is perhaps just as well to discuss it as the second phase of selection.

I will try to avoid too much involvement with the breed standard, and assume that you have some familiarity with the specific requirements. Although our AKC standard does not list any disqualifying faults for the breed, in careful breeding programs we must be much more selective.

Probably the first indications of characteristic qualities in a newly-born puppy are the coat texture and pigmentation. On the first day or two after the puppies are completely dry, it is easy to separate the straight coated pups from the curly ones. Usually the pups that have curly coats will later develop a heavier coat with a good undercoat. This coat will not necessarily stay curly as the pups grow, but experience shows that these puppies are more likely to develop the heavy, wavy, unique "Puli coat" than those born with a straight coat.

The pigmentation of a dog is quite evident at a very early age. The paws, nose, flews, and eyelids should be black or dark gray, and the nails should be black. Flesh color on the nose or paws and white or cream-colored nails are indications of bad pigmentation.

As the puppy starts to develop, we can judge the proportions of the body and the angulation and straightness of the legs. Viewed

Canadian Champion PuliKountry's Kocos Koukie (Ch. Nagykunsagi Csorgo, C.D. **X** Ch. Hidegkuti Kocos), owner-handled by Mrs. Louise Beerman. Photograph: Wainwright.

American, Hungarian Champion Gyalpusztai Kocos Burkus (Matyasfoldi Lurko Dongo **X** Gyalpusztai Morzsa). Breeder: Elek Farkas, Budapest, Hungary. "Koci" is turning in a most astonishing career as both sire and show dog. He was only 2¼ years old when he left his native Hungary. Seven years later he still ranked as the sixth top-producing sire of all time on the records of the Hungarian Kennel Club. Although he finished his AKC championship shortly after his arrival in the U.S., he has not been shown actively, to spare competition to his kennel mate, Ch. Cinkotai Csibesz. After the retirement of "Csibesz," "Koci" at the age of six years started an unparalleled show career, with a group placing his first time out at the Del Monte K.C. Show, Pebble Beach, California. A week before he turned ten years old he won the largest (to that date) Puli Specialty Show for the third consecutive year. He is shown here handled by co-owner Barry Becker. Judge: Mr. L. Skarda.

Hungarian, Czechoslovakian, Polish, Monaco, Italian, F.C.I. International Champion Pusztai Furtos Ficko (Ch. Gyalpusztai Kocos Burkus X Kondorosi Bajos Bogar). "Koci's" internationally best known son is pictured here at the age of 20 months, not yet in full coat. "Ficko," who is Top Producing Sire of all times in Hungary, by now has outstanding progeny in every country where Pulis are bred and shown. Owner: Mrs. Sara Nagy of Budapest, Hungary.

from the rear, hind legs are vertical and parallel. Usually when a pup has nice straight legs and an even gait we can reasonably expect that he will keep these good qualities when brought up properly.

The above mentioned points are generally true in the case of most dog breeds. However, it is a less well-known fact that the Puli's body should be *square* and, though our AKC standard doesn't mention it, the length of the body should be the same as the height. This quality is usually evident in puppyhood. When judging the proportions of a Puli, this point should definitely be taken into consideration.

Ch. Szatmari Kapuore Szultan Csibesz. He is Apors sire and was imported by Mr. & Mrs. Majoross of Painesville, Ohio, based on his sons' qualities. "Csimbo" became the foundation stud at the Majers's and Majoross's excellent new kennels.

Another important factor is the head. Its proportions, the length of muzzle, the presence of a clearly defined stop, the shape, setting, and size of ears, and the distance from each other and shape of the eyes can all be determined at a very early age. Unfortunately there is one thing that is difficult to judge in a young puppy and that is the bite. It takes an experienced eye to determine whether a puppy will have the perfect scissors bite when fully grown, or whether its bite will be overshot or undershot. As a rule, the lower jaw develops more slowly than the upper jaw and it is generally safe to state that those pups that appear slightly overshot at 7 or 8 weeks of age will have the desired scissors bite when fully grown. Any pups that are already undershot at the age of 7 to 8 weeks will definitely stay that way, or will worsen. Using similar logic, we may assume that pups which appear to have a level bite at that age will more than likely be undershot when fully developed. Because a bad bite is a hereditary fault, one can lessen the risk by examining the bite of the parents, grandparents, and littermates.

The most common mistake that even experienced breeders often make is selecting for their future breeding programs the heaviest, biggest-boned puppy of a litter. May I emphasize again, the Puli is a light-boned and very active dog; it is unlikely, therefore, that a heavy, big-boned specimen will produce ideal, light-weight offspring. It is false to suppose that bones larger in dimension are necessarily better in quality. Often heavier bones, instead of being more valuable through strength, have actually lost some of their flexibility. With a breed such as ours, where speed and agility are so important, this would be quite a drawback.

Selection strictly by the appearance of a single dog might give us a good show specimen, but unfortunately it doesn't guarantee perfect breeding stock. In order to have both, one has to combine all four methods of selection.

Hungarian, Polish, F.C.I. International Champion Pusztai Kocos Panna, another international champion offspring of "Koci's," is presently owned by Mrs. Stretton and Mrs. Horan of England. "Panni" is looking forward to an extensive show career in England, where Pulis were unknown until comparatively recently.

Champion Tiszaujfalui Pamacs (Ch. Gyalpusztai Kocos Burkus X Korosparti Delibab). Owned by Dr. Anthony Brunse of Encino, California.

ANCESTRY

Every dog, unless he is a product of line breeding or inbreeding, has two parents, four grandparents, eight great-grandparents, and so on with all pairings from different generations. The puppy will inherit most from his parents, somewhat less from his grandparents, and as we go farther down the line of ancestors the strength of influence will be less and less. It is, of course, false to suppose that 50 percent of all inherited visible characteristics come from one parent and 50 per cent from the other, or that 25 percent come from each of the grandparents. If this were so, all of the pups from the same litter would look exactly alike. Anyone who has ever bred dogs will be able to testify that nothing is further from the truth. There

Champion Hunnia's Tisza Tee, C.D. (Ch. Gyalpusztai Kocos Burkus X Tinker Tee), owner-handled to her championship and C.D. titles by Mrs. Lillian Humphrey, here finishing her title with a BOS under judge Mrs. Mickey Kish. Photograph: J. Ludwig.

Dorozsmai Fruzsi (Nagykunsagi Ulti Suttyo **X** Imrei Fruska) posed here by the author's mother. Although she never left Hungary, "Fruzsi" is presently ranking third top-producing Puli bitch in the U.S. She was bred only four times in her life, each time to Int. Ch. Pusztai Furtos Ficko. This breeding combination was planned, based on pedigrees, well before "Fruzsi" was born.

Champion Varosszeli Bogar (Ch. Gyalpusztai Kocos Burkus x Arpadligeti Cuki), imported and handled by Mrs. Eva Winkler of the Prairie Rouge Kennels of Pennsylvania. Photograph: Gilbert.

Champion Sasvolgyi Hunnia Panka (Int. Ch. Pusztai Furtos Ficko X Dorozsmai Fruzsi), owner-handled to her title by Mr. Barry Becker. Judge: Mrs. Helen Wittrig. Photograph: J. Ludwig.

Champion Sasvolgyi Pici Pamacs (Int. Ch. Pusztai Furtos Ficko **X** Dorozsmai Fruzsi), the first one of the "Frutos"-"Fruzsi" combination puppies to finish her AKC championship. Owned by the author. Photograph: J. Ludwig.

is a possibility of an equal influence on each individual feature from both sire and dam, but it very seldom happens. All of those characteristics that are repeatedly present through the line of ancestors will more readily be inherited. Unfortunately this is true about bad characteristics as well, and this is why we have to be very thorough in the examination and judging of the ancestors of the pair we plan to breed. Luckily for us, dogs develop fast enough so that we can observe several generations in a short period of time.

It is good practice to take the time and effort to see the litter brothers and sisters of the dog to be selected. What good is an outstanding dog for breeding purposes if all or many of his littermates are of inferior quality? Only after we have examined all of these close and distant relatives, and have found them to be more

Champion Sasvolgyi Hunnia Suba (Int. Ch. Pusztai Furtos Ficko **X** Dorozsmai Fruzsi) proved himself an excellent stud dog, house pet and show stopper for owner Mrs. Laura McKean.

Ch. Skysyl That's It (Adam) (Skysyl November Leaf **X** Ch. Kylends Watch It). Adam was retired at a relatively young age to spare competition to his kennel mate "Harvey," but not before he added a Best In Show to his impressive show record. Photo: Gilbert.

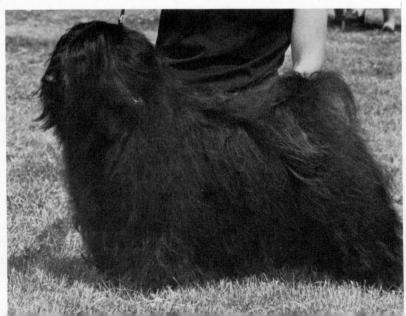

Champion Sasvolgyi Puszi Pajtas (Int. Ch. Pusztai Furtos Ficko X Dorozsmai Fruzsi), pictured here finishing her title and going BOS at, to that date, the largest Puli Specialty in the U.S. Owner-handled by Mrs. Deborah Hoffman; judge, Dr. W. Shute. Photograph: J. Ludwig.

or less of the same appearance, of good temperament, and free of all serious faults, can we hope to be certain of a litter of the desired quality.

To strengthen certain characteristics in a dog, breeders often turn to inbreeding or line breeding. (Both terms refer to breeding back to some relative of the dog.) This method is very helpful in producing excellent show specimens, but it is also the most dangerous way of breeding, since it must be realized that along with strengthening of the desirable characteristics that are apparent we may also strengthen and bring to the surface the hidden and undesirable ones. Careful inbreeding requires time-consuming study and an ample knowledge of the science of genetics. To inbreed

Champion Sasvolgyi Torkos Miska (Int. Ch. Pusztai Furtos Ficko X Dorozsmai Fruzsi) thrilled his owners, Mr. and Mrs. Glenn Cook, when he finished his title with a Best of Breed win.

Champion Sasvolgyi Hunnia Dorka (Int. Ch. Pusztai Furtos Ficko X Dorozsmai Fruzsi), owned by Schuyler McLaine of Los Angeles, California.

Champion Sasvolgyi Hunnia Borzas (Int. Ch. Pusztai Furtos Ficko X Dorozsmai Fruzsi) won a 5-point major while going WB at the Puli Club of America's Specialty in October, 1971. Owner: Mrs. Kelly McLaughlin.

Two-time winner of the National C.A.C. title and H.F.G.Y., Nagy-kunsagi Fustos (Int. Ch. Pusztai Furtos Ficko **X** Nagykunsagi Fodor) is owned and was bred by the well known authority of the breed, Dr. Imre Bordacs of Hungary. At the time of this printing, "Fustos" is the current favorite at Hungarian dog shows.

out of necessity or negligence is a sure way of ruining the reputation of a bloodline. Inbreeding is a complete study by itself, and I mention it here because in selecting the ideal specimen, we have to be aware of its advantages and disadvantages.

OFFSPRING

The true value of a selected stud dog or brood bitch can only be determined finally by the careful examination of the offspring they produce.

In respect to a brood bitch, we can make a first judgement of her after puppies of her first litter are old enough to be examined critically. If the pups are not up to expectations, we should select another stud for her next mating, preferably one that is known to have produced excellent offspring out of other bitches. If the bitch continues to produce pups that are in any way undesirable after trying two or three different sires, she should be taken out of the breeding program.

In the case of the male, we must be even more careful, as he can produce more than 100 times as many offspring as a bitch. This can be proved with a bit of basic mathematics. The average litter of puppies for the Puli is five. Assuming that in a given year a bitch was bred twice, then she produced ten puppies. In that year a well-publicized stud, who could also be known through his show career, could well be used as often as three times a week. During that year he would thus produce 780 puppies. In more popular breeds there are studs that have been used more than three times a

Sasvolyi Hunnia Cili (Int. Ch. Pusztai Furtos Ficko X Dorozsmai Fruzsi), shown here owner-handled to a major win by Mrs. Martha Williams of San Antonio, Texas. Judge: Mr. Larry Downey. Photograph: Twomey.

Champion Prairie Rogue's Burkus, C.D. (Ch. Kakaspusztai Bogar Cigany X Nagykunsagi Fitos). Owner: Lissy Robbins. Photograph: Robbins.

Champion Kakaspusztai Bogar Cigany (Ch. Tiszaufalui Pamacs X Tiszadobi Csopi Moniko) is another third-generation descendant of Ch. Gyalpusztai Kocos Burkus. "Bo" turned the center of interest on himself by going BOB from the classes numerous times. Usually shown by Jane Forsyth, he is pictured here owner-handled by Mrs. Eva Winkler of Prairie Rogue Kennels, of Palmerton, Pennsylvania. Photograph: Gilbert.

Prairie Rogue's Bo Rag-A-Muffin (Ch. Kakaspusztai Bogar Cigany **X** Nagykunsagi Fitos), following his sire's footsteps, is shown here going BOB from the classes under judge Mr. Booxbaum. Owner-handler, Mrs. Susan Ann Reiss. Photograph: Gilbert.

week throughout their prime years. (As a general practice a bitch should not be bred twice a year throughout her life.)

Because of this important productivity factor, most experts working in the field of inheritance derived a method of selection by offspring in much more detail concerning the sire. According to scientific studies, less than 10 percent of all males can be considered ideal stud dogs. But using this 10 percent properly can be of the greatest help in improving the breed. After the male has been tried with five to six bitches and produced unquestionably good puppies, he can be considered a good "proven stud" and bitch owners should be referred to such dogs.

Of course, it would be a mistake to judge either sire or dam only by the offspring that are known through shows and personal

White Oaks Kis Pajtas (Ch. Tiszaujfalui Pamacs **X** Ch. Imrei Kocos) is owned and bred by Dr. Anthony J. Brunse of Encino, California. Handled here by Barry Becker. Judge: Mrs. Helen Wittrig. Photograph: Alfred Stillman.

Champion Star of Hunnia Bogancs (Gyalpusztai Bundas X Ch. Gyali Csopi) is handled here by the author for co-owner Dick Velthoen. Photograph: J. Ludwig.

contacts. To get a reliable picture of a sire or dam, we have to take into consideration all of the puppies produced by that dog or bitch.

Each of these four methods represents a part in a filter system. Although the order of importance may be debatable, each performs a specific function in filtering out undesirable characteristics.

It should be pointed out here that absolutely no compromise should be made when selecting a Puli for a definite breeding purpose. A Puli that is structurally acceptable but has a much lighter coat color on his face and legs than on the rest of his body, or one that has a coat of intense solid color but also has sloping pasterns or is straight in the stifle, or the dog that is of good conformation, has solid color, but is of poor temperament, is a bad choice. One may have to search for months or years to find the overall quality required for breeding stock. But patient, careful selection will pay off in saving the breeder or prospective breeder from years of trial and error and many disappointments.

I believe that a little concentrated study of the above methods of selection and the willingness to learn more than just the names from pedigrees about the history and ancestry of our dogs will help our breed considerably and will hopefully encourage Puli breeders to outline some kind of breeding program on paper well before a contemplated mating time.

Ch. Sasvolgyi Puszi Pajtas, "Minka." Top-winning Puli bitch (Phillips System) 1973, 1974. No. 13 Working Dog, No. 40 All Breeds 1974. She won Best Of Breed at the Puli Club of America spring 1975 specialty show. "Minka" is the second Puli bitch in the breed's history to go Best In Show.

Chapter 6

THE NATIONAL PULI FANCIERS' CONVENTION

Credit and appreciation are due to those who have helped this breed get on its feet in America and have continued helping its advancement. Without taking away from the worthwhile achievements of the majority of the breeders and individual Puli owners, we must mention those who have on occasion held back the advancement of this breed. As in every breed, we will unfortunately find some in this category. The more popular a breed becomes, the more "leeches" appear for such various reasons as monetary gains, personal glorification, educational experience, various psychological reasons, etc. One would have to be a psychiatrist to list all the possible reasons. But besides these "hangers-on," consider the difficult start this breed had at the beginning in the United States.

When World War II broke out, the disbanding Research Center of the Department of Agriculture at Beltsville, Maryland, auctioned its Puli stock to private owners. These dogs were in kennel clip and for all intents and purposes the only Hungarian sheepdogs in the United States. For a long time the vast majority of the Puli owners never saw a Puli in its full-blooming coat, not to mention the classic corded coat. Several old-time dog show judges told me that there was only one corded Puli shown in the midwest area of the United States in the late 1930's.

For 20 to 25 years after the breed was introduced into the United States, printed technical material on the Puli was non-existent, mainly as a result of World War II. This made it difficult for even the well-meaning, serious minded breeder, since without the adequate information, it is very hard to give advice to new owners, very hard to create a base for quality, and even harder to fight personal beliefs. To love a breed alone is not enough to really help it.

Breeders scattered far apart could not even compare their dogs with those of the others on a competitive basis. This unfortunate situation led to some breeders introducing changes in the structural make-up and appearance of the Puli. Although there was a Puli standard to use as a yard stick, it was, like most standards, not detailed enough to help the average person create a mental picture of the ideal specimen of the breed.

We have been told many times that the human element in the interpretation of the Puli standard, and the American penchant for doing things our own way, were responsible for the wide differences between different bloodlines. This might be true, but it should only be true to a limited extent. The breeder's interpretation of the standard and his knowledge of what is desired and what is not desired in his breed should not vary from kennel to kennel, influenced alone by the human element. Acknowledging the possible slight variance in the individual breeder's interpretation, there is still no excuse for the wide discrepancy, and often weird differences, between Pulis coming from different bloodlines.

Many decades ago the original purpose of holding a dog show was to help breeders, through open competition, to evaluate their stock and their breeding procedures in relation to the quality of the stock of others. Competition could also suggest which bloodlines could help correct the faults inherent in their breeding program. Through the help of the knowledge and the unbiased opinion of the judge, future mates to one's own brood bitch or stud dog could be selected, and ribbons and prizes were awarded as tokens of achievement in advancement of the breed.

A dog show judge was to act as a stepping stone between the present and the future of the breed; for better or worse, his decisions would influence the trends which the breed would follow. Any achievement could be realized only if the judging was uniform from week to week and from show to show. How could one ask for uniformity in judging when some of the breeders did not produce two Pulis that were alike? Breeders could blame themselves for the questionable quality of judging so often encountered. For some,

Ch. Cinkotai Csibesz with the trophies he collected during his show career.

showing a Puli had degenerated into a race to collect ribbons, silver hardware, and occasions for posing for "win" pictures.

Judges who asked important questions from breeders and were honestly interested in learning more about the breed got different answers on the East Coast than those given on the West Coast.

If more ideal conditions were ever to exist in the U.S., all of the Puli people needed the guidance, strict scrutiny, and competent authority from experts whose integrity was beyond question. This was needed not only for breeders and judges to learn more about this breed (to enable us to honestly measure the value of our stock), but also to establish a scale to measure the worth of different breeding theories.

Since the Puli Club of America seemed too busy in popularizing the breed only on the pet owner's level of interest, it became apparent that there was a need for a Puli breeder's forum. Because of the high Puli concentration and population in California, it came as no great surprise that the first National Puli Fanciers Convention was organized under the auspices of the Puli Club of Southern California, Inc. This convention proved to be so successful that it has since then become a bi-annual event at which Puli breeders and owners gather from every part of the globe. Well-known judges of the Puli, as well as judges of other breeds, sit in the audience at these conventions to learn more about this fascinating breed.

What could have been more natural than to invite the leading authority on the Puli and a man from the breed's own native country to give us the guidance that was much needed? Dr. Imre Bordacs spent only a few short weeks in the U.S., but his visit will still be felt by all Puli enthusiasts for a long time to come.

Although not thoroughly familiar with the Puli situation throughout America, or its relative position to other breeds, he managed in his short speech to touch upon the essence of everything that I am trying to say in this entire book. His speech should be the creed of all Puli breeders, and it should be framed in gold in every Puli owner's home.

DR. BORDACS' PRESENTATION

NOTE: The following presentation was made by Dr. IMRE BORDACS (of Budapest) at the FIRST NATIONAL PULI FANCIERS CONVENTION (Hollywood Roosevelt Hotel, June, 1968).

The attachment of the Puli to his master is really something to behold. It is probably just because of this attachment that the owners and breeders of Pulis are so vehement in their love for this animal. The Puli owners and breeders are a great family whose prize possession is that friend who has for about 7 to 8 thousand years borne the name Puli.

It was this attachment and love that motivated the Puli Club of Southern California to be the first to organize a Puli convention in the New World, far from the country of the dog's origin. It is my understanding that the convention's aim is to promote the breed and to discuss scientific breeding practices. The Club has been

Dr. Imre Bordacs of Hungary, internationally known authority of the breed, was the main speaker of the first Puli fanciers' national convention with one of his favored Pulis.

able to attract people of all walks of life and from far regions of the country. It is due to the Club's efforts that for this convention someone has been invited from the country of origin, Hungary, to come to speak to you, and to tell you what is being done in Hungary and Europe for the breed. I would like to take this occasion to thank the Puli Club of Southern California for making it possible for me to come to this convention, and I would like to convey the greetings and very best wishes of the members and directors of the Hungarian Dog Breeders Organization (which is the Hungarian Kennel Club) and The Hungarian National Puli Club. They have asked me to personally transmit their heartfelt greetings and their desire that this congress will result in true success for the benefit of the American Puli breeders.

It is this meeting which should constitute a cornerstone in the history of American Puli breeding, just as the first Hungarian Cynological Congress gave future direction for equanimity and conscientious Puli breeding and has been the impetus for knowledgeable growth.

Before we get to the problems of Puli breeding, we must agree that however large *and* cohesive the group is, insofar as love and appreciation for the breed, there is a difference between Puli fanciers and Puli breeders. I am sure here in the U.S.A. we will also find individuals whose love and appreciation for their own Puli is so great that they are sure he is the most beautiful and most intelligent. His possible faults become dim before their eyes, and they would be willing to even change the standard requirements to fit their individual dog.

The true Puli breeder is quite different in this respect. They are by far not as delighted with their own Puli, rather they put themselves to the task to determine the ideal, and strive to approach it with their breeding. This constitutes in breeding circles passion, sport, and noble competition.

What I am about to tell you is mainly intended for the breeder. However, the Puli fancier will also appreciate knowing how many problems have to be met in order to achieve the breeding of a really excellent bloodline, and with this, attempting to turn Puli fanciers into enthusiastic but objective breeders.

I am deeply honored that I have been given the task to speak before so many experts: Puli breeders, Puli owners, and enthusiastic participants; to tell you about principles of the past and present that we have followed either by choice or maybe even unintentionally, but which directions we will have to follow purposefully in the future, in order to serve the best interests of Puli breeding within the different regions of this world; and to hope to reconcile these practices. We wish to achieve in the shortest possible time that *this*, the most ancient Hungarian breed, the Puli, shall give evidence in conformation as well as inner traits to the superior intelligence, lovable demeanor and possibly least pretentious behavior, thereby popularizing his fame all over the world and gathering more and more friends among dog fanciers, dog breeders, and dog owners.

The Puli has for many thousands of years definitely been a herding sheepdog. For this reason selections have been made for countless years mostly for inner traits. First consideration was given to his ability to complete his tasks. Therefore, not too much care or importance had been given, in the beginning, to color, coat and many other body forms to which today we strictly adhere. (I am afraid in some cases even too strictly.) One thing however is certain: Size has *always* been important. The ancient Magyars have always insisted on the small size in the Puli, for we find the larger sheepdogs, whose task it was to guard the flocks, were well known to them, personified in the magnificent Komondor, a breed distinctively different already in ancient times. With such breeding precepts it is therefore quite understandable that such traits as temperament and obliging readiness to learn, that will manifest itself in every case, bred into the Puli for centuries, can be observed even in Pulis that have never known other homes than city apartments. This, therefore, we don't have to belabor because it will be noticeable in this breed even in dogs of extreme differences in conformation.

Around the turn of the century and in the first decades of this century, equal importance has been given to the outer appearance. The color has now standardized and breeding of black, a whole range of gray and white solid colors has evolved. However, the appearance of (chocolate) brown has always denoted foreign implication. The present form of ears has also become a requirement, and the dogs with raised ears have been separated from those whose ears lie close. An important step was taken when in the

Miss Elizabeth Csengeri, right, with the author's wife rating some
puppies at Hunnia Kennels. Miss Csengeri was invited for her visit
in the U.S. by the Puli Club of Southern California, Inc.

thirties, the Puli standard appeared, which determined the size of the Puli, and divided it into 4 groups. The color remained unchanged and only the white spot was restricted. This constituted a meaningful advancement at that time and in my opinion it would have been a really determining advancement had the breeders with expert knowledge and determination followed up on these breeding practices and separated their breeding stock into the 4 size groups. This however was not done. The dogs were bred without real programs or restrictions. It was unimportant how big the progeny grew. He would in any case fit one of the 4 sizes.

Such breeding practices were also to be found outside of Hungary, where the dogs imported before the second World War were bred without the benefit of direction from the country of origin, determined goals, or influx of fresh bloodlines, to the vim and determination of each individual breeder, under completely different and foreign environments.

The result of this is well known to almost all present here. In Hungary this aimless breeding has been terminated by the breeders themselves. After long discussions, sometimes reaching far into the night, and after many scientific deliberations, the reviewed and revised Puli standard has been published with the help of the governing bodies of the Hungarian dog associations. This standard, without doubt, determines the ideal Puli type. Besides other requirements, it establishes definitely the height of the Puli at the withers. It was absolutely necessary to do that, so we could start from a fixed point. Since that time some years have passed, and our breeders, adhering to these standards, have achieved a breeding stock in which 75 percent represents this type. It is lamentable that the foreign countries, because of lack of communication and fresh bloodlines, have not kept pace with the Hungarian improvements of Puli breeding, and in some places Puli breeding has taken paths of different directions. In my country, this problem has been all but eliminated, and we can also find conformity to this direction in some foreign breeding groups, where the breeding goals have been recognized and efforts are being made to adhere to them, struggling against individuals who wish to follow the easy paths.

This convention has been called to find accord and agreement. What shall we do to promote the similarity and conformation of appearance? The Puli standard shows us the way by prescribing the ideal form of the Puli. Here we must first of all determine: what is the Puli standard? And then shall we follow its direction?

The Puli standard is a guidance, a model, a pattern of the ideal Puli, that the breeders must approach. This should therefore not be taken as an exact requirement. Many will feel that from now on all Pulis have to look as the standard prescribes. This is not true, and it has given fuel to many a heated argument. The standard is to be used as a guide line to the conscientious breeder in his breeding practices, and to the judge when he performs his duty in judging.

After determining these facts we may now come to the following:
1. The general appearance
2. The coat
3. The color
4. The movement
5. The size
So now let's go into these points one by one:

1. The General Appearance
The Puli's exceptionally lively temperament must be enhanced by a body that is nimble, resilient, and muscular.

The ideal form of this requirement is known not only to dog breeders but to everyone interested in any kind of animal breeding. Such a body must have elasticity and be able to effect fast movements, turns, and must have a pleasing countenance. Such a body must be well proportioned. The head well covered with a long coat should be well rounded, which excludes a long muzzle. Only in such a classic evenly-shaped head can the bite form a scissors position.

The Puli's ears are characteristic. They are of medium length and V-shaped. When pulled forward, the tip of the ear should reach the inner corner of the eye. The ear must have a medium set because any other set would tend to disfigure the head's outline. For this same reason, the ear may not be too light, too gay, or too drooping. The movement of the ear therefore is not upward, but rather backward. The forehead is well-rounded, with a well-arched stop line. The eyes are somewhat almond shaped. They are never too deep-seated or protruding.

The neck should be well proportioned and should raise the head intelligently above the backline. The withers are perceptible.

One of the most decisive requirements of the Puli is the ideal body. The body should be tight and the length from the point of shoulder to the point of rump should be equal to the height at the withers. This means the Puli's appearance should be square in profile. The intrusion of foreign genetic elements are often revealed by an elongated body. The loins are short and tight. The shoulder blades are moderately angled, and lie snug to the chest. The tail should almost appear as a continuation of the body. A droopy tail should not hinder the Puli in his lively movement. The length of the tail reaches to the hocks. The natural positioning of the tail is such that it will curl to the midline of the back, the coat on it falling to both sides of the rump. It is acceptable if the tail curls over the back and falls to one side or the other. A tail carried in such a manner is, however, never as stable. A heavy coat sometimes camouflages an otherwise faulty, loose tailset. When the hindmost tail vertebrae are correctly curved, it will enhance the correct tailset. The extremities should be proportionately balanced and sinewy. They should well support the body, at the same time enabling the Puli to make rapid change of direction. They should be parallel when viewed from the front or rear. The stand is medially broad. The paws are tight and close, because only this enables a quick, resilient movement. All parts of the body should be well covered with proportionately long, profuse coat.

2. The Coat

In former times, the shepherds didn't pay much attention to the coat, and its formation was entrusted to nature. The classical Puli coat developed as a result of environment. This coat would best protect the Puli against the hardships of weather and nature, and served best in not restricting the Puli's movement. This is how the felty tassels or cords evolved that protected the Puli from the rigors of winter frost and precipitation, while during the summer heat these cords often were shed in parts to allow freer air circulation. The cords, however, were never shed on the head or rump areas. In my opinion, overemphasis has been given lately as to the length and profuseness of the coat, which, although impressive, often hides major faults and shortcomings. What then are the possible Puli coat formations?

a. The ideal type is the flat cord that covers the whole body with proportionately uniform ribbon-like tassels that are approximately the width of $\frac{1}{2}$ inch.

b. Another type is that which does not form cords or tassels, but mats up into uneven bunches, mainly toward the rear of the body. This type of coat is not as desirable because it is hard to keep clean. The surface of the skin is not free to properly ventilate and could be the cause of health problems.

c. An opposite to this is the round, overly-thin cord. This type of cord is often not even a natural formation and it is probably not indigenous to the breed. It is possible to tear the aforementioned two types of coats into these too narrow cords. But these thin cords are not desirable because they do not fulfill the function of body temperature regulation.

d. In the fourth group we include the completely open straight coat which lacks all tendency to cord into either round or flat tassels and will not retain the undercoat, so necessary for the correct formation of the coat. This coat is usually silky in texture and shiny in appearance, and is very likely the result of foreign genetic involvement. As such, it is highly undesirable for breeding purposes.

How does the Puli coat occur in so many different forms and why? The Puli coat consists of a top coat and a woolly undercoat. The relative proportion of these two governs the development of the Puli coat. While an abundance of top coat tends to encourage the cord formation, an overabundance of undercoat tends to encourage matting. Therefore, what constitutes the ideal Puli coat? Perhaps the best way to describe it is the one that needs the least amount of human intervention so that it should not hinder or inconvenience either the Puli or his master with its upkeep. And one that with the least amount of labor can be kept clean. It should not mat excessively, for this will hinder the Puli's free movement as well as be detrimental to his health and cleanliness. But on the other hand it should not be too open or too narrow corded so as to interfere with the dog's heat exchange mechanism but should enhance his physiological well-being to the fullest. This unique coat formation has been greatly instrumental in the establishment of the good reputation of the Puli to be among the most rugged breeds not easily prone to health or skin problems. The ideal type of coat

Dr. Erno Kubinszky of Budapest, Hungary. The well known veterinarian and international all-around judge is shown awarding Best Senior Sweepstakes at the P.C.S.C. Specialty at Santa Barbara in 1970 to Champion-to-be Tish's Kis Fekete Kaloz (Ch. Nagykunsagi Csorgo, C.D. **X** Ch. Princess Tish of Beverlywood, C.D.). Handled by Barry Becker.

can be recognized even when cords are lost due to shedding for reasons of temperature variations or work conditions, etc. The remaining short coat appears to be more substantial, wavier and sometimes even curly.

3. Color

The color is a very important factor. As I have mentioned in the beginning, centuries ago the shepherds were more interested in establishing the inner desirable traits than that of the color. The original color of the Puli was probably the dull rusty black in its various shades, and Pulis with a white spot on the chest or white coat on their paws must not have been uncommon. This ancient trait must be responsible for the fact that even today this dull or rusty black is the dominant color of the breed and that we sometimes encounter small white markings on the chest or paws or between the pads. In judging the Puli's color, more emphasis should be placed on the pigmentation than on the actual color of the coat. What do we mean by that? All hairless parts of the body must be black with the exception of the pads which may also be a dark slate gray. The areas of the skin that are covered with coat must always be slate gray. (This includes even the white coated Puli). The iris of the eye should always be dark, coffee brown. Therefore, the deeper the pigmentation, the more desirable the color. With this we have determined the Puli's color. What are, therefore, the solid colors possible when limiting ourselves to black or slate gray pigmentation? First of all, black. Secondary, the whole range of gray all the way from the deep black through the dull black, rusty black, all shades of gray all the way to pure white. (Of course, we mean a solid color, whatever its shade!) Excluded therefore are all shades of brown that occur in conjunction with pigmentations other than the required black or slate gray. The often appearing salt and pepper effect caused by the even distribution of white or light gray individual hairs within the coat is not to be considered a fault and it is a very often occurring Puli coat characteristic.

I'd like to devote a separate chapter to the question of the white color. The white Puli is accepted and is considered today equal to the black or gray. We must, however, give very special attention and strict consideration to the white Puli's pigmentation. The exposed skin areas of the white Puli (nose, eyelids, flews, pads) must be without exception black or at least slate gray, and the skin under the coat must also be a shade of gray. The appearance of yellow markings must be considered as excluding as are the white spottiness or parti-coloredness in the black or gray Puli. Therefore, if it is recurrent, it should be considered a major fault, and when these spots have definite outlines they should be considered disqualifying faults. The authenticity of the white Puli was often questioned. I must here state categorically that the white Puli definitely exists. We should, however, not be misled by accepting white individuals that have been bred to this color by the accidental or willful mating of the Puli to the Maltese or small Komondor.

Mrs. Sara Nagy of Hungary. This well known breeder and judge of Pulis poses here with Champion Thundermount Arpad (Acsi of PuliKountry X Star of Hunnia Furtos) during her California judging tour.

An experienced judge or breeder will have no difficulty determining this foreign influence if present. Such foreign influx can be easily determined when looking for traits usually characteristic of the other two breeds. Since we know that white or grayish white Pulis existed in the ancestry of our breed, we should not be surprised when black Pulis with many generations of known black ancestors will sometimes throw a well-pigmented pure white Puli. Now let's examine the question of spottiness. We often encounter the white spot on the chest. We now have to establish a limit to the size which the standard does not yet consider a major fault. According to the standard, the area must not exceed 2 inches in diameter. Such a spot goes in conjunction with a non-pigmented pink skin beneath. Spots on any other parts of the body, as well as yellow spots in case of the white Puli are to be considered serious faults, and if there is a definite outline to it, or it occurs on more than one place, it is disqualifying. Occasional darker shading in the gray Puli should not be considered a fault. The albino Puli is to be excluded from both breeding and exhibiting. Naturally, the different colors are to be bred separately, recorded separately, and judged separately.

4. The Movement

There is something very special about the way a Puli moves. In his work he is not required to run long distances constantly. The main importance is on the speed of his reaction, and especially on the ability to change direction "on a dime." While excitedly waiting for a command, he seldom stands still but is performing almost a dance-like bouncing movement. When he takes off, he'll gallop full speed, and only when he finishes the given task does he come back with a leisurely normal trot.

The Puli's natural gait is not the long strides of the Kuvasz or German Shepherd. His sudden change of pace and direction is spontaneous and reflex-like. The joints of his extremities are developed in a way to accommodate this quick movement. His shoulders are about as angulated as those of the other working dogs; his gait is not far-reaching. It is more important that the move be quick-stepping, alert, and determined.

5. Size

I have purposely left the question of size to the end because at this time size is of the greatest importance, and is the center of attention of the international Puli scene. Here arises the question "why was it necessary to combine the four sizes into one?" The old standard grouped the Puli into four different size categories. This aided in the possible degeneration of the breed. The problem was easily recognized by the Puli breeders, while many Puli fanciers and owners have failed to recognize its importance to this day. The second World War had disastrous effects on Puli breeding. A great part of the breeding stock perished while others changed hands without registry. Even before the war the fact of division into four sizes had detrimental results, where the general Puli traits and appearance were concerned. It gave contingency to hide the manifestations due to the possible influx of alien blood. Whatever size the progeny was, it would fit into one of the four size categories. It was a frequent occurrence that a small Puli threw large progeny or vice versa. I must explain at this point that according to the international judging method that is being followed in Hungary, a dog may receive the rating of "Excellent" when only one fault is present and the dog otherwise is outstanding. However, if the judging certificate shows more than one fault, this automatically excludes the dog from the rating "Excellent." Therefore, by the mere fact that size was disregarded as a fault, this rule was already broken, and other faults were handled with more leniency. Under this, I mean such faults that go hand-in-hand with the extreme changes in size. Such as, an over-sized Puli will often lose the characteristic agility and stamina, while an undersized Puli might become too fragile. The stabilization of size was therefore an important factor in eliminating all-around faults. The validity of this decision has been attested to by the appearance of greatly improved stock at recent international shows held in Hungary. To the best of our knowledge this lack of control existed also in many countries outside of Hungary. This, coupled with the fact of diminished influx of fresh blood from the country of origin and the fact that due to circumstances no help was given in the form of direction from this body, the direction of breeding was left in the hands of Puli owners and fanciers.

We would be willing to accept these different sized Pulis and the establishment of different standards for these different sized Pulis if governing bodies could be maintained to assure the separate breeding, registration and judging of these various size categories. This, however, is only a utopian idea, because should we try to do this at this time, it would only tend to confuse the issue and might result in undermining those efforts that have brought improvement to the breed during the past decades.

Now we get to the often-discussed question, on the question of size, what is our position, as the country of origin? How much is taken into consideration at dog shows, and at breeding stock qualifying inspections? And what way does it influence the value of the individual Puli? The difference between a dog show and a breeding stock inspection exhibit is that while at a dog show the dogs are judged for their appearance and beauty mainly, at the breeding stock inspections more emphasis is being placed as to their value in breeding. It is true, however, that a dog that has won many honors at dog shows will often be sought after and will be frequently used at stud. At dog shows, size will only be decisive if two or more otherwise equally good Pulis will compete. At such times it is imperative that the dog that approaches the ideal size most closely will be handed the ribbon. Size, however, is a much more decisive factor at breeding stock exhibits where the selection as to the value of stud dogs and brood bitches is determined. The question arises now of what to do to approach our goals. We must pledge ourselves to strict adherence to the standard's requirements. We mustn't allow that efforts of the conscientious breeders be set back by either Puli owners partial to their own Puli, or by such individuals whose only interest in the breed is the monetary remuneration. We must not allow, under any circumstances, the standard to be adjusted or modified to fix the individual properties of any given Puli. Rather, we should strive to approach in the progeny the ideal standard through scientifically programmed breeding. Every conscientious breeder should endeavor to achieve the ideal Puli type by either the introduction of new bloodlines or by scientifically applied, careful, extremely selective inbreeding. The most positive approach to the stabilization of size is the use of ideal-sized stud dogs. Let me present the question. What would happen if no ideal size was prescribed? Before long we would be faced with a population of Pulis from the smallest midget-Puli to the largest, almost robust looking, coarse individuals and the Puli population would soon be losing the traits we so dearly cherish in our breed; such as, for example, that lovable, affectionate "perpetual motion" quality. Therefore, let's not stop halfway. Let us not be satisfied that we have a Puli and believe that this is the best and most beautiful Puli in the world. Let us breed and improve our stock from generation to generation. How can this all be achieved? We have to entrust the direction of breeding to technically well-informed breeders and experts who are able to see the truth without emotional involvement, and will act to the benefit of the entire breed—not only in their individual interests. The breeding controls must be improved and special attention must be given to the exclusion of serious and disqualifying faults as prescribed by the standard. We must examine not only the individual dogs but their parents as well. We must find the reason why the progeny has become better or worse than its parents. We must be more vigorous in the elimination of inferior breeding stock. We must always use the best, most desirable type stud, disregarding personal feelings. Good outcrosses to new bloodlines are ideal, but at the same time it is important that several separate bloodlines should be maintained. The stud must always be superior to the brood bitch, as only then can we expect the progeny to be superior to its dam. It would be desirable to hear an expert's opinion on any individual Puli before it is being taken into breeding to assure that more and more breeders be acquainted with the properties that constitute the ideal Puli as described by the standard, and what the goals are that they must be mindful of.

With respect to all the aforementioned, I would like to assure all American Puli breeders of the close cooperation we in Hungary wish to offer. We are all working for the same objectives, and that is to keep this valuable Hungarian sheepdog true to its unusually good qualities and high reputation, even though in many cases he has been deprived of his original function. Our utmost desire is to maintain the Puli in the coming centuries as that very special being he is.

For this we Hungarians wish to solicit the help and cooperation of all the friends of the Puli and would like to assure all of you that we will extend all the help possible to those who are striving for the advancement and progress of the breed. With this in mind, I would like to close, and would like to wish further success to the Puli Club of Southern California and to the Puli breeders of America—the valuable work this convention has set itself to accomplish.

Chapter 7

PERSONAL EXPERIENCES
WITH PULIS

WHO UNDERSTANDS THE HUMAN WORD
by Ferenc Zentai

Michael Czako is a shepherd in Czehled, Hungary. He has practiced his profession for about 35 years. The cooperative farm where he works has 3000 sheep, of which 300 are Michael's responsibility; rather, they are the responsibility of Michael and his two Pulis—eight-year-old Ficko and his son, two-year-old Rigo. Both of the Pulis are registered and have an impressive pedigree to show their ancestry. Standing on the side of the highway, we fell into conversation with this experienced shepherd.

"The shepherd is not a shepherd without his Puli," he said. "The Puli gives invaluable assistance to his master. He takes the biggest load of work off his shoulders . . . of course, only the good Puli—because there are some bad ones too . . . but then, in most cases it isn't the Puli's fault but the man's . . . Because you see, a Puli has to be taught with a lot of patience until he understands the human word . . . Just listen!"

He looked at Rigo. The Puli, understanding the movement of the eyes, stood up and was already anxiously watching the shepherd. "Go Rigo! Bring them here!" At that, Rigo flew over the brook and began to approach the distant flock in a great circle from the left. First, the lines on the left started into movement. Then, as Rigo neared the group, the ones on the right began to move too. Rigo, while running, changed direction, and within three minutes the flock was in front of us . . . and Rigo's reward? An appreciative

This Hungarian stamp commemorated the International Conference of Breeders of Hungarian Sheep Dogs in 1966.

The four top-winning Pulis in the U.S. during the years 1965, 1966 and 1967 as they appeared on the cover of *Dog World* magazine's February, 1968 issue. From left to right: American, Mexican, Canadian Champion Nagykunsagi Csorgo, C.D.; American, Mexican, F.C.I. International Champion Cinkotai Csibesz; American, Mexican Champion Matyasfoldi Kapuore Bitang and Champion Puli-Kountry's Apro, C.D.

petting on his head and the kind words "Good little Puli! Good boy, Rigo! You'll really be something if you keep it up like this!"

"Which one of your Pulis do you remember the most?" we asked Michael. ". . . well, perhaps the Moric," was his reply. ". . . he was two years old, too, another son of Ficko. Once a Greek merchant bought a large number of sheep from the farm and he fell in love with Moric. He wanted him, too . . . I got 500 forints for him. It was hard to give him up as he was a wonderful one, that Moric . . . Since then, he has learned Greek, too . . . The Puli understands the human word in many languages."

Perhaps so. Perhaps this is the key to the extreme intelligence of this faithful partner of the shepherd—the Puli. These men treat them as children, with great respect and even greater love. And they believe—beyond the shadow of a doubt, they believe—that the Puli understands their every word.

. . . translated by Klara Benis from "A Kutya," monthly publication of the Hungarian Kennel Club, Vol. XXIX, August 1966, No. 2.

"PERGO," A PULI OF THE PUSZTA
by Sandor Palfalvy, M.D.

It was a beautiful sunny May morning. From the front of our house, I watched the two Lipicai horses who were pawing the ground restlessly and giving Joe a lot of trouble in holding them back. I was waiting for Feher Miska to come and play with me. Joe was waiting for my dear father to take him to the Nagyperkati Ranch. I had always wanted to go to the ranch because my father and mother talked of it so often, but my father's usual explanation was "Just what business would a child have there?" and that was always the last word. Even this morning (and I was about 8 or 10 years old at the time) I could hardly believe it when my father came out of the house and said, "Come on, hop up there. I'll take you along."

I forgot about Miska and playing in a hurry . . . and perhaps one of the happiest feelings of my life was born just then. Something so long hoped for had finally become a reality. I sat on the sand-runner proudly, like a prince starting on a tour of his land. There was no talk as the two fiery horses flew with the sand-runner. Behind the sunlit dust cloud, our house and the village slowly disappeared.

THE PULI IN PRINT

AROUND THE WORLD

Puli Club poster depicting Puli publications from around the world.

The author's wife demonstrating the two types of grooming to Miss Eva Gabor and Miss Betty White with Champion Gyalpusztai Kocos Burkus, Champion Tatarhegyi Borka Panna and their puppy during the taping of the nationwide *Pet-Set* television program.

Then we left the road and proceeded on the horizon-encircled meadow.

The picture is still vividly alive in my mind. Far in the distance some white-washed houses seemed like tiny toy buildings. A few jegenye trees (perhaps similar to our poplar trees) directed their candle-like crowns toward the sky. A few horsechestnut trees gave color to the endless green of the meadows. It was so still and peaceful. Not even the turning of the wheels or the rhythmic sound of hoofs was noticeable. And it was no wonder! We were traveling on the most luxurious velvety carpet God ever made. In the distance a white shadow became evident and we took our direction toward it. We could not see a living soul, near or far.

All of a sudden this peacefulness was shattered by a clamor that broke to the skies. It came from a little black spot running so fast that within seconds it was making circles around the sand-runner. It was jumping, barking, showing its teeth, here and there snapping at the wheels and jumping up and down in front of the horses. He was obviously trying to tell us that we were unwanted, that we were intruders in his domain. His tremendous shaggy coat was flying around him like thousands of little flags, and he danced around our wagon and horses with such bewitching speed and agility that it seemed as if one of Hell's little devils was loose on us. Even the horses slowed down with obvious respect and tried to kick sideways to avoid the possible contact with those very, very white teeth.

I gave my whole attention to this threat and looked around only when the wagon stopped. From the shade of a big tree, a white-haired old man got up. Lifting his hat, he greeted up—"God bless you." The white shadow seen from a distance was there in front of us —it was a peaceful flock of sheep. The angry little threat gave a few more high-pitched sounds. When the old man mumbled something like "coki te" (hold it), he settled down by the tree, looking almost ashamed.

My father shook hands with the man. I stayed on the seat, looking at the little black thing now peacefully sitting by the large tree, shaking his curly tail here and there. I didn't dare get off. I was convinced that the moment I set foot on the ground the little devil would take me to pieces. My father kept urging me in vain. Finally the old shepherd came to the wagon and assured me that all was well. "Pergo wouldn't hurt anyone. Come on down, little master! He is as peaceful as a day-old lamb!"

Well, I believed it—and again, I didn't. "If he is so peaceful," I said, "why did he want to bite the wheels of the wagon and why did he bark so furiously?"

The old Marton, with that very typically shepherd-like quiet voice said, "Pergo didn't want to bite anyone. He just tried to turn the wagon back. That he barked—well, that is his job." Finally convinced, I got off and settled down well between my father and the old Marton, hoping that they would save me from any danger that might come. They were deep in talk. Over what, I wouldn't know. I had eyes and ears only for Pergo who was completely ignoring us. When the discussion was over, out came sheep-cheese and snow-white bread and we started to eat. At this, Pergo decided to come closer. My heart started to beat faster again. But old Marton began talking to him . . . I still remember the words . . . "Come here, Pergo, the little master will give you something—but then, behave yourself." Pergo came over to me, his funny little tail constantly shaking. "What comes now?" I thought. The old shepherd motioned to me to give him some of the cheese. Hesitantly, I lifted my hands toward Pergo. He gently took the cheese and proceeded to lick his mouth in every direction.

I realized there was no more danger, but I still had no thought of petting him . . . So went our lunch on the puszta with my father, the old shepherd Marton, the driver Joe, and Pergo. Then something happened again. Old Marton said to Pergo, "Go, run around." Pergo took off like an arrow. Within seconds he ran around the flock, driving them so close to each other that they could hardly move. Then he came back to the shepherd, sat, and gave a few short yips as if to say "The order is done." As he was sitting there, I had the feeling that he was nothing but a tremendous mop of hair and a red tongue . . . that's all. Old Marton asked, "Well, little master, are you still afraid of Pergo?" My answer was far from definite. "No . . . I'm not . . . but say, Uncle Marton, what kind of a dog is Pergo? I have never seen one like him in the village."

Old Marton looked as if I had jabbed him with a needle. His usually quiet voice snapped. "Pergo is a Puli. A Puli—not a dog. They should teach you that in school. If they didn't, well, then you shall learn it now from this old man. Never forget it, because a Puli is not a dog, it's a Puli. This is as true as the sun is in the sky, little master."

"Pergo is my hands and feet, my eyes and ears. I am 82 years old. I can do no running. I couldn't keep the flock in order. Pergo knows the shepherd's job . . . perhaps even better than the shepherd himself. Believe me, without a Puli a shepherd is less than half a man. And one more thing, little master—perhaps you will think this is foolish talk, but you can believe it because an old man tells you so. The teacher at the school says that the human is the smartest in the world . . . well, they can teach that, but with my 82 years I

Mystic's Botond (Star of Hunnia Koma X Mystic Samantha Punny-Wurth) with young handler Lindsey Williams of San Antonio, Texas, shown winning BOB from the classes.

am convinced that isn't true. The Puli has more sense than a man because—and little master, listen to me well for I am a man 82 years old, so the long life speaks from me to be true as I say—Pergo is only 3 years old this summer and for his 3 years understands perfectly everything and has learned everything that I, the man, speak to him in Hungarian. Yet I, an 82 year old man, am still so stupid I could not learn the 'Puli language.' Believe me, not only is there a Hungarian, German, Italian and French talk in the world, but there is also a 'Puli talk.' The Puli even at the puppy age understands the Hungarian or German talk, but we humans all through our lives couldn't learn the Puli language. That there is such a language every shepherd knows . . . I am willing to swear to it . . . but we just aren't smart enough to learn it."

So far was the old Marton's lecture. He only said once more, "Think about it, and you'll realize that it was no foolishness what I said." Suddenly Pergo had received a halo in my eyes and I looked at this mop of hair and red tongue as if it were a miraculous thing. I believed old Marton's talk, especially since after his last words, Pergo gave a few short barks, as if saying "Amen."

It was about fifty years ago that I first saw Pergo and heard the words of old Marton, but since then I pledged my life to the Puli. Good old Marton and Pergo are long, long gone—but the picture and the words live in my memory as vividly as then . . . We are sitting on the large shepherd's cape and I am nibbling on the cheese, listening to old Marton's words . . . "The Puli is a Puli, the Puli is no dog, it's a Puli." Even the Puli-talk sings in my ears, the way Pergo said "Amen" after the old shepherd had spoken.

And now, when I myself am slowly at "the end of my bread," I remember this episode of my youth, and as a memory, I myself have to quote the words of the good old man . . . "Perhaps you'll think it foolish talk what I say—though a life speaks from me . . ." And now, in my old age, to all of what Uncle Marton said, and to which Pergo in Puli words answered "Amen"—I too, in human language can only repeat . . . "So as is—be it so" . . . which translated to Latin means "Amen."

THE BREADWINNER
by Sandor Palfalvy, M.D.

This happened in the Spring of 1935, at Kispec (Gyor Megye,

Hungary), during one of my visits to the home of Joseph Kovacs, landowner. After I attended a member of the family who was recuperating from a mild illness, we were chatting with Mr. Kovacs on his front porch, when one of the "hands" came up and said, "A man is here to see you, Mr. Kovacs." "Send him here," he said. After a few minutes a man in his forties, clothed in his "Sunday black," appeared and greeted us with "God bless you." . . . but I'd rather record the whole conversation, as it speaks for itself.

Kovacs: "What can I do for you, son?"

Man: "I came from Lovaszpatona, where one of the shepherds said that you are looking for someone to take care of your sheep. I'd like to take the job, if you'd hire me."

Kovacs: "Tell me, son, do you have a Puli?"

Man: "Oh, yes. How could I be without one? How could there be a shepherd without a Puli?"

Kovacs: "Well then, how old is your Puli?"

Man: "He passed three years this fall."

Kovacs: "That settles that. You are hired . . . And, say, just what is your name?"

Man: "Andras Sipos, from Kisden."

Kovacs: "Where have you worked before?"

Man: "At Zirc, for many years. Now I have moved back to Kisden as my father died and my mother is old and someone has to take care of her."

Kovacs: "All right, son, go out to the 'tanya' (farm) and tell Mr. John that I sent you, that you are the new shepherd, then go look the sheep over."

Man: "Thank you, Mr. Kovacs. Then, I'll be on my way. God be with you."

He left happily. I looked at Mr. Kovacs, not understanding, and asked, "How does it happen you hired this man before even asking his name or where he worked before?" "Believe me, Doctor," said Mr. Kovacs with a smile, "his name and the place where he worked before is important enough. But, the most important question of all was settled first . . . that is, whether or not he had a Puli and how old his Puli is. Everything else is secondary. His Puli is assurance for me that the flock will be in good hands. The man is not as important as the Puli."

On my way home I wondered, and ever since I have thought over that conversation. I have come to the conclusion that Andras Sipos, Hungarian shepherd, owed his bread, job, and the future to his Puli. I don't think that I am mistaken . . . what do you think?

THE FIFTY FILLER STAMP
by Margaret H. Curran

It was only the enlargement of a stamp at the bottom of a poster of The Puli in Print Around the World—the 50 filler commemorative stamp of Hungary. But the big man in the plaid wool shirt had been looking at it for a long time. As I came up behind him, he turned and said quietly, "I saw that happen a long time ago."

The light of a memory of his homeland—one that he had stored away for well over thirty years—was in his face. "In Hungary?" I asked, moving toward the picnic benches.

"Yes . . . in eastern Hungary . . . in the township of Hajduhathaz." He leaned back, resting his elbows on the table. As I watched that

"The fifty filler stamp," part of a set commemorating the various Hungarian breeds.

MAGYAR POSTA 50f

mobile face and heard that gentle voice quicken with the excitement of reliving an experience of long ago, I too was vividly caught up in the past. Here is Stephen De Bodnar's story, exactly as he told it to me.

"I was on a field exercise with a Hungarian machine gun company. About a hundred of us were marching that day. It was through grazing land, and on one side of the road a man had his herd of cattle feeding."

He paused a moment to explain that the Hungarian cattle were large and white—something like a Brahma, but without a hump. "All of a sudden we heard a rumbling noise like a locomotive and saw a huge bull not three hundred yards away.

"One look was all we needed. There are few things a man on foot dreads as much as a raging bull. We headed for the trees on the other side of the road. The trees weren't very big . . ." he laughed at the thought as he added, "and by the time they were full of men they were shaking just like we were. We knew they couldn't hold us for long!

"Across the road, the herd and the man didn't even move. It was almost as if they didn't even know we were there. Below us, we could see the bull pawing the dirt and hear the deep-throated rumble that meant he was getting ready to charge.

"Then the man raised his long stick and pointed. From out of nowhere, it seemed, six black Pulis came racing. As they reached the bull they split—three to the left, three to the right. The first two jumped for the bull's nose and hung on. The bull raised his powerful neck and shook his head from side to side until he shook them off. Immediately the next two Pulis jumped for his nose, one from the left, one from the right. They, too, hung on until they were shaken off. Then the third pair took their place. This relay in pairs, one on each side, kept on and soon the bull was tired.

"Then—and only then—did the man move. He walked, nice and easy, up to the bull. The Pulis gave room. He swung his stick and hit the bull two sharp raps between the horns. The bull, with a toss of his head, moved away.

"There was a quiet kind of dignity about the herdsman as he stood for a moment looking up into the trees. Then he spoke for the first time.

"Now, gentlemen, you may come down."

MARCI
by Lois Powers

(Twenty-four years ago Dr. Sandor Palfalvy was one of the medical examiners in an incident which he reported in the July 1, 1965, *A Puli*. Klara Benis kindly translated his account to provide me with the pertinent facts upon which this story is based.)

Autumn surrendered to winter as flakes of snow brushed the village white. Shivers of the north wind tossed snow clouds high above the village houses as if to warn the villagers to make ready for the cruel months of winter. Inside his home, Michael Szucs piled several more pine logs on his fire, rubbing his hands together in appreciation of the warmth of fire and home, but the warmth inside only intensified the cold outside. He returned again to the frosted window as he had many times during the last few days, hoping to discern among the snow-laden pines a moving flock of sheep coming back for the winter. But as before, the mountain side was undisturbed, except for winter's approach.

Mr. Szucs had watched dozens of flocks come home from the high, green meadows of the Carpathian Mountains during early autumn, but his flock alone had not returned, and he could not understand his faithful shepherd's unusual tardiness. Old Jano, the aging shepherd whom Mr. Szucs had inherited from his father with the flock of sheep, had always infallibly sensed nature's calendar. For as long as he could remember, Jano and his Puli assembled his flock of sheep at spring's promise to go into the summer meadows, and each November, shepherd and Puli ushered his flock back to winter's safekeeping in the village. But this November did not bring Jano back. It was not like Old Jano to be late and Mr. Szucs was troubled. He trusted his faithful shepherd and his Puli, but his most valued possession, his splendid flock of sheep, over five hundred of them, seemed to have vanished. Worry became alarm. "I can wait no longer. Each day I hope to see my sheep and Jano, and each day I see nothing."

The troubled farmer trudged through the falling snow, from house to house, summoning friends and relatives to search for his vanished flock. The men organized into pairs, sectioned off the formidable mountain terrain, and began the search, but the steep vertical cliffs, always a challenge even in the best weather, concealed the mystery of the lost sheep.

The search continued, and days passed without discovery. The discouraged Mr. Szucs knew that the frustrating search had to come to an end. The villagers could go on no longer. A gray sky and snapping wind threatened more snow. He had no choice. He must tell the searchers to return with him to the village, fully aware that when he did, he was pronouncing a death sentence upon his defenseless sheep.

The farmer stared down at the earth as he watched winter's evidence mount into piles of drifted snow. When he glanced up, he detected two men in the expanse of snow and pine. He watched the black specks swell into the encouraging shapes of his friends.

"Michael," they shouted into the wind, "we have found your flock, about five days walk from here, higher in the mountains."

"Thank God," Michael responded, "but why is Jano so late?"

"Jano was not with the flock, Michael. The flock is guarded by a small, tenacious Puli. And that Puli would not let us near the flock. He barked furiously, bit at our heels every time we came near. He wouldn't even let us guide him home. We had to come for help, Michael. We couldn't get near that Puli. He's the most protective animal I've ever seen. The flock is his, and he would not entrust us with its care."

The darkening sky warned the men that the trip to the high mountains needed the sanction of daylight. The next morning, Mr. Szucs, four friends and several mountain patrolmen began the ascent to the high country to recover the sheep. As the sled stretched parallel lines in the snow, the distance between Mr. Szucs and his flock of sheep diminished. But nearness did not ease his troubled mind. What had happened to Old Jano and how could he get the Puli to relinquish his sheep?

Mr. Szucs tried to remember what Jano called his Puli. He knew the Puli only slightly because Jano spent the summer in the mountains, and during the winter he kept the Puli in his shepherd's quarters. And too, Mr. Szucs did not speak Hungarian. Though his parents were Hungarian, he lived in Romania and spoke only Romanian. He listened to hear Old Jano call his Puli, but the sounds of his memory were inaudible. Then his probing thoughts were interrupted with the cry, "Michael, there they are. Look at that Puli!"

The men were captivated by the animation of the little Puli as he

Puli jewelry created by Rick Humphrey and offered by the Puli Club of Southern California, Inc.

circled the wayward flock, keeping the sheep and lambs together. The Puli's shaggy black cords caught the wind and streamed backwards like wings, while at the same time he was pursued by the snow flurries of his own creation, made from his momentum against the powdery surface. And then the Puli sighted the men. He barked, marching defiantly forward to caution them that he was in sole charge of this flock, and they dare not endanger his sheep and lambs.

And in that moment, Mr. Szucs' memory provided him with Old Jano's magic command. "Marci, Marci, gyere ide, Marci!" he called out. The tenacious little Puli did not recognize the voice, but he knew the command. His fury left him as quickly as it came. Old Jano's words transformed the fiercely protective Puli into a gentle, docile creature. Wagging his tail, Marci chanted a strange song and danced a unique little dance at Mr. Szucs' feet as if to say, "I'm

Champion Tatarhegyi Borka Panna (Pajtas Ekes **X** Istenhegyi Cinka
Panna) pictured here completing her title under judge Mr. R. Ward.
Owner-handled by Klara Benis. Photograph: J. Ludwig.

glad you finally came. It's been hard alone, but I did it. I cared for the flock when Old Jano couldn't."

The tall men, silhouetting the lonely sky, stood in silent admiration of the small Puli as he turned over "his" flock to its rightful owner. Then Marci, Mr. Szucs, and the other searchers began the long downward journey back to the village with the sheep, and the mountain patrol went on to look for Old Jano or clues of his disappearance.

Days later the patrol returned to tell Mr. Szucs what their search had uncovered. "Michael, we have found Old Jano. Under a large pine, inside his little hut, we found him . . . that is, we found his fully clothed skeleton on a pile of hay not too many miles from where we found Marci. All of his belongings were there, his cans, his pipe—all undisturbed."

"We sent for medical examiners from Ceytarce," continued another, "though we were certain it must have been Old Jano. The examiners determined Old Jano's death at five or six months ago. They believed he died from natural causes—a shepherd to the end, probably assigning his Puli to complete his last task."

"God bless him," Michael uttered, "but do you mean Marci guarded the flock all that time? There wasn't a single sheep missing, not even one sheep hurt. How could that little 'sheepherder' have survived in that rugged mountain region? By what ingenuity could he have guarded the sheep night and day for half a year? This is incredible!"

Incredible, perhaps to Mr. Szucs, but he had not known Marci as Old Jano had. Although Mr. Szucs could hardly envision the Puli's heroic achievement in the alien environment, Old Jano, no doubt, would hardly have been surprised. He would have known his majestic little Marci would serve him to the end, leaving no task undone—even one as difficult as this.

Chapter 8

CARE AND TRAINING

HOUSING

In spite of their sturdiness and protective coat, the majority of Pulis today are living under more domesticated conditions than their ancestors. Normally they prefer to be outdoors, but they also prefer to be close to their human companions. It is up to the owner to draw the line: to let his Puli sleep next to his bed (or on it), or next to his bedroom window on the outside of the house. They do not need to be pampered, but they need some protection against dampness, cold drafts, and extreme heat. They will be as content with a dog house outside as with a corner of their own within the house.

All dogs should have a corner or an area they can call their own. This area should be as permanent as possible. One does not move a doghouse to a different part of the yard every day. Similarly, one should not move his dog's pillow to a different room of the house every night. But more important than that, do not force a Puli to stay overnight inside the overheated house when he is used to staying in the yard, as he will be uncomfortable all night. On the other hand, do not force him to suddenly sleep outside on a cold winter night, when up to that point you have let him stay with you in the bedroom. In otherwords, be consistent in regard to quartering your Puli.

The owner of the famous Chicago restaurant "The Bakery " used to live on the East Coast with his three Pulis. All of them stayed in the house most of the time, and he could not think of having it any other way. One unfortunate, disastrous day his house burned down and all three of his Pulis with it. Haunted by the memory of this, he blamed himself for the accident and for letting the dogs stay in the house. Years later, after moving to Chicago, he purchased two new Pulis. The new house rules, based on the previous bad experience, called for the dogs to be outside at all times. Knowing how severely inclement the weather can be in Chicago, this might sound extreme for the average pet owner. However, nature is the best provider if we let her provide. His dogs at barely one year of age had a full, completely developed coat of a density such as I have never before or since seen on any other Puli. And both of his Pulis are as healthy and happy as can be.

If your Puli stays outside most of the time, I would recommend building an elevated platform of wood construction for him, preferably in an area where he is protected from rain and snow.

Champion PuliKountry's Luv Moppet (Ch. Erdalsoi Adu Betyar Matyi X Ch. PuliKountry's Bordacs Baby). Owners: Bill and Judy Sanders, Dallas, Texas. Photograph: Twomey.

Champion Csardas' Achushla of Sczyr (Ch. Matyasfoldi Kapuore Bitang X Sczyr's Grey Babe) with owner-handler R. Breckenridge of Iowa.

Choose a location from which he can see his entire territory. It does not necessarily have to be higher than 5 or 6 inches above the ground nor exceed 3 feet by 3 feet in size. Dogs usually enjoy sitting or lying down on such a platform, and it is also good to have air circulate under it to prevent mildew. Dust and dirt will fall through the boards, helping to keep your dog clean and above the ground draft. Dog houses should also be raised a few inches above the ground for the same reason.

The only time a Puli needs special attention is when he is wet, be it after bathing, swimming in the lake, or from a lengthy walk in the rain. Do not let him chill while wet! The Puli's coat is water repellent to a certain extent, but once it is thoroughly wet, it does not provide the same protection against wind and cold.

Older Pulis should be especially protected from extensive heat. The coat acts as fair insulation against both cold and heat, but our modern-day Pulis who live more protected lives than their fore-fathers are usually more sensitive by the time they grow old.

FEEDING

The Puli is a sturdy little fellow who does not need to be pampered, either in his feeding or in his housing. By the nature of his duty, he is used to being outside day and night, through most of the year and through most of the extreme weather con-ditions. Classically, he ate a minimal amount, usually the shepherd's leftovers, and he returned to the village with the flock when the snow started to cover the ground and would enjoy the wider variety of table scraps only during the winter months.

With the abundance of the commercially produced and packaged foods and vitamins especially prepared for dogs, today's Puli is in more danger of being overfed than underfed. No attempt will be made to determine the right amount of food to feed a Puli, for that is regulated mainly by his age, daily activity, climate, environment in general, and his individual size and metabolism. The main objective in feeding is to mix the various amounts of basic food and mineral elements to produce a balanced diet. A growing puppy will need more body-building ingredients such as calcium, phosphorus, iron, etc. than would a fully-matured, active dog, which needs more energy-producing foods. Again, an old dog will need a different diet (almost calcium-free) that is easy to digest. Owners should consider that the Puli is throughout life supposed to be lean, hard muscled, and never fat or sluggish. A distinction should be made, of course, between dogs that are lean and wiry and those that are under-nourished and sickly-looking.

The most important period in a dog's nutritional life is puppy-hood, and especially when the puppy is separated from the dam. At this time, the amount the puppy eats is so little that it is hard to create a complete mixture of all the essential nutrients since the bitch's milk is so rich and complete. Special attention is required of the new owner when feeding the freshly-weaned puppy. Breeders should always give detailed instructions to the owner of a

Champion Star of Hunnia Misty Baba (Gyalpusztai Bundas **X** Ch. Gyali Csopi) is pictured here going BOS at the 1964 Specialty of the Puli Club of Southern California. Owner-handled by Mr. Joseph Heiden. Judge: Mr. O.C. Harriman. Photograph: J. Ludwig.

new puppy on what food he has been eating and what he should be fed. This is a learning period for the new owner, while for the puppy it is the most critical growing age. The owner must feed the puppy everything the puppy needs for proper nutrition but, on the other hand, must carefully watch that the puppy does not become a roly-poly butterball. To carry extra weight on those pliable little leg bones can be as dangerous to a puppy as a rickety under-nourished period. As a general rule, puppies should be fed three times daily until the age of six months, then twice daily until a year of age; thereafter, one feeding per day is enough. This one feeding can be in the morning or at night, whichever fits the family schedule best, but the important thing is that the feeding occur at a regular time each day. Vitamins should be added regularly to a puppy's food, especially up to the age of two. Milk is not harmful, but is unnecessary after 9 to 10 weeks of age, and often causes diarrhea.

The Puli is not a fussy eater unless you spoil him. Do not leave his food with him longer than fifteen minutes at a time. If he has not eaten it by that time, pick it up and give it to him only at the next feeding time. By then he will be hungry and will eat it. Try not to vary the food too much, and mix everything well, or you will notice that the puppy will pick out his favorite food and leave the rest. Some Puli owners get so worried about their "starving dog" that they keep offering better and better treats to him so that the dog will eat. A smart Puli will realize this and will stay on a hunger strike until his favorite dish is offered. The regular feeding times are most important with such finicky eaters. If you need to put weight on your dog, do not leave food available to him all the time, as knowing the food is always there, he is more than likely to eat less. If he knows that there is nothing else to be offered until the next feeding, he is much more likely to clean his dish up at once.

A Puli that has to go on a diet for being overweight is another problem. He will act dramatically starved, playing on your sympathy. You must, however, limit his portions drastically, particularly the kibble. To satisfy his hunger, a dog needs bulk in his food. This can be accomplished by chopping lettuce into very fine pieces and mixing it well with small amounts of lean ground beef. This diet will fill up the puppy's stomach, yet contains a minimal number of calories.

GENERAL HINTS ON HEALTH CARE

It is best to get into the habit of checking your dog at regular intervals from puppyhood. Check his eyes and ears; open his mouth and look at the throat and teeth. This is excellent training for the puppy, to get him conditioned for standing for examination in the show ring. This is also the age when they chew on everything. You will be surprised what can be found in little puppies' mouths; littermates' torn-out coat hairs wrapped around the teeth, pieces of wood or of plastic toys between them. Examining the dog from the beginning will enable the owner to recognize early signs

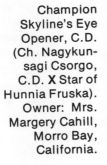

Champion Skyline's Eye Opener, C.D. (Ch. Nagykun-sagi Csorgo, C.D. X Star of Hunnia Fruska). Owner: Mrs. Margery Cahill, Morro Bay, California.

of abnormal behavior symptomatic of the onset of more serious illness. Loss of appetite, persistent coughing, loss of sparkle in the eyes, and lethargic behavior are all early warning signs. Take his temperature regularly, and also at the first sign of a change in his eating habits. Use a rectal thermometer; insert it carefully, and leave it in about two minutes while taking precautions against injury by holding the dog stationary. Normal temperature is about 101 degrees F. for a grown dog. Puppies could be slightly higher. If temperatures range up to 102 degrees, there is no reason to panic, but when it approaches or exceeds 103 degrees, immediate attention is required and a trip to your veterinarian is often indicated.

IMMUNIZATION

Opinions differ widely on the subject of puppy shots. I start out with the first permanent distemper, hepatitis, and leptospirosis shots at eight weeks of age. No puppy is allowed to leave our kennel without it. The second half of the permanent D.H.L. is given at the time recommended by the vet., usually from 8 to 9 weeks after the first shot. From then on, they receive booster shots. Do not neglect these! Dogs going to shows should be immunized twice a year; dogs staying in the backyard need only be immunized once a year. Rabies vaccination is required by law. Some rabies vaccinations are good for two years, others only for one year.

SUMMER OR HOT CLIMATE CARE

It is not essential to change your Puli's diet for hot weather, or because of warm climate. During the winter, however, dogs use up more fat because of the cold; during the summer they need fat to build fatty tissue under the skin to help keep it from drying out and to lubricate the growing coat. Unsaturated fat, such as safflower oil or peanut oil, should be included in the Puli's daily diet all year round. In a very dry climate such as in the Arizona or California desert area, I recommend increasing the fat intake during the summer months to the point where the sign of a consistently soft stool gives warning to retard the fat intake slightly. The measured amount can vary widely with individual dogs or their normal diet. One teaspoonful of shortening at each feeding is my dog's daily minimum fat intake.

External treatment of the skin or coat under normal circumstances is not required. However, frequently-bathed show dogs often show tendencies toward overly dry skin and dull coat. Lanolin products are a helpful aid in controlling this. Lanolin in aerosol cans is easy to store and a real help in applying the desired light, even coating of the skin. The rule to follow when applying lanolin is to get it to the base of the coat and then massage it into the skin.

In the case of a persistently dull, lifeless coat or of dry scaling of the skin, your veterinarian should be consulted. Skin and coat problems are more often than not caused by parasites (external or internal), or by ailments requiring diagnosis to determine the proper course of treatment.

FLEAS

The life cycle of the flea begins, in your view, when he lands on your dog. He lives on the dog's blood. The female flea lays her eggs in the dog's coat or in his bedding or favorite nesting spot. From the eggs hatch wormlike larvae that subsist upon excreta of adult fleas and on other animal debris. Upon reaching adult form, they again return to the dog to feed upon blood and continue the life cycle. To rid the dog of his fleas, the life cycle must be broken, preferably at all stages simultaneously.

The unhatched flea eggs are the hardest part of the life cycle to cope with. The dog's house, kennels, and his favorite napping places should be regularly sprayed with insecticides. Malathion-based chemicals in aerosol cans are widely used. Weak chemical solutions, most of them originated from chlorine, are on the market for the saturating of gravel runs or lawn areas. The most important thing in using these solutions is to regulate their strength so that they are strong enough to be effective against fleas and their eggs but not so strong as to irritate the skin or paws of the dog.

There are many products available to kill fleas that are on the dog. Flea soaps are too strong for the skin of most Pulis. Concentrated dips, thinned more than recommended for most dogs, will do the job, as will aerosol products.

It is important to protect your dog from fleas at all times, as fleas are the cause of a wide variety of skin irritations and they carry bacteria into the blood when puncturing the skin to feed on the dog. They are also one source of canine tape worms.

WORMS

A dozen or so varieties of worms infesting dogs are known and their treatments differ widely. Puppies should be checked every second week up to six months of age; adults, at least twice a year. Many of the worms or their eggs are not visible, and a stool sample should be taken to your vet for laboratory analysis. Let your veterinarian worm the dog, or let him prescribe the medicine for you to use. The correct dosage and the method of administration can mean the difference between success and failure.

CLEANLINESS AND FIRST AID

Ear cleaning

Remove excess hair from the inside of the ear and clean the ears with a cotton swab dipped in mineral oil or any of the available commercial ear-cleaning products. Common sense and regular visible checkups will indicate how often such care is required.

Eyes

Eyes should be cleaned with damp cotton. Some dogs have an abundant eye discharge and require more frequent cleaning than others. Unless the eye discharge comes with red skin around the eyes, or it is persistent in nature, it should be considered normal. Do not let this discharge accumulate on the eyelids; its chemical nature can cause temporary loss of hair around the eye or more serious skin irritations. Special cleaning fluids are available at pet shops.

Cuts or wounds

I always keep at home, and carry in the grooming kit, a disinfectant spray such as a weak solution of hydrogen peroxide. I either spray or swab with a Q-tip directly into the wound to clean out and sterilize cuts or wounds.

Upset stomach—Diarrhea

To counteract upset stomach caused by travel or a new diet, I use charcoal tablets or Kaopectate. Diarrhea, unless it is of serious nature, can be stopped by replacing the dry dog food with cooked rice or by adding bone meal to the daily diet.

Fattening a thin dog

The fastest way I've found for putting weight on a dog is to feed it a nice bowl of rice and broiled breast of lamb.

Constipation

One teaspoonful of mineral oil is normally sufficient for relief.

Poisoning

Speed is essential in countering a poison. If the type of poison is known, use the recommended antidote or induce vomiting by using a solution of salt in water and pouring it into the pocket of the lip at the corner of the dog's mouth. Go to the nearest veterinarian. If none is available, your family doctor can give you advice over the telephone.

Champion Nagykunsagi Apro (Matyasfoldi Lurko Dongo X Borsodi Ancsa) handled here by Klara Benis for co-owner George S. DeBodnar. Judge: Mr. Charles Hamilton. Photograph: Bennett Assoc.

Skunk Spray

Wash the dog with tomato juice! The red color of the tomato juice in the coat will give you a problem later, but such a bath is the only effective means of removing the odor.

Electric Shock

If your dog has chewed on an electric cord, wrap a dry rag or towel around your hand or use a rubber glove to pull the plug from the outlet. Hold ammonia under the dog's nose and apply artificial respiration. The head should be lower than the rest of the body. Place the dog on his side and press his rib cage and release in two to three second intervals, or use mouth-to-mouth resuscitation (after insuring that the dog's mouth is held shut so as not to leak air) and blow into his nose while covering both nostrils with your mouth.

Dogfight

Number one rule: Do NOT reach between fighting dogs! In the excitement, even your own dog may bite you. If possible, separate fighters by pulling on their tails at the same time. A bucket of water is the surest and fastest means of separating battlers. If the dog's throat was damaged or his inhaling is heavy after the fight, oxygen may well be administered.

THE CARE OF A BITCH IN WHELP

It is assumed that a bitch is in top condition when she is being bred. A Puli bitch should not be bred before fifteen to eighteen months of age. This is a slow-developing breed that stays in top condition well beyond the average years of other breds. The bitch's booster shots of DHL and rabies should be up-to-date.

The normal gestation period (pregnancy) is 63 days from the date of mating. If two breedings take place, the first tie should be considered the starting date.

During the pregnancy, the bitch should not be allowed to become fat; she should receive the normal amount of food, but its quality should be increased. Her food should be higher in protein, well-balanced, and multiple-vitamins should be given daily. In addition, it is a good practice to give her di-calcium phosphate tablets through the pregnancy, and preferably during at least part of the lactation period.

About two weeks from the due date, prepare a whelping box. This should be large enough for her to comfortably stretch in, yet not too large, since the puppies should not be allowed to wander away from her. For an average size Puli bitch, a box three feet square is adequate. The height should be one that she is able to clear without difficulty, even with a full belly. About 10 to 12 inches is recommended.

Get her used to this box by placing it in her favorite corner of the house, service porch, or garage. The box must be well-protected from draft, cold, and heat, as well as from excessive noise. Preferably, placement should be under something such as an old table or a shelf. If such cover is unavailable, be sure that the whelping box is in a corner where the usual household traffic is minimal. Once you have found a good corner, do not relocate the box. Feed her there; pet her there, and make it a generally pleasant place for her. Praise her whenever she settles down in the box.

Line the bottom with many layers of newspaper, and on top a heavy blanket or a towel. During whelping, however, it is best to use only the newspaper lining, since the newborn puppies can easily become entangled in cloth.

Do not be alarmed or surprised if your bitch begins her whelping earlier than expected, as many bitches have their litters as much as a week early. They can, of course, be late as well. However, if a bitch is more than one week overdue, take her to a veterinarian. Before whelping, a bitch should be prepared by cleaning her exceptionally well in the vaginal area and on the belly. The hair around her nipples should be trimmed very short to assure that the puppies do not get entangled in her coat when they nurse.

When the time of whelping comes, some Puli bitches will prefer to have the owners right there with them, while others will make sure that everyone is out of the house or sleeping before starting labor. They seem to have a great ability to hold back labor until the appropriate situation exists. Very few healthy Puli bitches need assistance in whelping. Only on one occasion in my experience did I need to call the veterinarian and following his advice given over the telephone, I was even then able to cope with the situation. But a word of caution here: *DO NOT* panic and run to the veterinarian the moment your bitch gets ready to whelp. Unless definite medical attention is needed, you are asking for trouble by moving a Puli bitch from her home. They are quite emotional and a frantic car ride, a new environment, and strangers present could have a very bad effect on the natural, instinctive whelping process.

However, just to be on the safe side, have a pair of clean scissors at hand and small spool of fine thread.

Do not interfere with the bitch's whelping by constantly pushing her aside to see what is going on. Wait patiently until she stops her activity around the new puppy, and only then see if all is in order. After the puppy is pushed outside by the forces of labor, the bitch will open up the puppy's sac with her teeth, slowly pulling it back and off the puppy. Then she will proceed to chew the umbilical cord and eat the afterbirth (this contains the extruded portions of the placenta, embryonic membranes, and umbilical cord) before the next puppy arrives. If the sac is intact, yet the puppy is already separated from the dam, it is important to take it gently in your hand and pull on it to tear the sac open so that the puppy's head will be free for breathing.

Often the bitch will stop to rest while the puppy is still hanging by the cord. Do not be alarmed by this; she will get to it as soon as she regains her strength. Do not assist the bitch in cutting the cord unless it seems absolutely necessary, since she most often uses the remaining cord to pull out the afterbirth and to ease the next puppy closer to the opening. If it is necessary to cut the umbilical cord, do it at least 1 to $1\frac{1}{2}$ inches away from the puppy's navel.

The situation should be the same with each puppy. Do not attempt to prevent the bitch from eating the afterbirth unless she obviously rejected it and left it in the whelping box. This is a natural process and helps her in restarting her normal body functions, as well as initiating lactation and being a source of nutrition for her.

A vaginal discharge usually continues for several days after whelping. This should give no cause for concern. However, it is a good idea to take your bitch to a veterinarian the day after whelping to ascertain that all the afterbirth has been expelled.

PUPPY CARE

During nursing, the dam should remain on a special high quality diet with more than the usual amount of milk being made available to her. Little needs to be done for the puppies in the first four to five weeks unless the dam does not for some reason have enough milk. However, at four to five weeks of age, supplementary feeding should be started. First, cereal, (pablum, oatmeal, etc.) mixed with milk can be used. This is followed in a few days by fresh raw ground-beef mixed with puppy chow or cereal.

By the time they are six weeks old, puppies can be fed the same food as their mother. Somewhere during this period the dam's instinct tells her it's time to wean the pups. She will at some point then eat an excess amount of food, chew it, and regurgitate it in front of the puppies. This partially digested food looks like a small

Champion PuliKountry's Csopi (Ch. Buksi Sajo von Funfhausen X Ch. Hidegkuti Kocos) shown here by Mrs. Ruthlee Becker for owners Ray and Lois Powers. Photograph: Henry Schley.

meat loaf. Do not be alarmed. The bitch is not sick. This is not vomiting, only her excellent natural instincts at work as she prepares her pups for solid food. Let the puppies eat it. (You would be confusing the mother if you hurriedly cleaned it up and scolded her for it.)

Paper training the puppies can be started at a very early age. You will notice that within the whelping box, one corner seems to be always dirtier and damper than others. Place layers of newspapers in that corner, and towels or blankets in the others. Shortly, the pups will all use the paper for eliminating and the towel area for resting. At about four to five weeks of age, the puppies will start jumping out of the whelping box. Start removing the towels to a corner outside the box, and the pups will more than likely return to the newspaper area to mess and will keep the towels or blanket clean. At this point you can slowly make the newspaper area smaller and move it farther away from the playing area and sleeping quarters. Good luck!

Before sending the puppies to their new homes they should be checked for worms and should receive their first DHL vaccinations. If the dam's vaccination is up-to-date, the pups are protected during nursing; however, after weaning they have to have their own protection! DO NOT GAMBLE WITH THEIR LIVES!

GROOMING
Grooming the Corded Coat

Regardless of which grooming method we choose, the grooming procedure begins at an early puppy age. If you chose in the beginning to cord your Puli, the only tools you will need are your own fingers. Place the puppy on a sturdy table of comfortable height (grooming tables with hitching posts are best). First try to divert the puppy's attention, and make an enjoyable event out of the grooming session. For the first few grooming sessions, do not force the puppy to stay for long periods on the table. After the puppy feels safe and comfortable on the table, lay him down on his side or let him stand still, as you prefer. Start grooming at the feet, and work your way up the legs. Lift his coat and determine whether the coat is falling into even-sized tassels over his entire body. If you find areas in which the coat is either matted or scratched into a ball, hold on to the outer end of the coat (at the natural ends of the tassels) and part the tassels with your fingers, all the way to the skin. If you do this regularly, either once each week or once every second week, your puppy's coat will have an excellent start. The interval between grooming sessions will be determined by the denseness of the coat of the individual puppy, the geographical location, or the season. Puppies in colder climatic conditions will naturally grow their coats faster and heavier than those living in the sunny warmth of California or Florida.

If you are one of the lucky ones whose Puli will cord automatically into nice even-sized cords, your weekly coat checkup ends with checking. If you regularly find mats, or if your puppy scratches large areas into balls of fur, separate the coat into even-sized cords at the matted or disturbed areas, and wet him down. Soak the coat

Champion Belzebub Gezengus ("Gombi") and Champion Cinkotai Csibesz, a faithful pair; "Gombi" is pictured here at 8 and "Csibesz" at 11 years of age.

thoroughly to the skin with water, especially at the spot on which you have just been working. Place the puppy in a clean area where he can run without picking up dirt, and let him drip dry. If your puppy has the proper coat texture, you can see the progressing formation into cords by the time he is half dry. At this stage, do not use a blower type hair dryer as the blower will force the cords apart, requiring you to start the entire procedure over again. If it is cold outside, keep the puppy in a warm room until completely dry, or place him under a heat lamp.

It is important that you do not separate the coat into tassels that are too small, so try following the coat's natural formation as much as possible. As the puppy and its coat grows, these tassels or cords will become thicker and more pronounced. From the age of eight months to a year, the coat will really start reacting to your care and will be noticeably less work and more eye-appealing. During this period, place special emphasis on keeping your Puli free of grass cuttings, sawdust, or any other kind of dirt that can become entangled in the cords of its coat. If this happens anyway, brush him with a soft bristle brush, trying to keep the cords as undisturbed as possible. After the cords are well-formed, it is relatively easy to keep a corded Puli clean. You can brush him more vigorously if needed; you can use a vacuum cleaner if you can accustom him to the noise, or you can bathe him without the danger of disturbing the cords.

On a mature, fully-coated Puli only occasional separating of the cords should be necessary, as new growth dictates. Separate those cords that seem to have grown together at the skin and spray the area with warm water.

It is important that the ends of the cords be open at all times. Use a slicker brush if necessary, but do not let the ends curl back and double up in the cords. Not only will the ends start growing back into the cords and double up in thickness without getting any longer, but the coat will also appear matted and the Puli will lose its neat appearance. The ends are easy to check and, unless your Puli is running in and out of water all day, this should not give you much cause for concern.

For the show ring, groom your Puli thoroughly. After bathing and drying him, lay him down on his side. Hold up his cords with one hand and bring them down with the use of a brush in your other hand. Use a stronger bristle brush or pin brush for this procedure.

Start at the feet and brush upward. After you are through with one side, turn him over and repeat the procedure on the other side. Before going into the ring, I brush my Pulis once more, reversing the direction. Start at the top line and brush vigorously in the opposite direction of the natural fall of the cords. Let him stand up and shake himself. The real secret of grooming is in the brushing. You have to develop a method wherein you are brushing the coat without tearing it. This is true with either method of grooming. If you are campaigning a show Puli, combed or corded, you can not afford to tear out a bag full of coat before each show.

Learn to rotate the brush from your wrist. It is more likely that you will notice if you are tearing the coat when you put the power into the brush from your wrist. If you move your arm from the shoulder as you brush, you are automatically putting too much force into it. Watch some professional handlers brushing at a dog show; one of them can brush a poodle for thirty minutes without filling the brush with torn coat.

Grooming the Combed Coat

Whether your Puli is a show dog or house pet, the earlier you teach him to be at home on the grooming table, the more trouble you will save yourself. Teach your puppy to enjoy grooming. The combed method particularly will require patience from the Puli, for he must spend time quite regularly to keep his coat in the desired condition.

In the first few months of the puppy's life, you will only need a soft or medium-hard bristle brush. Set your grooming schedule according to your Puli's coat condition. Brush him only as often as is absolutely necessary. If he gets matted only behind his ears and around the base of his tail, brush him only in these places. If he gets matted only every two weeks, do not brush him every second day. It is easier to tear the puppy coat than it will be to tear his mature coat.

Lay your puppy down on his side and start brushing him from his feet upward. Hold the coat up with one hand and let the brush bring the coat down layer by layer. Work your way up to the back. Brush the tail and the loin area, leaving the head for last. Brush the head from the muzzle towards the eyes, paying much attention to the lips and the eyes. In case you run into matted areas do not try to open them with the brush. Tear up the mats in the manner described for corded coat grooming. After the mats are separated into small tassels, continue with the grooming. In the case of stubborn mats, soak the matted area in coat oil, or work some lanolin into the affected area before attempting to open it with your fingers. Mats that are left in the coat for prolonged periods may have to be cut apart with a mat splitter. To split a mat with a splitter, place the mat splitter under the mat at the skin, and carefully start cutting parallel to the natural direction of the coat. Be certain to move the splitter in the direction the coat is naturally falling in order to cut the least hair.

The older the puppy gets, the more often he will require brushing. After his mature coat begins to grow in, you will have to change to a pin brush. If you decide to keep your Puli in the combed grooming it is even more important that you learn to brush your dog without tearing his coat.

For the show ring, start preparing your dog's coat at least a week before the show. Go through the coat carefully and clear up all the matted areas. Brush him only at the spots where matting or considerable cording occurs. The day before the show, brush him thoroughly from bottom to top as previously described. Before you go into the ring, brush him backward and fluff him up with a soft brush. Let him shake himself, and you are ready to go into the ring.

Many Puli owners make the mistake of brushing their dogs at the easiest places to reach, rather than at the places that need the most grooming. They will brush, for example, on the shoulders because the dog's shoulders can be reached regardless of the position of the dog. As a result, the dog will eventually have much less coat in the shoulder area and will appear unbalanced. Remember that frequent, unnecessary, or vigorous brushing can have a disastrous effect on your Puli's coat. In America I have seen many overgroomed Pulis with a lifeless, thinned out, dry coat. The number of overgroomed Pulis in the United States greatly exceeds the number of completely neglected ones anywhere else in the world.

BATHING

Prepare your Puli for his bath before you dump him in the tub. This is done by thoroughly examining him, as follows:

First, check the ears for excess hair and wax, removing the hair with your fingers. This can be done without causing discomfort to the dog by dampening a piece of cotton or Q-tip in a mineral oil and wiping the inner parts of the ear with it. Do not put alcohol in your dog's ear. After the ears are clean, place cotton in them to prevent soapy water from entering during the bath. Odor coming from the ear is usually the indication of infection requiring a veterinarian's attention.

Next, clean the areas around the eyes with a sponge and luke-warm water. Place a few drops of mineral oil under his eyelids to prevent the shampoo from getting into them and causing great discomfort. Never use boric acid or any other preparation to clean the eyes.

Then lift up the paws and trim the hair between the pads. This not only helps to keep the pads tight but also gives the dog better traction on the smooth concrete or hardwood floors that he usually encounters at indoor dog shows. Trim the excess long hair from around his paws. For this procedure, stand your dog up on his four feet in a natural pose. Hold the scissors at about 45 degrees to the horizontal and clip around his paws. Make sure you follow the line of the paw in an even, smooth circle to make a completely round cut where the hair touches the ground. Check his nails. Toe nails should not touch the ground when the dog is standing still. If you exercise your Puli regularly on hard surfaces he probably will not need nail clipping, but if he spends much of his time on a grass lawn or carpet you will need to clip or file them occasionally. Buy a good quality nail clipper specially made for dogs. Do not try to use clippers made for human use; our nails are flat and thin, whereas dog nails are round and hard and the two types of clippers do not work on the same principle. Try to avoid cutting into the quick of the nail. If you do cut into the quick occasionally, stop the bleeding with styptic powder* before proceeding to the next nail. Unless you use a power file, filing the nails is much more time consuming, but the result is more rewarding, as you can shape the nails smooth and round without the danger of getting into the quick.

Finally, before putting your Puli into the water, check his coat once more for matting, because, corded or combed, the mats tend

* aluminum sulphate or the double sulphate of aluminum and potassium known as alum

to tighten up when wet and you will have a harder time eliminating them after the bath.

There are probably as many theories about how often to bathe a Puli as there are Puli owners. Suggested as a basic rule is: Bathe him only as often as it is absolutely necessary. Dogs are like kids. Some are born with the instinct to be clean. Some will walk around the entire back yard to avoid a puddle or wet grass, while others will playfully sit in the same puddle or roll into the wet, muddy grass. You are the sole judge of how often your Puli needs bathing. But, unless the dog is really sticky or soiled, avoid using shampoo or soap. Most dirt will readily come out with lukewarm water and gentle pressure. If you can no longer avoid bathing your dog, or if you are preparing your Puli for a show, place him in a tub of water, thoroughly wet his coat, and let him soak for a few minutes. The procedure is much the same for both a corded or combed coat.

After he is well soaked, let the water out of the tub. Pour shampoo on the full length of his back, from the head to the tail. Water the shampoo, preferably with a hand shower, into the coat. Massage the shampoo into the skin gently. Work it into the coat in much the same way as you would in washing a wool sweater. Squeeze it through the coat systematically, so the coat is completely saturated with suds. When bathing a corded or combed Puli, never use a rubbing circular motion to work the shampoo into the coat; if you do, you will have a tedious job getting out the mats that you have just rubbed into the coat. If the Puli has the proper coat texture and you are keeping it combed, you will have to fight matting anyway, without making more work for yourself. If your Puli is corded, keeping those cords evenly separated is enough of a job without fighting the mats you created in the bath tub. Rinse the shampoo with the hand shower, preferably with strong water pressure. Then start at the head, lifting it up by holding onto his chin, and begin rinsing above the eyes, letting the water run down the back of his head. Separate the coat with your other hand and rinse it layer by layer, going down the dog from top to bottom. Repeat the shampooing and let the dog sit with the foamed-up shampoo in the tub without water for five to ten minutes (in order to let the shampoo act on the skin). I use only a medicated shampoo, because I have found that medicated shampoos are least likely to dry out the skin, and because they take less of the life out of the coat. Some people prefer hair conditioning cream rinses to put the life back into the coat that shampoo has taken out, but I prefer to leave the natural lubricants in the coat and dispense with corrective measures.

The importance of the final rinsing can not be emphasized enough. After the second shampooing, you have to rinse the suds out of the coat in the same manner as I described earlier. You have to rinse the entire dog from top to bottom three or four times, or until the rinse water that is draining out is as clear as pure drinking water. Rinse out the tub and fill it up once more with clear water; let the dog submerge in it so only his head is above the water, to make absolutely sure no shampoo has remained in hidden areas of his coat. The smallest amount of shampoo left on the skin can make the skin dry and the coat dull for weeks afterwards, and the skin will become irritated at the dry spots and cause your dog to scratch, rub against walls and furniture, or wriggle on his back, defeating the whole purpose of giving the bath.

After the last rinse, let the water out of the tub. Make your Puli stay in the empty tub to drip long enough to avoid wetting the floors all the way to the drying area. If you can manage it, throw a large bath towel over him before he starts shaking himself, and lift him out of the tub wrapped in the towel. Soak up the excess water from the coat with towels, again paying particular attention not to use a circular rubbing motion. The drying process differs somewhat between the two types of grooming. I place my corded dogs in a warm area in a wire cage, padding the bottom of it with two or three heavy bath towels to soak up the drips, and let them dry the natural way. Frequent bathing or using the wrong type of shampoo can occasionally cause the cords to tighten up like steel wire. When this happens, I use a gentle blower to dry them, while loosening up the tight cords with the airstream. In this process you cannot put the blower down next to the cage and leave the dog to dry, as he will sit in the corner of the cage and the blower will dry only a small area. In this small area, the cords will be loose to the point of almost opening, while other areas will stay tight. Therefore you have to place the dog on a table and move the nozzle of the blower constantly around the dog until he is completely dry.

When drying a combed Puli, you can use any of the hard-blowing commercial dog dryers. I let the combed coat dry completely before I use a brush on it. Brushing the coat while drying tends to straighten each individual hair, thus causing it to look like a faulty straight coat. Combed dogs can also be placed in a wire cage on thick towel padding to dry in the natural way much as described for the corded coat.

I very carefully watch the dogs that I must bathe more often than I would prefer and at the first sign of dry skin or dry coat, I spray them with a pure aerosol lanolin product (such as St. Aubrey, Mr. Groom, or Professional Groom) or brush some caked lanolin into their coats and massage it into their skin. In case of dandruff-like flaky skin, I work baby lotion into the affected skin area. I do not know whether it is the sturdy nature of the Puli's skin or the effect of the baby lotion, but I have been lucky enough in most cases to eliminate this flakiness within twenty-four hours unless the condition is the result of parasites or a more advanced skin infection.

You may be one of those exceptionally lucky persons who owns a Puli with the inborn instinct to keep clean at all times. If you have a backyard fully covered with thick green grass and a washable hard surface, and if you are willing to hand feed your dog, you might be able to keep a Puli clean without ever giving him a bath. Yes, it can be done! I have been introduced to retired and still active Best-In-Show winning old English Sheepdogs that have never been in a bathtub. Eliminating the bath does not mean you do not have to clean them at all. Dozens of drycleaners are on the market, and there are even spot cleaners specifically developed for dogs. Or if you want to be really old-fashioned about it, you can brush your Puli's coat perfectly clean with a mixture of corn-flour and vinegar. In the case of the white Puli, cleaning chalk works best. Advocates of these cleaning methods maintain that the only way to keep a dog's natural coat texture is by eliminating the necessity for the water and shampoo treatment. After heart-to-heart talks on the subject with my barber, my wife's hairdresser, and my doctor, I am inclined to believe the drycleaning advocates. But to date, I have never seen a Puli that was inactive enough that I would even attempt to keep it clean solely with drycleaners.

EARLY MENTAL DEVELOPMENT

The elementary responsibility of a breeder does not stop with assuring full bellies for the puppies. Beyond the tender loving care that the nursing bitch should receive, and the vaccination, worming, and general physical well being of puppies, the psychological health of the puppies is of utmost importance and they need guidance toward emotional health.

When one makes the initial decision to breed a bitch, he had better be ready to take full responsibility for those lives being brought into this world. It is carelessness and negligence if in this day and age puppies show undernourishment or lack of physical care after weaning. But even if they go through a short period of undernourishment, as dangerous as that is, there is still a long developmental period when you have a good chance to make up for the early mistakes in feeding. If one neglects the emotional development for any period during the first three months of the puppy's life, permanent damage is inevitable. They have to go through a systematic socialization period in order to begin relating to humans. As a rule of thumb, a very minimum of fifteen minutes a day should be spent with each puppy from the day of whelping. Figuring a litter of six, this accounts for an hour and a half every day that you must spend giving the pups individual attention. If you are not willing to sacrifice this much time for your puppies, over and above the time you spend on feeding and cleaning up after them, you should not breed your bitch.

Research scientists and operators of experimental kennels have spent countless years seeking a better understanding of the emotional stability and socialization of dogs. Many books have been published on the subject in the past few years. Probably the most noteworthy for easy home application of principles are *Genetics and The Social Behavior of the Dogs* by doctors Scott and Fuller and *The New Knowledge of Dog Behavior* by Dr. Clarence Pfaffenberger. The first one is written in scientific language; the latter is written in layman's terms and is more-or-less a practical adaptation of the Scott, Fuller book. By reading up on the subject of socialization, you can learn simple practices to employ in early-age preparation of puppies for emotional stability in life. Do not try to rationalize or fool yourself by saying that you will cut down on the required minimum time by spending time with the show prospects out of a litter and thus waste no time with those destined to be merely *pets*. First, unless there is a definite color defect or other obvious fault, you cannot tell in the first few weeks which of

Champion Thunder Mount Arpad and Champion Thunder Mount Acsi (both by Acsi of PuliKountry X Star of Hunnia Furtos), pictured here winning Best Working Brace at the K.C. of Beverly Hills Show, June, 1971. Handled by owner-breeder Miss Augusta Plank. Photograph: Henry Schley.

the litter are your future show dogs and which you will have to sell without registration as pets. Furthermore, the puppies you sell as pets are as much representatives of the breed in the eyes of the general public as your *Best In Show* prospect and they deserve an equally normal emotional start in life.

In temperament, there is no "absolute" measurement of what is required of a good Puli. One keeps dogs for protection, for companionship, for a child's playmate or for assistance in certain types of work. The Puli can easily serve in any or all of these roles. The various duties possibly to be demanded of him later in his life will also require a basic emotional stability. It is a long-standing misbelief among novice dog owners that guard dogs or attack-trained dogs should be mean to all humans from an early age. This false idea was probably planted in the minds of the general public by unethical "dog producers." It is not rare to hear such a breeder say, when one of his puppies is revealed to be nervous or shy: "He probably won't be a good show dog because he does not like strangers, but he will be a good guard dog." Yes, he will likely be the uncontrollable type of guard dog that will fiercely protect you from your best friends, and may possibly turn upon one of the family for some trivial cross.

Puppies growing up without adequate human contact are more likely to develop into unpredictable, overly-suspicious, shy animals. The fear-biter, the dog that attacks innocent bystanders without warning, or without any apparent reason, or bites the hand of a child who wanted to pet him, is marked as a dog that grew among his littermates as in a pack of wolves, either in an overcrowded commercial kennel or in a private home without the tender loving care puppies require. I am not saying that a dog's temperament is not influenced by hereditary factors, nor that behavior cannot be ruined later in the dog's life, but I would venture to say that the vast majority of Pulis with undesirable behavior in maturity were ruined in the first few months of their lives.

On the other hand, the Puli that will walk away with the first stranger, or will lick the hand of a burglar breaking into the family house is as undesirable and un-Puli-like as his nervous counterpart. Our breed standard spells it out in plain English: . . . "Sensibly suspicious of strangers." This phrase has probably been misinterpreted more often than any other, in the entire *Complete Dog Book* of the A.K.C., by Puli owners, dog show judges, and by exhibitors alike. In short, DO NOT confuse "sensibly suspicious" with shyness or mental instability. Owners trying to rationalize the panic stricken behavior of their nervous house pet to a visitor who has been just bitten are far from being right. Nor is the judge right who walks up from the rear of a Puli in the ring and starts the physical examination by checking the testicles, and then disqualifies him for shying away as a result of his abrupt approach.

What are we really looking for in Puli temperament, and how can we help the puppies achieve it by our treatment during their early development?

We are looking for a well-balanced, mentally stable dog that will be pliable to train for practically anything we want him to do. The selection and basic training starts on the first day of his life. The concept of the entire socialization period is built on one basic idea. Make every occasion of human contact a pleasurable experience for the puppies.

Although the newly born puppy's senses are not fully operative, they will react to touching and your body temperature. They should be handled daily for a few seconds at a time from the first day of their lives. Turn them on their backs in your hand. The puppy that fights this defenseless position like an overturned bug, and unable to relax in this position even after the first few days, will invariably turn out to be the puppy that will be easier to frighten, or that will freeze in new situations. Rubbing the tummy very gently with your fingertips, stroking the back and sides and making this routine a pleasurable experience is the first step in building the contact between human and dog that will develop into unquestioned trust. This practice in socialization is limited to handling and contact in the first three to four weeks.

The real training can start when you first start feeding them, by giving the puppies fresh, finely-ground beef out of your hand, thus strengthening the socialization bridge even more. At this time you can introduce a sound signal, by calling them to the feast. Like all other commands or signals later in their lives, it is important to be consistent. Always use the same words. "Here puppies," "Come on puppies," or anything you wish. Within just a couple of days, the association of this sound with the pleasure of eating will get them up and coming when they are called.

Up to this point the puppies' world was limited to their whelping box. At the age of a month, they should be taken to a strange place one by one just for a few minutes at a time. This is the time to really begin observations. The puppy that will get up and start exploring the new surroundings on his own will be the pup that will cope with all new situations in life. He will be self-assured, confident, and sensible. Some puppies will sit down wherever you place them (not necessarily frightened, but reluctant to move around) and will begin barking or yelping. More than likely, those dogs will be noisier than the rest of the litter throughout their lives. The ones that show any signs of being frightened should be coaxed and encouraged. Use your puppy-calling sound-signal or roll their favorite toy in front of them. Do anything just to help them overcome their fear. If they do not relax in the new situation within a couple of minutes, pick them up and let them relax in your hands. Place them back in the pen with the others and try it again later. Repeat this until they get the idea that there is nothing to be afraid of. Praise them lavishly whenever they do what you want them to. Your tone of voice should be enthusiastic, soft, and encouraging, They soon learn that coming to you when called will bring them hearty praise, even when it does not bring food.

At six weeks of age, the time one spends with the puppies individually should be increased. The puppy must be taken out of the mother's area and should be far enough from his littermates that their noise will not distract him. These sessions should present something new for the puppy to cope with. Make the tasks easy for him at the beginning. Take the puppy to a corner of the yard where he will not be distracted. Put a small collar on him and step back a few feet. Always wait for his first reaction. If he continues to play or walk toward you, praise him. Next, snap a discardable leash or a short piece of rope on the collar and let him drag it around until he gets used to it. Then pick up the end of the tether and start calling him. At this age, one very seldom runs into the persistent resistance against the leash that we experience if breaking to the leash is postponed until the puppies are several months old. If a puppy sits down and balks, DO NOT force him, DO NOT drag him! Let him sit as long as he wishes, and when he gives up, let him go wherever he desires. Just hang on to the end of the leash and follow, praising him while he is moving. Stand, sit, retrieve and other easy routine tasks can be set up during these sessions. (Do not over-exercise any of the puppies at this age.) If he sits for you for a few seconds at the beginning, show him that you are happy. You are not *training* at this time in the true sense of the word, you are helping him to cope with all the new situations he can encounter. At about six or seven weeks of age, the puppies should be paired and locked up in a crate for a few minutes at a time, slowly increasing the interval. Later, they should be locked up alone. Again it is important to start out with a few seconds, and to increase the time very slowly. Give each puppy a bone or a toy to chew on while in solitary confinement. If they are willing, let them nap in there. From my own experience, I leave the puppies with their mother longer than any of the above-mentioned books recommend. Puppies, like little monkeys, learn to imitate, and this breed is still closer to nature than many others. I have studied dams, and with puppies between six and eight weeks the good mother will really spend time with her puppies teaching them to fight for what is rightfully theirs. She scolds them if they fight with each other too seriously. I have personally seen mothers teaching their puppies how to hunt for birds and cats when they were nine weeks old. There is no danger to the puppies in learning from their mothers how to hunt if at the same time they have an established contact with humans and are beginning to learn to obey.

The word NO should be completely eliminated from this early training period. "NO" should be the key word for the absolute no-no's later in life. In teaching, repeat what you want the puppy to do; do not tell him what you do not want him to do. The first few times a puppy does one of the few absolute no-no's (of the house rules) use a loud NO!, and at the same time shake him by the skin on the back of his neck. This severe treatment should be used sparingly, and only for "major crimes," such as chewing on electric cords, flowers, bed sheets, making puddles on the living-room floor, etc. Most importantly, use the neck shaking and the loud "NO" only when you catch him in the act. Do not yell at him when you discover some of his mischievious doings minutes or hours after he performed them.

Many puppy owners are urgently inclined to start either dog show training or serious obedience training at too early an age. Let the puppies have their "childhood." Pulis are especially fun-loving, active puppies. Do not expect them to stay in a sit command for minutes or hours at a time. If they learn the meaning of the word "sit" at six or eight weeks of age, you are already ahead of the average dog.

Leaving the puppies with their mother and littermates longer will require special attention on the part of the breeder, to make sure that they do not establish an order of dominance. The puppy that is too rough with his littermates should be scolded by the neck-shaking method when he tries to dominate others. The one that is cornered should be removed from the others and should receive special attention. At this age, the puppies should be protected from

Champion Bridget of PuliKountry, C.D. and Champion PuliKountry's Bordacs Baby (both by Ch. Nagykunsagi Csorgo, C.D. X Ch. Hidegkuti Kocos), bred by Robert and Anne Kennedy, are shown here going Best Brace in Show with co-owner Mrs. Anne Decker handling. Photograph: Henry Schley.

almost all failure. If the smallest one is having a hard time getting out of the whelping box to run after the others, help him get out. The puppy that consistently fails in his first attempts will soon become afraid to try solving even a simple problem.

Even the simplest training requires the development of a spirit to solve new problems as they come along. If you use common sense during these critical weeks to protect them from early failures, you will build their self-confidence to the point where they will be anxious to try to cope with new situations.

The above briefly described method is overly-simplified and very unscientific. The average Puli owner does not need to create a laboratory type, controlled atmosphere to prove that a problem puppy can be made a useful member of the Puli population. Those who are interested in a more detailed or more scientific exposition of behavior studies can find books to fill a library on the subject.

By no means do I want to create the feeling in the reader that Pulis should not be disciplined or obedience-trained later in life. On the contrary, I advise everyone not to let a Puli grow up to be spoiled and uncontrolled. The critical development period of pups should be studied by all breeders and puppy owners in order to get the most satisfaction of them in their later months. At this age, gentleness and understanding are as important as consistent, firm commands in their later obedience training.

HOW TO TRAIN YOUR PUPPY FOR THE SHOW RING

Before we can even talk about the show ring, the puppy has to be leash-broken. The best time for the puppy to begin his preliminary training is between the ages of six to twelve weeks. At this age, leash-breaking is practically effortless and is no strain on the puppy. First, put a small light leather collar, without any attached tags, rings, bells, or any other noise making device, on the puppy's neck. If the puppy fights it, leave it on only a few minutes and slowly work up to where the puppy will tolerate it all day. After he has completely accepted the collar, attach an old worn-out leash or two to three feet of light rope to the collar and let him drag it around. This part of the training should be done when you can keep an eye on the puppy at all times so that he cannot get tangled up and scare himself in the process.

Champion Princess Tish of Beverlywood, C.D. (Star of Hunnia Dongo X Wayside Karpathi Magda) shown by owner Richard Greenbaum to BOS at the P.C.S.C. Specialty at the K.C. of Beverly Hills, June, 1968. Judge: Major Godsol. Photograph: J. Ludwig.

After the puppy has accepted the idea of having the little extra weight dragging behind him, lift up the end of the leash, and at first let him go wherever he wants to go. During this process try to keep ahead of him and call to him and encourage him to walk. When he does a few steps on his own, praise him. During the first few lessons, do not force him by dragging the puppy around with the leash. Do not let his mind associate the leash with unpleasant forces pulling him back and forth; this can set him back in his training. These first training sessions should not last more than a few minutes each. After each session, make an effort to keep up his spirits by playing with him and giving him some tid-bits he likes.

In my opinion, when training a show dog or even a joyful companion, the most important thing to remember is not to break his will or spirit, but to make him enjoy every step of the training. Make a game of it. Naturally, this "game" can be more and more controlled as the dog gets older, but it can still be fully enjoyable for dog and owner. Leash-breaking an older dog takes an entirely different approach and dozens of obedience books are available for you to select a method that suits you.

Since the Puli is an exceptionally easy breed to train, you do not have to be as forceful with him as many of the obedience books recommend.

GAITING

After the dog moves around correctly on the leash, start training him to gait. Gaiting, by the way, is not just a more disciplined walking on leash as many novice exhibitors believe. Gaiting is the first step wherein the combined efforts of dog and handler are equally required. You have to teach your Puli to walk on a straight line with his head up, tail over his back, and all this in a gay manner. The method to achieve this can vary with each dog and owner. You can modify your bicycle so you can attach a special harness to force the dog to walk with his head up or simply wave a piece of liver in front and above his nose while walking him.

Hold the leash in your left hand, look straight ahead and pick a speed that is most advantageous for your dog. You may have to try different speeds until you find the one at which your dog gaits mostly smoothly. For most Pulis, this is the maximum speed at which the dogs can walk without breaking into a gallop.

You have to get them used to walking at this speed all the time. I have to point out that to be fast is not the most important thing in gaiting. Some exhibitors act in the ring as if it were a dog race on leash. You have to study your individual dog and determine at what speed he looks his best and get him used to walking in the ring at this speed, regardless of how fast the dogs ahead of you or behind you are moving. This is where the handler's adaptability is needed.

The handler has to adjust his steps to move his dog with the speed best for the dog, not at a pace to suit himself. He must also maneuver his dog among the other dogs in such a manner that his dog is not forced to change speed while gaiting around the ring along with the others before the judge and without at the same time disturbing or inconveniencing other dogs and exhibitors. It is relatively easy to move a dog at a chosen speed when the dog is moved individually, but experience and teamwork between dog and handler will truly shine when moving around the ring together with a number of other dogs and handlers.

STANDING

Teaching a dog to stand can also begin at six or eight weeks of age by holding the puppy with one hand between his front legs and the other hand holding him between his hind legs. Just stand him like that for a few seconds. After the puppy stops fighting this exercise, increase the time to a minute or a minute and a half. If he is standing relaxed, let go of him with the hand holding his rear, and just hold him by his collar. Finally let him go with both hands for a few seconds, eventually working this no-hands part of the exercise up to a minute in duration. When he is familiar with this much, get him used to posing while he is standing. First, hold his chin up in the position that you want it, and let him stand like that. Later, position his legs the way you want them. Finally straighten the backline and position the tail. Each of these additional steps must last only a few seconds at a time. The most important thing is not how well the puppy performs the first few times, but how happily he performs! As soon as he shows signs of being bored, praise him, give him his favorite toy or a tid-bit and let him go on his merry way. Practicing for only a few minutes, in sessions spaced several hours apart, is best. Do not try to teach the total standing or posing exercise to your dog in one or two training sessions.

The correct pose for a well-proportioned Puli is as follows: Set his front legs vertical and parallel to each other. Lift his head to achieve the desired neck angulation. Set his hind legs by dropping his rear to assure that his topline is level. Slowly move his hind legs until the hocks are vertical. In this position the Puli, if he is perfectly proportioned, should show from the side view an approximate 45 degree shoulder slope, well bent stifles, straight and level back, tail curling over his back on one side and (disregarding the head and tail) an overall appearance of a square body.

CONDITIONING

Your young dog can walk on a leash, gait, stand, and pose, yet

Champion Hunnia's Ricsi (at 3 months of age) with 4-year-old Kati Kossuth winning BOB over an entry of 19 Pulis (all others with grown-up handlers) at a San Fernando K.C. Sanctioned Match under judge Mrs. Dolly Ward.

he can fall to pieces at a dog show unless you condition him to the noise, to the closeness of other dogs, to being touched and examined by strangers, and to the many other disturbances he will encounter only at a dog show. To condition him to noises, you can start at any time. Take him to supermarket entrances, theatre entrances, or even to a baseball game. Once he is assured that the noise is nothing to fear, he will learn to relax and behave in any situation. To get him used to other dogs, the best method is to take him to fun-matches, or to leave him in a boarding kennel occasionally for a day at a time. After he realizes that there are other four-legged ones on this earth, take him close to other dogs while on a leash. Preferably pick the biggest dogs you can find at a match. Walk between and around them. Praise him; pet him; do anything to help him keep his confidence. Later, when he can stand and pose, set him up for strangers and let them go over your dog while you are holding him. It takes ten to fifteen seconds at a time, and your dog will soon behave like a "pro." If he stood still while being examined, praise him and let him go. To get him used to being handled and examined by strangers from puppy-hood on, place him for a few minutes in the lap of every willing person who comes visiting.

Another conditioning that is many times neglected, even by some no longer novice exhibitors, is to get the dog used to the type of ground he is going to walk on in the ring. You can practice and your dog can turn out a perfect performance three minutes before you go into the ring on a hard surface, then you walk into the ring where he has to walk on dried or freshly cut grass, or on a rubber mat or roofing paper taped to the floor (at most inside shows), and you won't believe that you have the same dog at the end of the leash that you had a couple of minutes before. He may act as though he had never before worn a leash. After the first few matches or shows, you and your young Puli will get used to the noise, disturbances, and occasional tenseness of dog shows. You will master the trick of keeping your dog's constant attention and you will be able to keep him alert all the time while in the ring, constantly showing his best to the judge and ringside spectators.

Once you walk into the ring in front of the judge, the training period is over, no more corrections! By now your Puli should know how to gait and pose and show himself. Your job is to keep him alert and happy from the second you walk in the ring until you leave it. The judge will examine your dog and will probably ask you to walk him straight away from him to the other side of the ring, then across the ring, so he can also see your dog move from a side view, and then again straight back toward him, covering a large triangular course. He may also ask you to move the dog on a track resembling a "T" in shape. In some cases he will ask you just to go straight down and back. Try to keep as calm as possible as you and your dog perform whatever is asked of you. First of all, keep in mind that this is a sport, and we do not compete for blood. If you are nervous, your dog will also be nervous in the ring. Many decisions have been made in favor of exhibitors who managed to stay more relaxed than their competitors, and as a result could get more out of their dogs during those critical moments. Since the majority of the owners showing young puppies are themselves novices in the show ring, I think it appropriate that this long list of "Do's" be followed by one of "Do not's."

The following are absolute "No-No's" while in the show ring:

1. Do not walk into the ring and greet the judge with an ear to ear smile on your face and loud "How are you?" even if you have just recognized him as your next door neighbor, and you never knew that he was a dog show judge.

2. Most judges will let you use anything to keep your own dog's attention in the ring. You can bait him with liver, biscuit, a small ball or toy, but be considerate of the other dogs. Do not throw pieces of liver all over the ring, and do not let your dog begin to bark over the ball you are holding.

3. While the judge is examining other dogs, keep one eye on him and the other one on your dog. Do not engage in conversation with people sitting outside of the ring, or with other exhibitors in the ring. You are there to show your dog to perfection and to win, and not to talk over yesterday's baseball game or your new litter of puppies.

4. Do not start a conversation with the judge. If he wants to know something he should know, he will ask you. If he is asking a question, answer him politely and as shortly as possible. Do not try to let him know that "this is the litter sister of the dog he put up two weeks ago . . ."

5. If you are among the lucky ones receiving an award, walk calmly to the number he designated for your dog. Do not scream and do not kiss the judge in your uncontrolled happiness, but do say a soft thank you when he hands the ribbon to you.

6. If you are one of those who did not place, congratulate the winners and walk out with your dog quietly. Do not make faces, nor nasty remarks, not even between your teeth. Do not tell the judge to read the standard before he judges this breed next time. And above all, especially do not broadcast to all at the ringside, expressions of your disapproval of the judge's choice by yelling something such as "Mother, how did you like THAT decision?"

7. Come happiness or disappointment, hold yourself together and pay undivided attention to your dog until you leave the ring. Do not let your dog fall to pieces because of your emotional reaction. You never know when the judge who is going to judge the next show might be sitting at ringside and is watching you drag your dog out of the ring.

If you manage to remember half of the above "do's" and "do not's" while in the ring with a dog on your leash you will be doing better than the average dog show exhibitor.

DOG SHOWS

Dog shows are great fun and a recreational activity for the entire family. If you think that you would like to enter the show ring with your newly-acquired Puli, here is some advice: Before your puppy will reach the eligible age to enter a show or a club Match, you should attend a few of them and carefully watch the procedure. Depending upon the type of match, puppies can usually be entered from the age of three months. Matches are organized by local all-breed clubs, obedience clubs, and by most Puli clubs if you live in a densely populated locality. Most matches are sanctioned by the

American Kennel Club. This means that they have requirements somewhat similar to those of regular dog shows. Matches are mostly for practice. Some are smaller, but the entries in some may equal or exceed the number in a regular dog show. While you are in attendance, watch how the dogs are handled and what procedures are followed in the ring. As soon as your puppy reaches the eligible age, take him to a couple of these matches. It is excellent training for handler and dog.

After attending your first matches, if you feel you would like to try the real thing, start preparing for it. First, write to The American Kennel Club, 51 Madison Avenue, New York, N.Y. 10010, for the free booklet "Rules Applying to Registration and Dog Shows." Read it thoroughly and study the sections carefully that apply to your dog.

Study the breed standard. Learn to evaluate your own dog. Naturally all Puli owners are prejudiced. You should not own a Puli unless you love it beyond compare. But if you are sincerely interested in showing your dog, and interested in the dog sport, you must accept the fact that it is possible that your dog has a fault. More than likely it has even more than one fault. The perfect Puli has not yet been whelped. Studying the standard just might make you more realistic about it.

Inquire about Handling Classes in your locality. If they are available, be sure to participate in them.

Contact the A.K.C. licensed Dog Show Superintendent or Superintendents in your area, and ask them to place you on their mailing list for the upcoming shows. They will send you a "Premium List" for each show, which usually contains all pertinent information regarding the show and includes entry blanks.

Fill out the entry form carefully. Once the entries are closed it can not be changed.

The classes you can enter your dog in at an A.K.C. sanctioned show are:

1. Puppy Classes: For dogs between 6 and 9 months of age.
   For dogs between 9 months and one year of age.
2. Novice Class: For dogs that have never won a first prize ribbon (except in Puppy Classes.)
3. Bred by Exhibitor Class: Dogs shown in this class must be bred by the exhibitor or by a member of his immediate family.

4. American Bred Class: For dogs bred and born in the U.S.
5. Open Class: This class is open for all dogs. Even Champions can be entered in this class, although it is highly unusual. This class is for fully-matured dogs who are after their championship points.
6. Winners Class: The winner of each of the above classes will compete in this class for the winner title. Depending upon the number of dogs competing in the various classes, the winner of this class could receive up to 5 points towards its championship.

The same classes are held for both sexes, but separately. After the winners are chosen in each sex, the Best-of-Breed Competition enters the ring. All Champions of record are eligible for this class as well as the Winners of each sex. The judge will select from this class the Best-of-Breed, the Best-of-Opposite Sex, and the Best-of-Winners. In case the Best-of-Breed is a dog, then a bitch will be selected for Best-of-Opposite sex. If a bitch receives the top honors, the best male will be chosen for the Best-of-Opposite Sex.

The Best-of-Breed is entitled to compete in the Working Group. There are six groups.

Group I: Sporting Dogs
Group II: Hounds
Group III: Working Dogs
Group IV: Terriers
Group V: Toy Breeds
Group VI: Non-Sporting

The Best-of-Breed dog is representing his breed in the group and competing for first, second, third, or fourth place in the group. Then each of the six group winners compete for the highest award of the day: The Best-In-Show title.

SPECIAL CLASSES

There are some classes that are not available at all the shows. Some of these classes are very valuable for those who are seriously interested in the breed.

Stud Dog

Stud Dog class is for dogs which have sired one or more litters and have had at least two of their offspring entered in the same show in the regular classes. The sire is judged on the merits of his get.

Major consideration is given to the similarity between father and his progeny. The puppies sired by and shown with him do not necessarily have to have the same dam.

Brood Bitch
Brood Bitch class is identical to the above, except that in this case the bitch will go into the ring with two of the offspring she whelped. The puppies do not have to have the same father, but should look as identical as possible.

Brace
Brace Class is for two dogs under identical ownership. Again the dogs are judged on the merits of similarity. The dogs are usually shown on one lead and should exhibit team effort to walk and show the same way. This class is very popular among Puli exhibitors, mainly on shows where there are a large number of Puli entries. Puli braces have been doing some exceptional winning.

Team
This class consists of three or more dogs under identical ownership that are shown on a single lead. It is very rewarding to train three or four dogs that look identical and behave and move alike.

JUNIOR SHOWMANSHIP
Children who show interest in exhibiting their own dogs can enter in this class. This class is mainly to teach a child sportsmanship and showmanship at an early age. The winner is judged strictly on the handler's ability (the dogs are not judged). Any breed of dog is eligible as long as it has been entered in regular classes at the same show.

Pulis are exceptionally good with children and are often seen in this class with their little masters. After a few practice sessions, children outclass some adults in showmanship. The team effort can really shine when a child walks into the ring with his or her favorite Puli. Pulis have a tendency to be happier and show themselves better with a child. Adults sometimes get nervous in the ring and this usually upsets the dog. In contrast, a dog entering the ring with its human playmate does not receive the nervous vibrations and as a result it behaves more naturally and at ease.

WHAT A JUDGE LOOKS FOR IN A SHOW RING

What a judge looks for in the show ring varies widely. The Puli Club of Southern California, Inc. conducted a survey among judges to find out. The most impressive and surprising answer on the majority of the returned questionnaires showed that judges consider "Type" above everything else. And that is the way it should be. (We see judging once in a while that gives us the urge to sneak a similar breed into the ring to test the judge's ability to pick the real Puli type.) Soundness is secondary, but not less in importance. A mongrel can be sound, and a good mover, but it does not necessarily look like any breed. On the other hand, one can have an impressive looking Puli, excellent in type but lacking in soundness, in muscle power, and a questionable mover. Bone structure is next. If the skeleton of the dog under its heavy coat is sound, put together well in every respect, it is very likely that the dog will also be a good mover.

Showmanship cannot change a dog's overall qualities, but it can bring out the dog's best. Too many dogs are poorly shown, and that is the owner's fault. With relatively little effort, the overall show-manship could be improved considerably. There are handling classes in most cities, usually offered by local clubs. A short course can make the difference.

PROFESSIONAL HANDLERS

Every living soul who is able to move around, and can move his or her hands, should be able to handle a dog in the show ring. If the relationship between owner and dog is what it is supposed to be and the Puli has a good temperament to begin with, the owner should be able to get more out of the dog than anybody else. For most of us, the real enjoyment of the dog sport comes when we step into the ring with a dog we can be proud of and do our best to show the dog to its best. People who are unable to handle a dog because of a physical handicap or the inability to control and train their own pet may need the help of a professional handler.

Professional handlers are licensed by the American Kennel Club and may or may not be members of the Professional Handlers Association. Most of them are what the title suggests, professionals of their field in every respect. Nevertheless, it is still a good idea to make a very careful selection. Watch them handle other dogs, watch

Champion Shagra Tasha, U.D., one of the best known Pulis in obedience circles, clearing the high jump during exercises. Owner: Mrs. Sandy Cross.

their style and ring practice, and check their kennel facilities before making a final choice. Many of them are specialized in some breeds that require a different approach from Pulis. Choosing a good handler for your particular dog can be as difficult as choosing a suitable mate for your brood bitch. Handlers can be found through dog magazines or show superintendents. Reputable handlers will welcome the most vigorous investigation by future clients. Do not be bashful; if you need a handler, do everything in your power to get the most suitable handler for your dog's particular need.

A final word of caution to novice show-goers. Sitting at ringside, one can hear remarks by poor losers to the effect that this or that dog won because a certain handler was at the other end of the leash. As a general rule, this is not so. In short, do not hire a handler to achieve a particular win. Hire a handler who can show your dog to its best advantage. The reputation of an exhibitor who hires different handlers for different judges usually travels faster and farther than the news of his dog's occasional win.

PULIS IN OBEDIENCE

The Puli's intelligence, agility, and alertness makes him well-qualified for obedience work. Pulis having excellent relations with their human companions usually turn in the best performances in obedience trials. In obedience work, it is even more important that handler and dog have complete confidence in each other and possess a positive attitude towards the task at hand, be it basic training or the highest degree in ring performance.

Dozens of books are available on obedience training, and hundreds of classes are offered yearly across the country to teach the beginner how to train his dog. The basic philosophy in training a Puli should be that your Puli knows how to do what you want him to do but you, the master, have to learn how to make your dog understand what you want. If one goes into obedience with this in mind, success is almost certain. In the obedience ring, the dog cannot fail; if anyone fails, it is the handler. Never, never try to train your Puli by breaking his spirit. Once you have broken the happy spirit of a Puli, he will never perform as well as one that was trained with understanding.

Through the past two decades, the Puli Club of Southern California has conducted obedience classes for Pulis only, under the leadership of various obedience trainers in the Los Angeles area. After the graduation of these classes, most of the instructors agreed that Pulis in general are easier to train than the average dog. They also agree that Pulis get frustrated faster by overdoing a particular exercise. It is debatable if the above is due to the Puli's urge to encounter new challenges or if it simply learns faster and gets bored by endless repetition of the same routine. My own experience in obedience seems to point to the latter.

Years ago we took part in one of these classes for Pulis only. We took three of our Pulis to each of the training sessions. My wife handled one, I handled another, and our Ch. Gyali Csopi was staked out during each class where she would sit nearby watching our activities. At the end of each training session I would untie Csopi and practice the same exercises we had learned during the 90 minute classes, but only for 5 to 10 minutes, total. At the end of the course, just to satisfy my own curiosity, I took Csopi in the ring,

Nine Pulis during long sit exercises at one of the Puli Club of Southern California sanctioned matches.

Champion Erdalsoi Adu Betyar Matyi learning to hold the dumbbell.

Thunder Mt. Myra Mae Plunket (Acsi of PuliKountry **X** Star of Hunnia Furtos), another young Puli doing well in obedience. Owner: Mary Jane Richert.

and she successfully graduated. Those who have observed me as I obedience-train my dogs will testify that the above unusual success of Csopi can not be attributed to my ability as an obedience trainer.

Naturally, no two Pulis respond to training in identical manner. They are as individual as human beings are, and methods of training have to be custom-fitted to each dog in order to produce the desired results. There are a few Pulis that will demonstrate a kind of resentment for being expected to perform. With such a dog, the method of instruction will have to be modified, from training them to understand what is required of them to making them aware that the master can also demand certain things. With the occasional problem Pulis, professional advice should be sought.

Champion Zelda Plunket, U.D. (Ch. Shagra Csiko X Angel's Mist) was high-scoring dog in trial two years in a row at the Santa Ana Kennel Club Show. Owner: Mary Jane Richert. Photograph: Schley.

In most cases, with the understanding of "dog teaching methods" on the part of the owner, the training will turn into a challenging period for both dog and owner, and one in which they as a team will want to excel.

The most satisfying and rewarding type of obedience activity comes through team efforts in the form of hurdling races and the various other types of drill team activities. Aside from the fact that these special events provide excellent publicity for the breed, it is badly needed to retain the Puli's inherent agility and wit for future generations. In the modern lazy age of electrified sheep herding, a fast action, fun type activity is highly needed in order to get today's Pulis off their silk pillows and running again. I truly hope we will see in the near future such "all Puli" teams forming in various parts of the U.S., especially in areas where the Puli population is fairly concentrated.

THE WORKING PULI

In today's jet-paced life, millions of dogs can consider themselves lucky if they get ten minutes of daily exercise. Seeing the pampered pets of our crowded metropolitan cities, with costume jewelry on their fancy collars, one is easily led to believe that the days of the working dog are over. This is not so in the case of the Puli. We can consider our breed exceptional because in looking at the world population of Pulis we come to the conclusion that a larger percentage of this breed is still being used in natural habitat than is the case with any other working breed. It is of serious importance that our breeders can, if they want to, breed to actual working species. If sheepherding studs are not available, their first generation offspring are, and almost anywhere that Pulis are known. The only way to keep this breed's full value is to maintain the working ability.

One way to keep this working ability in our show dogs is by keeping an eye on the available stud dogs. If one can find a working herder that is also blessed with outstanding conformation values, he should be widely publicized so bitches can be referred to him. Dr. Bordacs's Nagykunsagi Puli Kennel built its reputation in Europe on the fact that he constantly searches the plains of Hungary for working Pulis to breed to. To mention just one of Dr. Bordac's internationally renowned dogs, Ch. Nagykunsagi

Systematic exercise should be a part of the life of every Puli but is especially important for the show-goers. Champion Hunnia's Suba (Ch. Cinkotai Csibesz X Ch. Tatarhegyi Borka Panna) here takes part in the daily jogging of owner Bill Pohlmann.

Csorgo C.D. came from a herding sire and a home-bred dam. The dam was also from a long line of field-working, shepherd-owned Pulis. Miss Csengeri at one time estimated that about 50 per cent of the puppies from her Bukkabranyi Kennel in Israel go to shepherds. With today's readily available transportation, breeders should be able to reach the most suitable mates for their Pulis in order, without giving up any of their desired qualities, to maintain the healthy balance between the pet Pulis and the working Pulis.

Working does not have to be limited to herding. Pulis are easy to train and are willing to attend a variety of duties. Most of them are ready to do anything out of the pure enjoyment of being active.

Teamwork, precision, and high quality obedience training is demonstrated by the 1968 relay team of the Puli Club of Southern California.

Shaggyland's Sobri Joska II, C.D. goes over the high jump. Owned by E. Cowell.

Kis Lo's Hajra Furge Bandita, U.D. (Ch. Kis Lo Batos Csiko **X** Kis Lo Csardas Susty Damsel), another Puli bringing fame to his breed in obedience circles, had his C.D. at nine months and later earned his U.D. in the first three shows where he was entered in Utility class. Trained and handled by Gilbert Pearson for co-owner Mrs. Wilhelmina Ferrando.

Guarding is especially suitable, since Pulis are very alert, proven watch dogs. It does not matter what duty one chooses for his Puli; the important thing is that he have a specific activity for the dog, as the Puli is much too active a breed to be contented as a mere living-room pet. Pulis badly curtailed in their activities by being locked in a room might become bored and begin chewing on children's toys or on furniture and other household items to occupy themselves. I have never heard of a working Puli destroying living-room furniture out of pure boredom when left alone at a mature age. Puppies are different, as they turn to rough play or furniture-chewing somewhat more readily, bored or not.

The best substitute for herding work is daily performance of obedience exercises, long walks, or show-conditioning road work. The latest invention that is rapidly becoming popular among dog owners is the electrically-powered dog-jogging machine. This machine is currently relatively expensive, but has its advantages. Probably the most noteworthy is that it can be used every day regardless of the weather. The dog can also jog in an air-conditioned, filtered-air environment and does not have to inhale the polluted air of our large cities. To the owner's advantage is that he can watch TV while the dog is exercising.

The daily use of their brains is as important in training the Puli as the physical exercise. Basic obedience work is again the most desirable form. In lieu of formal exercises, let your dog bring your slippers, pick up the newspaper in the morning, or just make him find his leash before his daily walk. These are some of the very easy tasks that are better than having no daily tasks to be performed.

HERDING

One cannot visualize the fascinating way a Puli fulfills himself by herding; one has to actually view the spectacle, and to fully describe it in writing is impossible. The herding method used by the Puli is quite different from any of the methods used by any of the other herding breeds. Travelling through Europe recently, I had an opportunity to witness and take movies of the International Herding Trials in London, England. Just a few days later, I filmed some working Pulis herding in rural Hungary. The contrast was amazing.

Cattle-herding Pulis being recalled after turning the herd around.

The Collies and Border Collies in England demonstrated a very obedient, quiet, and methodic form of herding. They executed their every move on the sound of a whistle or a hand signal of the shepherd. They never executed a fast or abrupt movement, nor did they bark much, if at all, at the sheep. On the other hand, upon receiving the command to perform a specific duty, the Pulis took off with lightning speed and did not look back at the shepherd until his command was fulfilled. To turn a single runaway sheep about, Pulis do not bark at the sheep until they have passed it and are ready to turn it. Once they have passed the sheep, they try to get in front of it before barking in short but frightening tones. To turn an entire flock in a new direction, or herd them to a new area of the pasture, the Pulis go on the side of the flock opposite the direction of motion desired and bark in short high-

One of the hardest exercises to teach a dog is to attack a human being. Champion Shagghland Sobri Joska III, C.D. (Star of Hunnia Dongo **X** Ch. Palinkas Zsuzsika) is demonstrating personal protection done Puli style. Owner: E. Cowell.

pitched tones until the sheep are herded as required by the order given. After they complete the task, the Pulis walk back to the shepherd and remain at his side.

It was most impressive to compare the sheep's behavior and reaction to the two different herding methods. While the Border Collies stopped and waited for a signal from their shepherd for the next move, the sheep had time to look around and consider the possibility of escaping. The sheep broke away many times from the dogs during the trials. However, the Puli's noisy way of herding is more demanding, and seemed to me to be more effective. Once they got the runaways or the entire flock on the move, they did not give the sheep a chance to look around to find possible escape routes.

After my films were developed and were projected for the first time, the silent movie called my attention to another interesting factor, the Pulis' footwork. Their footwork seemed to be of major importance to the sheep. While walking around the flock, no matter how close the Pulis walked to the sheep, the sheep did not seem bothered by or afraid of the dogs. As soon as the shepherd raised his stick to get his dogs' attention, the Pulis started their dance, small hops into the air, and sheep grazing as far as two hundred feet away looked up and followed every move of the dogs from there on.

During the height of the early sixties size controversy in the United States, misleading personal opinions were published with expressed reasoning that Pulis used to herd larger animals had to be larger themselves to be able to herd effectively. I looked to settle this point once and for all and sought a farm where Pulis were used to herd cows. After numerous inquiries in Europe, I decided upon visiting a collective farm not far from Budapest, Hungary. After my arrival there, I interviewed the man in charge of the cattle section of the farm and asked him what size he preferred the Pulis to be that were entrusted to herding the cows. He smiled and said, "Gentlemen, you came to the right place! I happen to own the Puli that was just recently named the best cow herder in this part of the country, based on her performance during a friendly unofficial competition." With a wink, the man turned around and whistled toward the buildings. The words "her performance" stuck in my mind, and I expected to see an oversized Komondor-

Two Pulis keep the herd away from the deep-water well during the noon heat.

like bitch bound around the corner of the building. The man told us to excuse her coat condition, as she had recently had puppies and dropped most of her coat during the lactation period. By this time a tiny gray dog was flying in our direction, tongue hanging and tail wagging, landing in a sitting position in front of our guide. "She is the one," he said. "We will take her out with us to give a short demonstration." To my amazement, she was one of the smallest Pulis I had ever seen. When we arrived at the field, two other Pulis came to greet us. They were her puppies from a previous breeding, and both of their coats were dragging behind them. The three Pulis put on a performance that I remember well. They herded about two hundred cows under a wide variety of conditions. The dogs were commanded to herd the cows along an adjoining corn field for about a mile to show us that they would not let a single cow eat a single ear of corn. Up a hill, down a hill, into a small forest and out again, the Pulis did their duty with more ease than their sheepherding relatives. At the end of the demonstration, they herded the cows to a clear area where they usually got their afternoon watering from a deep well. After the vigorous demonstration, the Pulis got the order to keep the cows away from the water. It must be about the most difficult task in the world to keep a thirsty herd of cows from their normal watering place. The Pulis, thirsty themselves, managed to hold every one of the cows away from the water until they were recalled. And much to my surprise, the dogs when released from their post drank side by side with the cows. In Dr. Emil Raitsit's book, *A Magyar Pasztorkutyak*, published in 1924, there is an interesting account of a friend's years in the Hungarian Cavalry. ". . . Most of our enlisted men were from the families of shepherds. As a cadet I have often paraded with my proud possession, a Puli given me by one of my soldiers. Whenever a Puli appeared in camp, 70 to 80 "grass-root experts" would form a large circle around it and judge its merits.

"Let me share with you the experience of one of these 'judgings.' The 'judge' picks up a stone from the ground and teases the Puli by blowing and spitting at the stone held in his hand. If this sufficiently excites the dog and it begins its typical high pitched yipping, then it is a Puli!—This was the temperament (alertness) and sound test (testing what sounds the dog will make). If this test will not excite the dog, his coat can hang to the ground and he can look as pretty as a picture, but he is not considered a Puli—just a dog. Otherwise, his 'Puli soul' is missing and he is degraded to a 'dog.'

"The second test is with the water bucket. The 'judge' would throw a bucket of water over the dog until it is thoroughly soaked and its shape shows through his wet coat. If the dog has thin bones, rounded skull, and a narrow muzzle, then the Puli is good. If the muzzle is wide and coarse, then it is a 'dog headed' Puli. If the dog's legs are heavy boned, it is a 'dog legged' Puli. And if the Puli is both 'dog headed' and 'dog legged,' then it is again degraded to a 'dog.' The logical explanation to this is that as shepherds they have to be careful, as a heavy muzzled, heavy jawed dog would hurt the sheep.

"A shepherd's ideal Puli has to be thin boned, or rather light boned so that when it herds the flock in or out of the pen and one of the sheep stops, blocking the entrance, the Puli can run over the backs of the others to reach and turn around the troublemaker.

"Then, for the 'classification' (because the Puli is not like other breeds, his uses are versatile), the shepherd's boots (approx. 40 cm) are used as a measuring device. Those Pulis, up to, and under the top of the boots are used to herd sheep and pigs. Those taller than the top of the boots are used to herd cattle and horses. However, a Puli's height should never reach the knees (approx. 45 cm)!"

In her speech at the Second Puli Fanciers Convention, Miss Csengeri gave a detailed account of the modern-day herding Pulis of Israel. She usually releases a puppy to a shepherd at about six months, and only after completion of basic training and past the critical mental developing period. They begin the field work shortly. A Puli can handle 200 to 300 cows or 400 to 500 sheep, but the dogs work much better in pairs. They have a much easier time than their forefathers, as they work only six to eight hours a day, depending upon the season. They receive a small amount of food before work in the morning and get their main meal at night. A Puli may have the privilege of sitting on a horse behind a cowboy or "mounted" shepherd, and upon receiving orders, he jumps off, carries out the order, and returns to his place behind his master.

The Puli is still gaining in popularity among the shepherds in Israel, due mostly to favorable publicity and the legend they have built with their unselfish devotion to their masters. On one occasion, a shepherd forgetfully left some possessions in a field and he returned with his Puli to pick them up. As he reached the place, his Puli actually grabbed him and pulled him backward, then jumped forward to kill a poisonous snake. In Ben Ami, another farmer entered a cowshed and was pulled aside by his Puli, who then jumped in and killed a snake. In the Kibbutz Tirat Zvi, two Pulis work with a large herd of cows, and the men entrusted with their care testify that the Pulis are doing the job that was formerly performed by five men.

Mr. Schmoll, an industrialist, uses his show Pulis to herd cows on his country estate near Vienna, Austria. He told me that his Pulis take on an entirely different personality as his car approaches the farm. In Vienna, they are "sophisticated" city dwellers, not showing half the animation that they demonstrate in the fields. They are willing to go to the city to be near their master, but they consider the estate as their real home.

In the United States at this time, we unfortunately do not know of many Pulis having show and breeding background that are being used for herding. Although we occasionally hear about herding trials, it is not yet a well-accepted sport among dog fanciers. It is a good activity for Puli Clubs to explore. Many of the American-bred Pulis have demonstrated good ability and willingness to herd, but they never get the chance. Few imported Pulis actually come from the fields. Mr. Joseph De Lengyel purchased a Puli from a shepherd in Hungary, and Miss Marianne Jona of Palo Alto, California, owns Imrei Zsuzsi, a Puli bitch that was imported after it was learned that the dog was fully trained for herding. Zsuzsi was the star, and her own stunt dog, in a short documentary film made about sheep herding. It is a shame that she never had a chance to enter a herding trial in the U.S. to demonstrate her extraordinary herding talent. She would have added greatly to the Puli's fame.

Dog racing is getting more and more popular each year, even among fanciers of breeds that have never been meant for racing. The entries are larger and larger on sled dog competitions and tracking trials. Breeders and fanciers agree that to get a step closer to the dog's natural field is badly needed. Hopefully the day is close when owners of dogs of various working breeds will create activities to measure their dogs' specific abilities in their breed's unique function. That would be the real measurement of "canine excellence."

Chapter 9

INHERITED DISEASES

It is very unfortunate that modern science has not yet come up with a computerized method to replace nature's sometimes crude but effective method of selection or elimination of the weak and undesired. With the domestication of our dogs and the placing of them in the status of pets, we interfere with the laws of natural selection. In the case of the Puli, I do not even refer back to when the ancestors of our dogs were living in the wild state. As recently as forty to fifty years ago, when Puli bitches whelped out on the plains of Hungary during the summer months, while performing their work, shepherds did not have the time or the willingness to nurse the weaklings of a litter through their difficult times. The ones that could not keep up with the rest of the litter in development did not survive.

What does today's breeder do? A Puli bitch, for example, has seven puppies. From the first minute they are born, six of them are healthy, squirming, and nursing on their dam. The seventh one is different from the beginning; it is weaker, not as healthy looking, and gets pushed away by the mother. Sometimes the dam even sits or lies upon this one, as if trying to kill it. We go into shock when this happens, scold the bitch for her action, pick up the puppy, hold it to her mother's nipples, and force it to nurse. Or we even go to the trouble of feeding the puppy with an eye dropper or a miniature nursing bottle made for that purpose. We manage to pull the puppy through, and a few days later, proud of our achievement, we return it to its mother. All through the nursing period this puppy will remain the weakest; it becomes the runt of the litter and the favorite of the whole family because of its handicaps. The puppies are sold and the entire incident is forgotten. A year later, even the breeder cannot recall which puppy was the runt, but one day he may receive a sad letter from the purchaser of that puppy reporting that it has died from some kind of undetermined internal trouble. If the breeder is one of those rare ones who keep very detailed records on every single puppy, he will find that the puppy dying so mysteriously happens to be the little weakling. At that particular moment he will not be so proud of his achievement in saving that seventh puppy.

It is not my intention to list the hundreds of health hazards a dog can encounter during his life. I shall only refer to the hazards of the inherited diseases. Just as in the case of such inherited serious faults as bad bite, bad pigment, lemon-yellow or white eyes, etc., the breeder should be responsible for his product just as car manufacturers are responsible for theirs. All responsible breeders should offer, without request of purchaser, a written health guarantee with every single puppy sold with AKC registration, not only guaranteeing the puppy's physical condition at the time of the sale, but warranting against inherited faults and inherited diseases that might show up later. Do not misunderstand me, I do not profess that this proposed guarantee system would stop all faults and diseases overnight, since by the law of genetics they can be hidden in a line for generations before coming to the surface, but, if properly applied, it would reduce the occurrence of these faults and diseases. Further, it would certainly reduce the number of breeders who are rushing into dog breeding under the attraction of the smell of "easy money," but who never intend to stand behind their product. I do not maintain that it would be easy to arbitrate determination of how much of a fault was inherited and how much of it was influenced by environment, but formal acceptance of some responsibility would certainly be a step in the right direction.

HIP DYSPLASIA

Hip dysplasia is a disease that is present to some degree in all canines. It is basically a malformation in the bone structure of the hip assembly. It can affect either the hip socket, the head of the upper leg bone that fits into the socket, or both. The socket could become too shallow, flat, or uneven. The femur, or upper leg bone, can deviate in many different ways. It can have flat areas on it; its head can be too small for the socket or be positioned at the end of the upper leg bone at the wrong angle, or in extreme cases be missing altogether so that muscle alone is holding the leg bone to the pelvis. Depending on the amount of departure from the normal, the joint is affected by the malformation. The flat areas of the femur start working on the socket, or vice versa, and in most cases a calcification of the joint begins. Dogs can develop this disease in varying degrees. It could be so slight that it can be detected only by X-raying the dog. Or it can be such that the only thing one notices is that the dog has difficulty getting up on his hind legs at times, particularly on cold mornings. Sometimes it can develop to such a degree that the dog is in constant pain and has much difficulty in walking.

Scientists are not yet in complete agreement as to how much a dog's environment can influence the seriousness of the final development of hip dysplasia. But they are in complete agreement that at least the tendency to develop the disease is inherited.

Hip dysplasia can not be eliminated by selective breeding techniques in one or two generations. This fact is quite discouraging, especially to new breeders. But with very careful selection, by breeding dogs with normal hips only, the percentage of incidence of the disease can be decreased significantly in five to six generations. To clear our breed completely of hip dysplasia, the cooperation of all Puli Clubs and ALL BREEDERS will be necessary. Breeds wherein the "dysplasia panic" came to its peak fifteen to twenty years ago and wherein something was done about it through selective breeding are far ahead of us. To date there are only a couple of hundred Pulis that are certified clear by different knowledgeable authorities. We should praise the efforts of the pioneers among our breeders who tackled the problem years ago. They helped pave the way. The direction this breed is to take in the future depends entirely on the breeders. If from this day on no un-X-rayed Puli bitch would be bred to an un-X-rayed Puli stud, we could completely eliminate this crippling disease within ten years. And when all of our breeders are willing to pledge such cooperation, we will truly be able to say that we have complete harmony within the breed. Such a task would not have to be influenced by personalities, or individual likes and dislikes, or corded versus combed coat believers, or small versus big size believers. It would be the real proof that everyone in the breed is trying to better it. Are any of our Puli Clubs willing to undertake such a task? At this time it seems to be a utopian idea.

To establish the law about how much deviation from the normal in a dog's skeletal makeup is permissible, the Orthopedic Foundation For Animals Inc. (OFA) was organized. This organization is the leading authority to arbitrate and determine what is normal and what is an abnormal hip development for the various breeds. If asked they will examine your dog's hip X-ray and certify their findings if the X-ray is determined to be normal.

I have mentioned the OFA to show that in at least the case of one inherited disease, an authority has been established and an owner has a source where he can get certified proof in case a guaranteed dog's hips are in question.

At the present time, another alarming health problem of concern is that of missing teeth. In the last few years more and more Pulis have been found in the show ring with two, three, or more teeth missing. Many of these animals are progeny of recent breeding. Presently, there are Pulis with enviable show records that have as many as six teeth missing. One or two breeders attacking this problem will not help the breed considerably, but what could help would be judges who would not award ribbons to dogs with major dental faults. But even more effective would be the selective breeding techniques used by breeders so that dental faults and many other inherited faults could be eliminated within the Puli breed.

All Puli Clubs should encourage their members to keep accurate breeding records. These records could be made available to all interested persons and would be the beginning of assuring a healthy future for our breed. One can not see into the future or use a crystal ball to know whether a stud that is certified clear of a certain fault will not still produce that fault in his progeny. But certainly, if one starts out with X-rayed breeding stock, he has a head start over those who do not even bother to X-ray their stock.

I include the following list not to frighten the future Puli breeder but to show a partial list of some possibly inherited diseases. Many items listed are not known to be present in our breed at this time; however, individual dogs or bloodlines can carry these diseases without overt manifestation. Heredity might not be the only contributing factor in many of these diseases.

Nevertheless, the thoughtful breeder should use such a list in evaluating his future breeding stock.

1. Skeletal Abnormalities
    1. Hip dysplasia
    2. Elbow dysplasia
    3. Patella luxation
    4. Undershot jaw
    5. Overshot jaw
    6. Reduced number of teeth
    7. Taillessness
    8. Skull defects
    9. Proneness to rickets
    10. Skeletal abnormalities and achondroplasia (abnormality in converting cartilage into bone resulting in dwarfism)
    11. Otocephaly (malformation due to defective development of the lower jaw)
    12. Cranial defects
2. Endocrine and Metabolic Disturbances
    1. Diabetes mellitus
    2. Hemophilia
    3. Pituitary cysts
    4. Anterior pituitary disfunction
    5. Predisposition to kidney stones
    6. Goiter
3. Soft-tissue Anomalies
    1. Hairlessness
    2. Umbilical hernia
    3. Inguinal hernia
    4. Harelip
    5. Prolongation of the soft palate
    6. Abnormal larynx
    7. Trichiasis (irritation caused by ingrowing eyelash)
    8. Entropion and ectropion (turned-in and turned-out eyelid)
    9. Dermoid sinus
4. Sensory-organ Anomalies
    1. Deafness
    2. Cataract
    3. Glaucoma
    4. Microphtalmia (abnormally small eye)

5. Retinal atrophy
6. Retinal detachment
7. Optic nerve hypoplasis (incomplete development)
5. Urogential Anomalies
   1. Cryptorchidism
   2. Oestral weakness
   3. Cortical hypoplasia (incomplete development of the kidney)
6. Proneness to Disease or Neoplasia
   1. Proneness to eczema
   2. Distemper susceptibility
   3. Incidence of neoplasia (tumors)
7. Central Nervous System
   1. Epilepsy
   2. Hydrocephalus
   3. Tetany
   4. Trembling
   5. Ataxia (loss of muscular coordination)
8. Behavioral Abnormalities
   1. Extreme shyness
   2. Aggression
   3. Abnormal maternal behavior

BIBLIOGRAPHY

American Kennel Club, "Complete Dog Book," New York, 1964

Anghi, Dr. Geyza Csaba, "Magyar Pasztorkutyak es azok kulfoldi rokonai " Budapest, 1936 (Hungarian Sheepdogs and their foreign relatives)

Appel, Ruth, "Wily Pulik: the Eggheads From Hungary," San Francisco Chronicle, ca. Aug. 1, 1962

Becker, Ruthlee, "The Phillips System," PuliKeynotes, September, 1971

Beregi, Oscar and Leslie Benis, "How to Raise and Train a Komondor," T.F.H., 1966

Buzzi, Felix Geza, "Magyar Pasztorkutyak " Budapest, 1915 (Hungarian Shepherd Dogs)

Donaho, Catharine L., "The Puli in Alaska," Puli News, March 1964

Harsanyi, Zsolt, "The Puli," The Hungarian Quarterly, 1950

Kennedy, Anne, "Puli Grooming"

Kubinszky, Dr. Erno, "Veterinary Manual," Budapest 1960

Kubinszky Dr. Erno and Dr. Szel, "A Kutya," Budapest, 1955 (The Dog)

Lloyd, Freeman, "Working Dogs of the World," National Geographic Magazine, Vol. LXXX, No. 6, December, 1941, pg. 784

Mahan, Philip, "Commentary," The Puli, December, 1966

McLellan, Mrs. R. D., "The Incredible Puli," Dogs In Canada, November, 1957, Newsletters, Associated All Hungarian Breed Club of North America

Mohr, Dr. Erna, "Ungarische Hirtenhunde," Leipzig, 1956 (Hungarian Sheepdogs)

McDowell and Lion, "The Dog in Motion"

New Yorker, July 20, 1946

Palfalvy, Sandor, M.D., "A Puli"

Palfalvy, Sandor, M.D., "The Puli"

Pfaffenberger, Dr., "The New Knowledge of Dog Behavior"

Powers, Lois and Anne Kennedy, "What the Judges Think," Puli-Keynotes, 1971

Scott and Fuller, "Genetics and the Social Behavior of Dogs," 1965

Trautwein, Howard, "The Puli," American Kennel Gazette, L. McManus column, October, 1961

Young, Stanley P., "Other Working Dogs and the Wild Species," National Geographic Magazine, Vol. LXXXVI, No. 3 September, 1944

Ch. Kallopusztai Apor. This excellent specimen was recently imported from Hungary by Mr. and Mrs. Victor Majer of Painesville, Ohio. Apor became No. 3 Puli (Phillips Rating) in 1974 and is the first Puli to place in the highly competitive Working Group at the Westminster K.C. show. Apor is also a Canadian Champion and the winner of the coveted Best In Show title there.

Index